LET THERE BE
LIGHT

to Liz, Bethan and everyone at ABR Construction (UK) Ltd

Let There Be Light - (Pbk)

© Tony Gillan, 2001

ISBN 0953592081

Published by Terrace Banter, Scotland
Printed by Heritage Press, England

Thanks to Bob and Betty, Jen and Dave, Lorna, John and June, Pat and Paddy, Anna and George, Wilma and Dick, Jenny and Bill, Mary and Tony, all at Coventry, everyone in the index, Bob Herington, Jimmy Marshall and all at the Ivy House.

On a proof reading note, thanks to Sheila Seacroft

And on a musical note, thanks to Henry Race

Further recommended reading concerning all things Sunderland come in the shape of the following spiffing fanzines.

A Love Supreme, 1 Hodgson's Buildings, Stadium Way, Monkwearmouth, Sunderland. SR5 1BT (also at www.als.sunderland.com)

Sex & Chocolate, 1 Hodgson's Buildings, Stadium Way, Monkwearmouth, Sunderland. SR5 1BT.

The Wearside Roar, c/o Echo House, Pennywell Industrial Estate, Sunderland. SR4 9ER.

TERRACE BANTER
P.O. Box 12, Lockerbie, Dumfriesshire. DG11 3BW. Scotland.
www.terracebanter.com

LET THERE BE
LIGHT

Our diarist has agreed to take on the job of Information Officer at what will be Sunderland Football Club's Stadium of Light and is about to leave a dull office job.

Expecting to be at the club for only a few months, he will be there for five years.

Enjoy.

1996

July 7 Sunday

I left work at Newton Aycliffe Industrial Estate today on a wave of emotion. Three people actually said goodbye to me and one of them even looked up from his game of *Find The Frog* to do so. I shall miss that type of warmth and repartee, along with the chocolate Hob Nobs.

July 9 Tuesday

The big day. The Sunderland AFC Visitors Centre, a magnificent hut, was formally opened by Len Shackleton in front of an appreciative crowd and the local media.

Shackleton was one of the most talented footballers of all time, an icon, wit and sporting ambassador, so he must have been chuffed to watch *Look North* tonight and find that he was sharing the small screen with me, having a good old lurk in the background.

Despite his legendary status, I almost didn't let him in. I was expecting him to roll up in a limousine with Mrs. Shackleton on his arm. Instead he turned up in t-shirt and trainers with his mate Sandy (which meant that the flowers were redundant). He looked just like the other run-of-the-mill pensioners who had attempted to get in with their carrier bags to help themselves to the vol-au-vents.

So, although I came close to chucking out our guest of honour, I did not have a bad first day.

July 10 Wednesday

Only my second day of giving information to the public and they are already beginning to irritate me. Immediately I am frequently annoyed by the words 'You know what they should have done . . . ', which is usually followed by an absurd suggestion for a mirrored ceiling or a tartan pitch or such like.

Some of the questions I have had to field have been hardly less silly. 'How much will the drinks be?', 'What number bus should I get?' and 'How far apart will the seats be?' were fairly typical, although that last one was not entirely unreasonable, coming as it did from a bloke who was 30 stones if he was an ounce.

July 11 Thursday

Interest in the new stadium continues unabated, despite the fact that at present it is merely a big hole in the ground. I think that the large number of visitors passing through is testimony to the quality of daytime television as it seems that people would literally prefer to watch paint dry or grass grow than stay at home and endure another episode of *Murder She Wrote*.

I glanced through some of the names in the visitors book and I can honestly say that it will be a rather desirable museum piece before long. However, I must have been too busy to notice Whoopi Goldberg and Frank Sinatra signing it. I must be more alert in future.

July 12 Friday

It came to my attention today that there is a Newcastle United supporter working on our lovely new ground. If asked I shall say that we have allowed him to work the land as a feudal favour to the less fortunate.

He gave himself away when he walked through the wind, up to our Visitor Centre door pointing at our club flag with his lighter and making the playful threat, 'I hope there's enough gas in here to burn that.'

I smiled kindly at him, the only course of action because one has to consider that only a Mag would consider attempting to set light to a heavily damp and flame-proofed flag in a force seven with only a cheap and virtually empty disposable lighter to assist.

Still, he left me clearly very pleased with his little jape and waddled over the humpback bridge to celebrate with eight kebabs and an elocution lesson.

July 13 Saturday

Late this evening I was in a taxi queue in Sunderland city centre in the rain, but the obvious displeasure I was gleaning from this was increased by an annoying drunk who was slobbering his way up and down the line saying, 'Give us a kiss / 20 pence' depending on the gender of his victim.

He had accrued 60p when he was silenced by one bloke who would not humour him and who put him on the pavement with one hefty bop on the chin. This garnered the easy victor some polite and appreciative applause from the other more tolerant members of the queue who had hitherto suffered in silence, but our champion did spoil the moment a tad by telling the sot to 'Get out of town!' in an over dramatic manner. But we enjoyed his achievement nonetheless.

July 15 Monday

I managed to get hold of some lead today and as Monday is my day off I threw it in the boot of the car and sped greedily to the nearest scrap metal dealer. You can never plan too early, so on the way I was deciding where in Europe I would sun myself on the proceedings. It was with more than a tinge of disappointment that I emerged from the scrap yard clutching a mere £2.55.

The day only got worse when the car broke down again this afternoon. It was almost fortunate that this happened in Bob Fairlie's street. I say almost because he provided me with a tow rope, but only one which had evidently been used to berth the Queen Mary as it was as thick as the car. So I nicked his washing line.

July 16 Tuesday
In a quiet moment at work, I was browsing through the visitors book when I came to the inescapable conclusion that the names of Whoopi Goldberg and Frank Sinatra are probably bogus. I say this for two reasons. The first is that I have no recollection of seeing either of them in my hut. The second is that the respective addresses given for them, Witherwack and Ryhope, do not tally with the lavish superstar lifestyle that they lead, even if the bus shelters have been upgraded recently.

July 17 Wednesday
My other half, Liz, insisted on having her birthday today. For her prezzie I offered her the choice of perfume or a ticket to see Sunderland in Richard Ord's testimonial game with Steua Bucharest. She opted for the perfume, which was fortunate as we were in Boots at the time, a store that has proved to be a singularly unreliable outlet for match tickets in the past.

I went on my own in the end and saw a deeply uninspiring one-nil defeat, so I spent most of the evening being bored but at least I don't smell like a girl. Unlike Liz.

July 18 Thursday
An elderly couple approached me in my hut today. I braced myself to listen to their tales of watching Sunderland on the day that Sir Geoffrey Chaucer had opened one of the previous grounds on the day that we had beaten Wessex Wanderers before 80,000 spectators. However, they actually had a question to ask me.

'He's wondering what to do about his ashes,' shrieked the woman as she tapped her husband about the midriff with a 1996-97 fixture list.

I suggested that they should wait until he was dead before arranging a scattering and that he should not bother having them sprinkled on Roker Park as before long he would be part of the foundations of another branch of What Everyone Wants.

July 23 Tuesday
At the site of the new stadium I am surrounded by a number of lavish eateries. However, I have already decided not to dine at one particular café as the pitiful quantity of cheese put into the last sandwich I bought there suggested that it had been made with a catapult. The cooked meals are not great either although they do a lovely Twix.

I now frequent Red & White Taxis, who for some reason have diversified into fry-ups which is vertical integration I think. Anyway, I ordered the chef's

7

speciality, a sausage and egg sandwich, fried healthily in diet lard and beautifully complimented by Chop Sauce. The only drawback to all of this was that I barely had room for my Twix. Ooh, I can still feel it sliding down me.

July 24 Wednesday

At work today I received a telephone call from Lesley Coates forewarning me that a journalist would be coming round to interview me. I have always fancied the idea of locking intellectual antlers with a Malcolm Muggeridge or even a Robin Day, so it was a big old let down to find that my interrogator was to be lager-swilling *Sunderland Echo* hack, Rob Freeth.

Rob has gleaned many a scoop from overheard gossip in the Ivy House toilets. Then as the first question he directed at me was concerned with whether I would put the kettle on, it was clear which level of journalism we were at. 15 minutes, a cup of tea and a packet of Hob Nobs later, we had between us concocted an interview fit for page 12, column four.

July 25 Thursday

Tonight's *Sunderland Echo* contained very little to hold one's attention. The best thing in it being me. I was on page three, appropriately enough, at the top of our ladder pretending to hoist the flag that had already been raised several hours previously. I did look rather dashing and in control, not unlike Errol Flynn in *Captain Blood* with a bit of Hannibal Lector thrown in. Such was the importance of the article, that it was easily bigger than the feature about the daring raid at Pete's Perfect Pot And Pan Emporium.

My hope now is that having taken the trouble to speak to the media, they will respect my privacy and write about something else.

July 26 Friday

The Olympic games are now half way through and the United Kingdom's current total of gold medals, nought, is in its own way quite healthy as it represents the amount we had fully expected to have achieved by now. Even better news is that the International Olympic Committee has decreed that snooker be included by 2004, which should bag us a few more badges.

Better still would be the addition of darts, which would surely provide a rare British clean sweep. Imagine national pride swelling as three Union Jacks rise slowly yet gloriously up the poles, our trio of successful athletes bellowing out the national anthem, while also giving the podium a truly Olympian test of strength.

July 27 Saturday

The latest addition to the walls of my beloved hut is a framed photograph of Len Shackleton being the first to sign the visitors book. Above it is the helpful caption, 'Len Shackleton Is The First To Sign The Visitors Book'.

Upon seeing this, one blissfully ignorant young fellow asked me if *his* picture would now be adorning the hut had he been down quicker on that opening day and beaten Mr. Shackleton to the book. I said yes. It was quicker.

July 31 Wednesday

July ended on something of a downer when I had to go over to work early because some nasty intruders had broken into my hut and stolen some odds and ends. Sadly they neglected to nick the video with its accompanying cheesy music, but you can't have everything.

Since the Visitors Centre opened, several thousand people have passed through to examine the place and proceedings, so when the policeman asked me if I had noticed anyone who may have casing the place, it was a decent show of constraint on my part not to point out what a monumentally daft question he had just asked me. Well, restraint and the fact that I need to renew my tax disc.

August 2 Friday

Our fax machine arrived today, which meant that I had to spend this afternoon programming our name to appear at the top of each page that we send.

I went home with a glowing feeling of achievement, a feeling that lasted until about midnight when Lesley rang me to say that we had been burgled again, properly this time, which meant that the fax machine was among the booty and that my hours of technical expertise had been applied in vain.

The thieves were not entirely heartless because they did at least have the decency to steal the video along with its alleged backing music (actually a series of noises coincidentally meeting up and having a fight).

August 4 Sunday

News of the burglary of my hut on Friday night is now pretty much common knowledge, as I discovered while out on the razzle this evening. On about 15 occasions I was jokingly offered a cheap video. Although as we were in some of the city's less decorous pubs tonight, not all of these propositions may have been made in jest.

I may have to return if my lovely daughter Bethan continues to insert toast into our machine. Indeed it is a small mercy that the insertion of whole Asda baking potatoes is physically impossible. I was offered a food-proof model, but it was Betamax.

August 6 Tuesday

Tonight Paul Callaghan and I were press-ganged by Quippo the quiz master into competing in a quiz in the lavish surroundings of the Colliery Tavern in Boldon. The event was hosted by Paddy McDee of BBC *Look*

North, someone I have always wished to meet because I had heard that he stands at five feet eight in height but his legs are only 18 inches long, so I was most interested. These claims turned out to be exaggerated, although his general physique put me in mind of Queen Victoria.

Our team managed a respectable fifth place from 12, which was not at all bad considering that none of our specialised subjects came up i.e. football, soap operas, adverts and general shallow rubbish.

August 7 Wednesday

In the aftermath of the burglary the other day, there was today a major breakthrough in hut security when we put up signs saying 'Television and Video Are Removed From Visitor Centre When Closed', to which one wag responded with, 'Well they were on Friday night! Ha! Ha!'

He was followed by another minutes later who said 'Well they were on Friday night! Ha! Ha!', then by another one shortly afterwards who joked, 'Well they were on Friday night! Ha! Ha!', thus establishing the comedic pattern for the next few days.

There was no reprieve in the pub later either as the 'Do you want a cheap video?' jokes continued relentlessly. Hopefully I shall remember all of this quality patter for after dinner speeches.

August 8 Thursday

Today say further insurance against dull moments when the shop section of the hut took delivery of new SAFC merchandise. Not that there is ever a dull moment in my hut anyway.

The pick of the stock has to be the official SAFC yo-yo, a real Premier League toy, the quality of which helps one to absorb the fact that we have left the First Division behind. Southend United yo-yos are reckoned to have notoriously sub-standard string and you can barely 'walk the dog' with the ones from Oldham Athletic.

August 9 Friday

I had a call at work today to forewarn me that Bob Murray would be gracing my hut at some point today. He is the Chairman of the club and I must remember that.

The kitchen and bathroom magnate and all round swell guy eventually strode in while I was explaining to a bloke with big ears that there was really no need for us to incorporate an ironmongers shop into the new stadium. But to my consternation, the great man was barely in for two minutes. He merely peered out of the window at the seagulls for a while, had a bit of a scratch, then left.

As I had gone to the trouble of combing my hair and filing the muck from the doormat, I must say I was left feeling rather let down.

August 10 Saturday

It will be several weeks until any steel arrives on site, but today I was given exciting news of the six new cranes that will be arriving soon and jolly nice they will look too. A bloke in the site office called Dave Lennon told me and he wears a tie so I tend to believe him.

The biggest of them will have a jib of around 30 metres in length which will be a enormous asset to some of the sturdy work force as it will be capable of lifting huge amounts of steel and concrete as well as stretching over to the café to collect lunches. With this sort of lifting capabilities, even a 'belly buster' should be a comfortable load.

August 11 Sunday

While nipping out of the hut for a paper, I was treated to an inspiring sight in North Bridge Street. I saw a short, stout, oldish fellow in a 'bald is sexy' baseball cap. He was not so much spitting at the pavement as attacking it with hockle that would have produced cracks on a lesser kerb. What a spit!

He made an extraordinary hacking wrenching noise that could be heard from the other side of the river, and when he had eventually finished he merely shuffled away as though nothing had happened, taking his incredibly robust throat with him.

One could only be impressed with such high velocity phlegm removal, although the people who had watched the whole performance over a Chinese meal in the Shanghai Palace seemed to be reserving judgement.

August 12 Monday

Further infamy has befallen my hut and on my day off too!

The Echo finally ran a report about the burglary despite our best efforts to dissuade them. They mentioned the theft of our tables, chairs and television, none of which had been touched. Then they mentioned that we were robbed of a whole list of items that had never been there in the first place, such as a computer, a virtual reality machine, a Persian carpet and a Bounty Bar. In fact the whole article read like a fraudulent insurance claim.

To read of the mess in the car park was notable mainly for us not having one of those either, unless the burglars managed to make off with that too.

August 13 Tuesday

In the city centre today, I was striding purposefully towards St. Peter's Bakers where I was about to startle onlookers by devouring a hitherto undreamed of quantity of corned beef pasties, when I saw a man bounding out of Phoenix House. With a good amount of triumphant gusto, he leapt gleefully over the adjacent barrier then sprinted joyously down the street.

The reason for this rapturous gymnastic display, as he told his friend in a loud, cheerful voice, was apparently a successful application for Disability

Allowance. If government officials are as easy to mug as this, then I may just pop in and claim to be an amputee, perhaps filling in the forms with my teeth for that touch of verisimilitude.

August 15 Thursday

Bob Murray was back over at the site again today with an entourage of press, officials and assorted lackeys. He was there to lay a time capsule which will be dug up in a hundred years time to give our ancestors a glimpse of what life was like, although what they will make of ten fags and a packet of Toffos is anybody's guess.

This is probably an academic point anyway, as it shows some rather misguided optimism to suppose that a time capsule as valuable as this will be awaiting rediscovery on the verge of the next century, considering that the fax machine in the Visitors Centre did not see out the evening.

They were lucky to leave the site still in ownership of the spade.

August 16 Friday

I listened intently to two old blokes in the hut having an inane ramble about the price of cheese, literally, even though I knew it was a waste of five valuable minutes of my life.

'One pound forty', bemoaned one.

'Yeah, 28 bob, eh!' said his friend in precise mathematical agreement.

'30 pence for a *Daily Mirror* . . . '

'Yeah, six bob . . . '

And so it went on, with the second bloke pre-decimalising the entire shopping list of the first.

As is inevitable in my hut their conversation soon turned to footy, the first one opining on Sunderland's recent acquisition of Niall Quinn for £1.3million. Correctly, I defied his mate to work out that this was 26 million bob.

August 17 Saturday

The football season has at last swung into action with the cream of the Premiership games being at Roker Park, of course, where Sunderland engaged in a goalless draw of breathtaking quality with Championship favourites Leicester City, so expect blanket coverage in the Sunday papers. After one entire game we have ascended to the vertigo-charged heights of 12th and would have been even higher but for the alphabet.

We are also a point above Newcastle, a lead that will last at least until Wednesday, so I rang around the local tattoo parlours to find out how much it would be to have the league table printed on an appropriate part of my body.

August 18 Sunday

T'was another leisurely afternoon for me in Wearside's leading hut, doing what might be loosely considered to be work. The most difficult part of my job is to refrain from telling members of the public not to ask such monumentally stupid questions.

One big eared youth asked me, without any comic intent, how many corners there would be in the new stadium, to which I smiled genially at him and told him four, whereas a more appropriate response would have been, 'Twenty seven. How many do you think there are, thick arse!? What do they teach you in school these days? Go home and revise and stop sniffing!'

It's a nice thought.

August 21 Wednesday

Nottingham Forest away. Four-one to us. Ha!

August 24 Saturday

I came home at about five o'clock to be given the startling news by Liz that Sunderland had managed a draw at Liverpool.

I had an anxious three hours wait to confirm this until reliable eye witnesses returned to the Ivy House from Merseyside. Having only seen the result on three television channels, two newspapers, Ceefax, Teletext and in someone's bay window in twelve inch letters, as well as hearing it on just five radio stations, I felt entitled to be sceptical.

Eventually Tonka and Taff barged through the door and loudly announced that 'Boooaaaghhh!!!', which despite its ineloquence was enough verification for me. No doubt tomorrow's *Observer* will take 300 words to say the same thing.

August 25 Sunday

Yesterday's prophecy concerning coverage of Sunderland's game turned out to be untrue, the match report in the *Observer* being confined to 'Boooaaaghhh!!!'. This was not perhaps as articulate as usual but it successfully captured the mood.

I was in the pub as usual tonight because I am great, but I am beginning to find myself being recognised from working in the famous hut and resenting it. It is something of a niggle to be approached at closing time and harangued for information on retractable sprinkler systems and polypropylene fibre pitch protectors. It is a waste of time for my interrogators too because the chances of me being able to say 'polypropylene' after a harmful quantity of grog are less than remote.

August 26 Monday

Bank holiday Monday is a dreadful waste when Monday is my day off anyway. To compound matters, this was the day when we had to buy a new washing machine. Liz has refused to opt for filth no matter how cost effective it is.

No summer picnics for Bethan then; instead we whisked her off to Northern Electric where she spent the afternoon inserting her head into various tumble driers. She was enjoying this mindless pleasure until we had to enter the room where transactions are made, which to Bethan looked dangerously like a doctor's waiting room. I asked the washing machine man to put a needle in her for a laugh, but he was not keen.

August 28 Wednesday

A fat woman in a *Pocahontas* t-shirt and Kicker boots came bounding up to me at work today. 'It's about the Brownies', she barked (and I use the word unadvisedly) as the whole of the hut shook. I politely pointed out that there were no plans at this stage for a designated Brownie enclosure, but I would suggest it to the relevant department. However, it turned out that she only wanted to bring a pack of them over, and feeling slightly intimidated, I agreed.

'Good. I'll tell Beryl then,' she barked further. The expression on my face had obviously exposed my ignorance of who Beryl was. 'You know! Brown Owl!' she informed me with the most unjustifiable indignation at this. And me an information officer.

August 29 Thursday

It appears that various social groups would like their own specially designated section within the new stadium and it is obvious that some groups have more chance than others do. Pensioners, for instance, could well have their way whereas the Brownies are probably wasting their time.

Sensible suggestions include an area for swearing and belching, a corner for fat people, a place for people with particularly long legs, a section for people who would still find something to moan about even if we win the European Cup, and an isolated seat for Taff.

August 30 Friday

I was in the Ivy House this evening, having quite an animated discussion with Tonka about which member of our class at school could blow his nose the loudest, when I was interrupted by a woman in a bandanna.

She said she was worried that my genius was impeding my facility to live and love, that my whole-hearted approach to my art was dehumanising me, and that I should allow the warm light of friendship to melt the solitude of creativity.

It turned out that she had got the wrong bloke as I apparently have the same jacket as this creative genius who designs garden furniture in Witherwack. It was nice while it lasted, even if I had no real idea what she was talking about.

September 3 Tuesday

There was considerable excitement in and around my hut today, owing to the arrival and erection of the first pieces of steel yesterday, which means that our new stadium is not just a hole in the ground any more. Hurrah! Steel appeal!

'Look at that!' drooled one man to his mate as he ogled some girders. 'Steel!'

'Yeah, steel,' replied his equally salivating friend.

'Yep, that's steel alright,' reiterated the first.

'Aye, you're not wrong about the steel,' confirmed the second.

Having firmly established that there was indeed steel on site, they returned to work happily, congratulating themselves as they went on their perspicacity. They rang me an hour later to confirm that it was steel they had been looking at.

September 4 Wednesday

Among the many people at the hut today were three snotty school children who had reams of questions for me as they were doing a project on the new stadium. Had they known of the abject standard of the projects I used to hand in at school they might not have been so keen to seek my help, but they seemed quite satisfied with my answers.

By the afternoon though, rumour had spread around the school that I was available to help with projects, and one brat who was studying English came in to ask for an example of tautology. So I called him a half-witted, pea-brained, pig ignorant waste of an education, which he merely took to be an outpouring of abuse. Mind you, it was.

September 5 Thursday

For some reason, most of the questions I waffled my way around today concerned the whereabouts of the sun and people would not be fobbed off by me just pointing upwards for a bit. They needed to know whether or not they would have to wear a cap on the 16th of August next year. I do not know if it is extreme optimism or pessimism that makes them think they will have to combat blinding light and searing heat in the new stadium. Sunderland is hardly noted for either.

Others have complained that the atmosphere at matches will be tainted by the lack of discomfort and that they will probably have to sit in a murky puddle just to improve the general ambience.

September 6 Friday

Attention was diverted from the stadium this afternoon by one of nature's wonders.

A heavy burst of rain was quickly followed by brilliant sunshine with the result of an impressive rainbow. Everyone in the hut exclaimed in unison, 'Ooh look, an impressive rainbow!'

How right they were.

With an educated guess, I would have said that this rainbow's accompanying crock of gold would have been somewhere in Thompson Road. Even though I am a bit strapped at the moment, I had no thoughts of wandering round to collect it as I would not expect a crock of gold to last even as long as a new Ford Escort over there. It will have been spent in the Colliery Tavern by now.

September 7 Saturday

British Summer Time has officially ended which means that Autumn is now upon us and my flip-flops have been put away for another year. It is time to take stock of the year, of life, of friends and relations and of the future.

Well it is if you're a big puff. The rest of us just plant some marrows then get down to the pub.

September 8 Sunday

Sunderland were on Sky TV this afternoon and our goalless home game with West Ham will be forever etched on the minds of football fans everywhere as it was about the most boring game ever to be inflicted on a television audience.

The high point of the whole programme came before the game, when the cameras came to show a breathlessly waiting world the inside of my visitors centre. I am sure we did not disappoint.

However, to beam images of the hut to a satellite somewhere in the geostationary orbit, about 22,000 miles above the Earth's surface, then bounce the signal back through the thermosphere, stratopause, ozone layer and ionosphere, then into the Howard Arms, about 400 yards from where it started, seems like a bit of a waste of technology to me.

September 9 Monday

Unusually for a Monday, I had to go to work where I was introduced to a chap called Chris Collingwood who is the new ticketing manager.

He has joined us from Queen's Park Rangers, something that he told me through a clenched grin although I don't know why. QPR may have struggled of late, but compared to the engineering company that I left in July they can put out a far better side. In fact, they are probably not that much worse at engineering and I am not just being bitter because I left two packets of fig rolls there.

September 11 Tuesday

Andy Gordon lent me his video of Sunday's game. Understandably, I skipped past the parts that featured the actual football and rewound to the parts that might have featured me.

My hut was given a good airing, but the only part of me to appear on the screen was my indistinctive left elbow, but the good news is that Sky reporter Nick Collins began his spiel in front of my car, which could well have sent its value spiralling up to the £600 mark. As seen on TV and all that.

September 13 Friday

I discovered today that discussions have taken place to suggest ways in which to jazz up the visitors centre. One idea was to display the First Division Championship trophy in there, a notion that was understandably and almost immediately abandoned. I have to take the video home every night at present to beat the burglars and much as I like the thought of taking the trophy too, perhaps with some nice daffs in it to admire while I have my tea, it is not really practical.

Besides, I would only be tempted to be dangerously ostentatious with it, taking it with me to the Spar when I went out for gravy granules, or sitting with it on my knee on the bus down to the Ivy House.

September 14 Saturday

Dealing with the general public, as I do, I am continually surprised by the propensity of some people to moan. This afternoon, an old bloke asked me about the new pitch, to which I enthused about the reinforced grass roots and the thermostatically connected under-soil heating, which means that snowy white pitches and postponed games in the winter will become a thing of the past.

This was responded to with a 'Harrumph!' (I am not sure of the spelling). This whinging old buzzard had found disgruntlement on two counts. First, he feels that atrocious conditions are part of what makes English football the modern day gladiatorial spectacle that it is, a weak reason. Second is that he likes the orange ball, a preposterous reason.

A long day and we also lost one-nil at Derby County.

September 18 Wednesday

Tonka is in the midst of a week off, so he was keen to frequent a nightclub. We pondered where all of the poets, painters and philosophers might be. Obviously they are unlikely to go to a place called Pzazz, so we went there.

We did very well to blend in with the rest of the clientele, despite neither of us being a hairdresser or an apprentice welder. There seems to be a theme for the disc jockey's play list to follow, so it was a pity that we had obviously stumbled in on Rubbish Night.

September 21 Saturday
Steve Agnew stylishly sorted out Coventry City this afternoon, but before the game three of their followers came into the hut for a neb.

When the fixture lists were published, the first away game they pencilled in was Sunderland. It seems that our present home is such a dilapidated, seatless dump that waves of nostalgia were incurred in them, as they savoured the anticipation of standing for two hours without a roof to protect them and only mince and air pies to keep them going.

Sadly for them the weather kept fine, but at least the game was dull. Further proof of their masochism was amply demonstrated by their return to Coventry.

September 22 Sunday
Tottenham lost at home to Leicester City this afternoon.

I only mention this as I saw the only Tottenham supporter of my acquaint, lager swilling *Echo* hack Rob Freeth, who was expressing sporting sentiment along the lines of 'We can't complain, we were beaten by the better team.' These conciliatory notices were taken as a lack of commitment by Taff and he was incensed, which is not rare. He demanded to know of Rob what had happened to the traditional responses of being bitter and twisted in defeat, then punching the occasional child on the way home. Rob is evidently one of the new breed of supporters who have no respect for the game's sacred rituals.

September 23 Monday
As ever, my day off was a relentless slog of lying down, drinking tea. I had been doing this for about an hour when I was alarmed to realise that I could not reach the television remote control.

We do not have a dog, so I asked Bethan but she was too preoccupied with pretending that the dining room furniture was a corporation bus. This left me with only one reasonable method of retrieval. Psychokinetic energy. Yet even this did not work. In fact it proved to be singularly unwise as not only did the thing not budge an inch, but my eyebrows began to ache.

In the end I took up the last resort and went back to bed.

September 24 Tuesday
Excitement mounted at work today when I received a parcel which I knew contained our updated video. I was positively animated at the prospect of having different music to accompany the pictures. Quivering

18

with anticipation, I thrust the cassette into the machine and stood back to listen.

As the first chord struck, my heart sank immediately from an Olympian height as I instantly recognised the same old tinny, cheesy, cheap and nasty, soulless, grating, naff, galling and offensively godawful racket that has been assaulting my ears since July. In fact if pushed, I would go as far as to say that I am not keen on it. At least I have proved that if a point needs to be laboured then I'm your man.

Tonight we knocked Watford out of the League Cup, but I would have preferred some new music.

September 25 Wednesday

I strode out of my hut for a gulp of fresh air and to take in the panoramic splendour of Kingston Windows Ltd car park, when who should approach me with a jolly trot but Peter Reid. I did not recognise him at first, but he seemed pleased to see me so obviously he knew who *I* was.

'It's great isn't it!' he chirped with child-like Scouse enthusiasm. This would have been a resounding enough compliment for any car park, let alone the humble effort of Kingston Windows Ltd., had he not instead been referring to the fast developing new stadium.

I am well aware of the name-dropping overtones of this entry, but then how else would I get cheap double-glazing?

September 27 Friday

It was my birthday today, so Liz and I headed for London to see Redge and Rachel and to undoubtedly watch Sunderland humiliate Arsenal tomorrow. Tonight we had a vast Chinese meal followed by a copious glug down Drury Lane. How original.

Later in the lift at Covent Garden tube station, we had to listen to people eulogising over tonight's performance of *Cats*, the watching of which, they opined, was a fulfilling experience in a musical, dramatic and spiritual sense. My counter opinion, that it was shite, was commendably ignored as they had rightly deduced that my view had emerged from a position of lager and total ignorance.

However, it was still gratifying to see them being beaten up by the *Starlight Express* fans that skated off a train to ambush them.

September 28 Saturday

Sunderland's game at Highbury this afternoon was the first game started by the Arsenal captain Tony Adams since he publicly admitted to having a drink problem. The visiting supporters rewarded his bravery with a hearty chorus of 'Who drank all the beer?' and comments such as, 'Puff! He probably only drinks the same as us!'

He has joined Alcoholics Anonymous, who are clearly not as anonymous as they used to be if the mass media coverage of this is anything to go by.

In the match itself, it transpired that the traditional eleven-a-side game has been deemed passé by Sunderland, who showed great footballing innovation by cunningly having two players sent off in the first half.

The plan was not without teething troubles as we lost two-nil, but these masterly tactics will not be thwarted when we play against seven.

September 29 Sunday

For the journey home this afternoon, Liz and I were accompanied by Tonka, Taff and Gerard Callaghan, and a sorry looking outfit they were too.

At a few miles past Peterborough, a loud, grating, wheezing noise filled our carriage and just as we were about to debate the issue of why someone had pulled the communication cord, it was pointed out that this unseemly racket had been caused by Gerard snoring.

He was significantly behind on his sleep having snuggled down in Regent's Park last night as a result of having about seven pence for a taxi. If only more of my associates were as romantic and swashbuckling as he.

September 30 Monday

Having gone a gruelling 48 hours without either watching football or entering a pub, we descended upon the Ivy House to watch Newcastle play Aston Villa.

About 20 minutes into the game and just inside the Villa half, a Mag had clearly infringed the rules and as a result Taff began to resemble the Warner Brothers' Tasmanian Devil as he leapt up and screamed 'Foul! Free kick! Penalty! Yellow card! Send him off! DEATH SENTENCE!!!'

An impartial observer may have construed this as somewhat draconian for someone who had merely strayed offside, but the general level of intolerance was not far below Taff's own high benchmark and his eloquent outburst gained warm support, although not among those who favoured stronger measures.

October 1 Tuesday

Bitter-sweet emotions washed over me today when I ceased to be the best footballer of all the people in the hut. First came a chap I used to go to school with called Martin Madgwick, who is remembered not so much for the accuracy of his shooting so much as the velocity of it which dented several teachers.

But perhaps even more significant was the visit of former Sunderland and England player, Eric Gates. To immortalise the moment, I asked him to sign the visitors book, which would have been a more worthy souvenir had his handwriting matched his ball control. The name of 'Oric Carol' commands even less respect than that of Martin Madgwick these days.

October 2 Wednesday

I went down to Middlesbrough tonight for a guided nosey around their Riverside Stadium and jolly nice it is too.

I was shown to their boardroom where I immediately sat at the head of the table, not to fulfil delusions of grandeur, but so that I could pick my nose and leave the results beneath the Chairman's swivel chair.

Later I was down the changing rooms, where by chance I happened to sit on a section of bench used by Juninho on a match day. I had a clear opportunity to shove his flip-flops under my coat to take as an illegal souvenir, but I did not bother as they were way too small for me and would not have allowed much growing room for Bethan's feet either now that she is almost four.

October 3 Thursday

I was hovering around the site offices this afternoon and casting my simpleton's eye over an architect's drawing. The most interesting feature on it was the vomitory which is an opening for crowd access and egress. The word comes from the Latin *vomitoria* which was an entrance to a Roman amphitheatre.

This diary entry is dripping with culture, yet my interest was really only aroused by the proximity of the word *vomitory* to *vomit* and no entry should be dripping with that.

I shall have a further rummage among the drawings; there could be any number of nearly rude words awaiting discovery.

October 4 Friday

Another star descended from the heavens to grace my hut this afternoon in the form of Sunderland's gifted centre-half, Richard Ord. I did not notice him at first as I was preoccupied with gawping at his wife who was rather nice. In fact, I only realised it was him when I saw them getting into a car marked, 'This is Richard Ord's car so there!' or such like. Had I spotted him earlier I could have asked him when he would be sent off next.

October 5 Saturday

For the first time, I was actually inside the new ground today, or what there is of it so far. The East Stand had an especially eye catching vomitory, but I was most struck by the view from the back of the stand which overlooks the front window of the Colliery Tavern.

With the utilisation of a decent pair of binoculars and some quite complex communications technology, there are some interesting possibilities for cheating at dominoes. Perhaps the club should mention this in a brochure as otherwise the East Stand overlooks precisely bugger all.

October 6 Sunday

The plan that I formulated yesterday for a complex telecommunications system to cheat at dominoes with a wired for sound view of the Colliery Tavern was today thwarted by some devilish counter technology when they closed the curtains.

Yet, perhaps an even more important development than a man drawing the curtains in a pub, is the naming of the South Stand.

The Metro Radio Stand, as it will be, has been sponsored for an undisclosed seven figure fee. So it could be anything from nine million quid, down to £112.87½ and a bottle of Merrydown Cider.

The future looks rosy in all but cheating at dominoes and even this may turn out not to be important.

October 8 Tuesday

In another day of hut related jollity there was much debating, ruminating, pondering, humming and hah-ing as to where to sit in the new stadium when it is opened.

This morning the second most cynical bloke in the world came in. A perfectly healthy and able-bodied bloke, he was hoping to be struck with some sort of affliction by the beginning of next season, as wheelchair users can purchase a season ticket for half-price.

The number one most cynical bloke in the world came in the afternoon and declared a strong interest in acquiring a seat immediately behind a wheelchair enclosure, as he does not like the people in front of him to stand up during the game.

October 9 Wednesday

People are pretty close to fever pitch anyway when they enter the hut, but today the excitement was almost palpable with the news that the grass seed has now been sown. When I told people of this stunning development, they would let out an admiring gasp before rushing to the window to watch it grow, somewhat impatiently I thought.

The same two blokes who had been in on the 3rd of September to gaze lovingly at the steelwork returned today to give the same affection to the grass.

'Grass, eh. Who'd have thought it?' asked one of them as I sat there marvelling at someone who could be surprised by the presence of grass on a football pitch.

October 10 Thursday

For the second time this month, I felt the tingle of privilege that can only be brought about by meeting a celebrity. Hard on the heels of former international Eric Gates last week, a current international was today strutting around the hut in the shape of Eddie Harrison. Not that I am in the habit of name-dropping you understand.

Eddie recently turned out in goal for the England Firemen team against their Scottish counterparts at Anfield. This was a two-one win for England, a weighty triumph, even allowing for the fact that the Scots had come straight from putting out a large furniture warehouse. The 37 strong crowd certainly had the free admission's worth.

October 11 Friday

I was half watching a television interview with the actor Peter O'Toole tonight when he made a surprising announcement. Without any reason that is known to me, he declared himself to be a Sunderland supporter. Although, I felt slightly less bewildered when I remembered how much drink he has been through over the years, a basic pre-requisite for most Sunderland supporters.

I do not recall ever seeing him at the match, but it was easy to conjure up the scene of Laurence Of Arabia and Davie Dowell slumped over the fruit machine in the Ivy House singing 'Number one is Gary Rowell . . .' after a skinful of Hooch.

October 12 Saturday

There was no game today, but I still had to venture out to Roker Park for reasons so dull that I can't even remember them myself.

Whenever I enter that place I can always hear an unspoken sentiment of 'Who are you?' from my colleagues. Not without justification either as I am generally stuck in my hut out on the ranch. But there will be none of this aloofness when they remove to the new stadium. They will be coming to me cap-in-hand for information concerning the acquisition of a decent corned beef and onion pasty and, thanks to my intimately detailed familiarity with the happy hour times of the Howard Arms and the Colliery Tavern, I shall become a pivotal member of staff.

October 13 Sunday

One of the hut punters this afternoon was not uncommon in finding complaint with each and every aspect of the new ground. He was in mid-moan about the sky being too low when his wife told him to shut his whinging face and to stop being such a misery guts, much to the appreciation of the other pilgrims present.

Despite almost applauding her myself, I found myself questioning the expression 'misery guts'. I have always found guts to be a rather upbeat and cheerful integral organ, particularly when they have a liberal amount of Hula-Hoops and Wagon Wheels to be going on with. Perhaps I am just quibbling.

October 14 Monday

Middlesbrough were in town tonight. As expected, Fabrizio Ravanelli scored then carried out his unfailingly amusing goal celebration of pulling the front of his shirt over his head running to the corner.

It was therefore a big bag of fun when Craig Russell equalised and the gimmick was copied, not by a player, but by a little fat bloke who leapt out of the Roker end to perform in front of the visiting supporters, with a theatrical wobble of his little belly to embellish the show. He was chucked out of course, but the act itself will be worth its weight in free drinks.

October 15 Tuesday

Lesley Coates appeared in my hut today and delivered the most welcome of all annunciations. Standing in a shaft of light like the Archangel Gabriel, she foretold of the arrival of an updated video, which, more importantly, will have new backing music to accompany it.

This is a triumph for decency and common sense over a cheesy racket that even the Prodigy could not in any way spoil. However, I was not told exactly when this new video would arrive and I may be committed before then.

Meanwhile, another minor historical event took place this morning, when a plukey-faced youth came into the visitors centre and managed to correctly spell the word 'excellent'.

October 16 Wednesday

I was in garrulous form this afternoon as I dazzled an enthralled hut-full with my in-depth knowledge of concrete tonnage and holding-down bolts. However, I could not help but notice that the gazes were not directed at my face but at the midriff region, even though I was clearly the most handsome fellow there. Unable to resist curiosity any longer, I had to look for myself at what was going on down there. My immediate relief at finding that my flies were not undone was all but vanquished upon discovering that the lower four inches of my tie was submerged in my cup of tea. All I could do was wring it out as casually as possible and continue to talk about the pitch's upper root zone.

October 17 Thursday

There was an historically historic ruling in terms of history today, when the High Court decided that Mrs. Diane Blood could not use her late husband's frozen sperm to conceive a child.

The argument was over donor's consent which, the judge said, was not given. This begs the question; if Mr. Blood did not wish to be party to an artificial insemination, why was he doing THAT into a test tube? It also leave us to wonder what they will do with his sperm if not make babies, although I understand it is very good on squeaking hinges.

October 19 Saturday
Sunderland travelled about 350 miles to be thrashed in our game at Southampton, during which we let in three goals, the same amount of breaks in the leg that goalkeeper Tony Coton received. Rumour has it that this was not an enjoyable trip.

October 20 Sunday
A chap of my acquaint named Johnny Everett approached me in the Ivy House and asked for a favour. His dog recently expired whilst ascending Tunstall Hill in hot, but ultimately unsuccessful pursuit of a Morrison's carrier bag. Johnny being a fervent Sunderland supporter as well as an animal lover, wanted me to use my supposed influence to discreetly scatter the ashes over the pitch at the new stadium. I lied about seeing what I could do for him.

Thankfully he did not have the urn with him, otherwise he would have left me in the companionship of dog remains for the evening, and being on the childish side after a few drinks, I would only have sprinkled them in people's crisps.

October 21 Monday
'Twas a night in for me and being a reliably inactive sort, I spent the evening channel flicking.

A film called *The Beast That Drank Satan's Blood* unsurprisingly turned out to be of the horror genre, so I switched to another flick called *Thoroughly Unpleasant Happenings In The Graveyard At Midnight* which was more of the same. When the only other alternative turned out to be a movie called *Frankenstein Meets The Werewolf In A Transylvanian Laboratory Under A Full Moon In The Mist And In A Thunder Storm Too*, I began to feel that perhaps I was not being given the range of choice that a viewer deserves. As luck would have it I still have *Herbie Goes Bananas* on video.

October 22 Tuesday
I slept in this morning having not slept al all well last night. This was due to a combination of having watched the last 20 minutes of *The Hairy Hand That Maimed From Beyond The Grave With Surprising Efficiency* and eating cheese.

October 23 Wednesday
About a week ago I was asked to compose a piece for the match programme about the progress of the new stadium. Rather bravely, I wrote that the grass is beginning to show, which was actually a hopeful prediction as the seed was sown on October 9th. It was therefore with immense relief that I saw the first shoots appearing.

Over the last few days I have spent a good deal of time on the roof of the hut shooing the pigeons. It was either that or face the wrath of a baying mob of disappointed grass fans, lining up to call me a liar, a charlatan, a humbug and a builder-up of false hopes. My burgeoning reputation as an information officer would have been in tatters.

October 24 Thursday

I had a sneak preview of the match programme for Saturday coming and was rather peeved to find that the part so eloquently composed by my good self has been omitted. So all of yesterday's fretting was pointless. A veritable poke in the eye for lovers of literature and history.

A possible perceived flaw in my précis of the new stadium is that it did not entirely concentrate on the building procedure and was prone to digressions on how lovely the weather had been, where in the vicinity one could purchase a decent corned beef and onion pasty, and saying hello to my friends. The more small-minded of the critics seem to have picked up on this.

October 26 Saturday

We won at home to Aston Villa, but the problem concerning goalkeepers that I mentioned a week ago has descended into crisis.

Today's half-time penalty shoot-out between a fat Sunderland supporter and an even fatter Villa supporter should have used the services of one of the club's young up and coming goalies. But so acute are these difficulties that they were reduced to dragging me from the Howard Arms to stick me between the posts in a quite massive bright yellow jersey.

The initial thrill that I felt at being on the Roker Park pitch for the first time soon evaporated in the midst of my feeble performance before an uncomfortably large crowd. Although in my defence I must say that both penalty takers flagrantly disregarded the 'no blammers' rule.

October 27 Sunday

Today at work it was necessary to read, just to stave off the boredom. Having digested the contents of the newspapers, the last two chapters of a novel and the instructions on the fire extinguishers, I was left to peruse the comments section of the visitors book.

It contains engagingly original epigrams, lauding the new stadium, such as 'Quite nice' and 'Not bad', which were two of the better ones. Subtle and esoteric humour is not entirely overlooked however with comments such as 'Sir John Hall is a bucket of shite!' But even that could not match the romantic lyricism of my favourite message, 'I like the new ground me.'

October 28 Monday

It was Bethan's birthday today and among the multitude of loud and colourful gifts that she received was a video of the *Singing Kettle Wild West Show*, which was almost as unwelcome a present as she could receive as far as I was concerned.

The person who gave it to her does not understand. Perhaps they would if they were to be exposed to an unending repetition of *She'll Be Coming Round The Mountain*. Then they would change their tune (geddit?).

At least Tonka did not carry out his threat of buying her a drum kit and I did not thank him for this either, as he is the type to have his memory jogged by this and remember to inflict it upon us at Christmas. Nice bloke.

November 1 Friday

No less a personage than my old Latin teacher, Bernie Duncan, appeared in my hut this afternoon.

I pointed out to him that what he could see in front of him was not an entrance but a vomitory, which seemed to delight and animate him. 'Ah,' he beamed, 'From the Latin *vomitoria* which was an entrance to a Roman amphitheatre,' before going over to inform his friend who was also a retired Latin teacher and therefore equally impressed. Some people are easily pleased I suppose.

They vacated the hut happy with this development, probably to have a gang fight with some retired maths teachers, or to the Howard Arms to go berserk on pints of snakebite.

November 2 Saturday

Sunderland were cuffed three-nil at Leeds. I was not there and I have not so far seen any television coverage or talked to anyone who travelled, but there is no doubt that we actually deserved to win easily.

November 9 Saturday

There was no football this weekend, which was a pity because if we had played we would have won easily.

November 12 Tuesday

One of the directors, Mr. McDonnell, conducted a small press conference in the hut this morning to announce the 'Brick In The Wall' scheme, whereby supporters can buy a personalised imprinted brick in the new stadium, provided that your name has less than 20 letters in it.

The idea has gone down well with almost everyone apart from a bloke I got talking to in the Ivy House this evening called Vantratoriafentis Shostakovitch, who was most annoyed by the matter. Although old VS, as his friends are allowed to call him, has always been known to work on a short fuse.

November 13 Wednesday

Word has travelled rapidly about the bricks. All that anyone said to me in the visitors centre today was a hearty cry of *'Briiiiiiiicksss!!!!!'*

No one is interested in anything else at present. It would appear that bricks are cool, super, fab, groovy, hip and happening. Bricks are the new rock and roll. Bricks are life. Bricks are the future. Bricks are twenty-five quid from the hut.

Many of them are being given as stocking fillers, which, apart from being hard lines on the stocking is a sign of the changing times. If anyone had given me a brick for Christmas when I was a lad I would have thrown it back at them around the forehead area. These days they are clamouring for them.

November 14 Thursday

Brick mania continued unabated today, which must be a bit of a head turner for the marketing men. They are not Cabbage Patch Bricks or Bat bricks or Teenage Mutant Ninja Bricks. They are just bricks.

Of course there must always be a dissenting voice and it droned its whinging way into my ear just after lunch today. This bloke was having a right old moan about having to pay for a brick. I calmly explained that there is another scheme operating in conjunction, whereby people who have no desire to purchase a brick can seize the opportunity to not bother. A once in a lifetime opportunity. We really have thought of everything.

November 15 Friday

I managed to get myself on television again today, although it was in one of my less swashbuckling roles.

The club has struck up a reported million pound agreement with a company called Lindley Catering to feed and water the masses from next season, which was good news for all concerned except me. I was called upon to stand in front of what will be the South Stand, dressed as a waiter to pose for photographs with Bob Murray and the chairman of Lindley, bow-tied and with a towel draped unconvincingly over my left arm. Simultaneously grinning, freezing and masquerading as a wine waiter are all in a day's work for Wearside's leading information officer.

Better pies are on the way.

November 16 Saturday

We lost at Tottenham, but before very long we will have a better stadium than they do, with better pies and bricks with names on. Ha!

November 23 Saturday

The green shoots of recovery that politicians go on about are once more apparent at Roker Park. The mighty Sheffield Wednesday were flicked back down to South Yorkshire by an Andy Melville pile driver. Oh yes. So let's hear that final score again. Sunderland 1 Sheffield Wednesday 1.

Hang on . . .

November 24 Sunday

Misfortune befell my hut today. A line of visitors was gazing intently and lovingly at the beginnings of a cantilevered roof when they suddenly became a foot shorter. The floor had collapsed.

'Is that supposed to happen?' asked one prize thicko who appeared to think that we had acquired the visitor centre from Alton Towers. The good news was that this enabled me to throw everyone out into the street and close early.

November 25 Monday

Bethan fell off a dining room chair that she was climbing this evening, which was met with loud guffaws from me, as she is always doing things like that. I felt more than a tinge of guilt a couple of hours later when we left casualty with her arm in a sling after the doctor told me she had broken her wrist. No amount of Dolly Mixtures made me feel any better.

November 26 Tuesday

News of Sunday's accident has travelled fast. On my way to Roker Park today I saw a bloke on the corner of Wreath Quay Road selling t-shirts with the legend, 'I Was In The Hut When The Floor Collapsed'. The wheels of commerce move quickly round our way.

November 30 Saturday

Sunderland won 3-1 at Everton today. I hesitate to describe this as a shock result, but a bloke I know called Alan Charlesworth decided to have a party tonight

Gerard Callaghan and his better half Rachel were there and she was bemoaning the fact that she has failed to gain a single mention in this diary so far, so one can only surmise that her life has seen a depressing privation of honours and accolades thus far. She even contemplated showing her knickers to Taff to create a noteworthy event, but even that would not have been enough to secure an entry when pitted against the poetic quality of Alan's sausage rolls, which I had intended to write about in more detail.

December 7 Saturday
Sunderland's recent surge for the championship was hindered by a home defeat to Wimbledon. This was all very depressing, as was the failure of the referee, Mr. Burge, to send off Vinnie Jones. Admittedly Vinnie did not actually foul anyone, but the crowd had paid good money to see it.

December 10 Tuesday
The morning at work was quite a difficult one as I spent all of it agreeing with a succession of pensioners that it really was marvellous what they could do these days, but now it was all about money. I remember when Shack . . . etc.

December 15 Sunday
The nation placed down a tray of tea and sandwiches and plumped up the cushions at five minutes to four, because once again Sunderland were on television. This turned out to be even better than the game with West Ham on September the 8th, as we beat Chelsea three-nil (honestly). Chelsea seem to prefer to sulk when it gets as cold as this and so it proved.

The afternoon was marred for me, however, when I was harangued in the street by a man with a clipboard. He had whipped up a petition, taking a great deal of time and effort in doing so. The protest is not concerned with poverty, unemployment, Third World debt, crime, nuclear testing, housing conditions or even animal welfare. No, away with such fripperies! This particular demo was concerned with the new club crest.

I politely declined to sign the petition on the very reasonable grounds that I don't give a penguin's poo, but this only inflamed him further. 'I see! You've taken Murray's penny now have you!?', which was not an entirely unreasonable comment as I am actually not on much more than that.

December 21 Saturday
The shortest day. 24 hours. Beat that! (see June 21st for nearly the same joke, and may I say how nice it is to be able to use it on a twice-yearly basis).

And may I say how un-nice it is to lose heavily at Manchester United. It was not difficult to predict this and so I attempted to avoid radio commentary. To do this I went for a nose around the shops, but every one I entered had a radio and it seemed that each time I picked up another item to examine, we had let another goal in.

By the time I had finished examining items it was twenty to five and too late for a comeback, so I trudged off home to rue my decision to enter that pick n' mix shop.

December 25 Wednesday

As today was Christmas Day, we commemorated the birth of Our Saviour in the traditional manner - by all coming back to our house to see how much drink we could hurl down our necks and remain vertical. God bless us one and all.

Peter Caine's karaoke machine was a great success, although I now have quite some disdain for *Mack The Knife* after it had been brutalised on no fewer than four occasions by the untalented Gerard Callaghan.

The other negative element to the occasion was that Bethan could not get to sleep, so Liz suggested that I persuade our guests to wind down the karaoke in favour of witty and edifying conversation, there being a first time for everything and what not. She was not therefore best pleased to enter the living room and find me on it.

December 26 Thursday

I scraped myself out of bed then toddled off to the match where Sunderland were a fair lump better than Derby County and won two-nil.

There are those who insist that the new stadium is unnecessary and that Roker Park can be redeveloped, but retain its 'character'. Redge, who was with me this afternoon, begs to differ.

We had gone downstairs at half-time to savour the Premier League fare on offer, which was confined to Twixes, Mars Bars and Kit-Kats but nothing for grown ups. But the coup-de-gras of tawdriness and tat was when we walked past the infamous 'coconut shy', a row of men's heads gazing out at the panoramic view of the underside of the Roker End while relieving themselves, unseen below.

One gentleman in this exclusive row managed to make the event more gruesome still by waving to his friend with his free hand and bellowing to his friend over a blasé crowd of semi-interested onlookers, 'Kenny! *Kenny!* Gerrus a pie will ya!'

'The sooner we leave here the better,' was Redge's reaction.

December 28 Saturday

We lost 2-0 at West Ham, but surely no one will mind that at Christmas.

December 31 Tuesday

I came out of the pub with four friends tonight and we decided to brave the elements and walk back to our house. But Fate intervened when a five-seater taxi pulled up in front of us. What joy! I decided there and then that 1996 was going to be a happy and glorious year from then on, although as there was only an hour and a half of it left by that stage, it was best not to get too carried away with this notion.

It turned out not to be an especially accurate prophecy anyway. When I got home I found that our Hogmonay supply of Twiglets was woefully

31

inadequate and that what was left was soon to be routinely scoffed by Redge and Taff. I shall try not to let this spoil 1997.

1997

January 1 Wednesday

New Year's Day, so Liz, Bethan and I lay in bed until lunch time and then lounged around the place eating biscuits, partially watching Sunderland's two-two draw with Coventry City on television and partially watching *Willy Wonka And The Chocolate Factory* on the other television. The football coverage was not much cop, but that's Ceefax for you.

Having therefore successfully kept the flame of tradition burning brightly, we then really moved into top gear by putting a cheese and tomato pizza in the oven and boiling the kettle, though I must admit that when all this was over I had to go and have a bit of a lie down. The only down side to all this was that my New Year's resolution, to take things easy, has already been transgressed.

January 2 Thursday

Back to work at the sacred place the infidels call the Sunderland AFC Visitors Centre, although it remains the Hut to those of us more intimately acquainted with it. I was accompanied by my new radio headphone set which fully enables me to ignore the general public by blasting my ears with the hot sounds of the Shipping Forecast. Bad news for Dogger today I'm afraid.

January 3 Friday

I arrived at work, bursting at the seams to pass on new stadium related information to an insatiable public. Jackie, who runs the shop end of the Hut, was there before me and ready to regale me with the tale of how she had to be taken to casualty last night with a swollen jaw. Eeeurgh!

The swelling had gone down by this morning, but I was perturbed to find that the jaw was back in complete working order with no prospect of it being wired up. Jackie is a lovely woman, but I had a hangover and my ears needed liberation by wire.

January 4 Saturday

This afternoon I gave a guided tour around our half-built new stadium to hypochondriac and all round pessimist, Peter Cain.

After I had persuaded him that the West Stand, an imposing edifice consisting of thousands of tonnes of concrete, steel and rivets (as well as having 30m foundations), was unlikely to collapse beneath the weight of three people, we took the stairs up to the top, pausing to check his heart rate after each three steps.

'Well,' he articulated, 'I wouldn't want to be the first person to be killed in the new stadium.'

Which is not unreasonable, although I resisted the temptation of asking him if being the second would be any better.

Later I went to a pub in Washington to watch Sunderland draw at Arsenal in the FA Cup, courtesy of a Norwegian satellite being utilised in a legally dubious manner. All the lads down the Ivy House tonight thought I was pretty darned hard. Replay next Wednesday.

January 5 Sunday

I was out with the chaps tonight and we formulated ideas for 'Jaunty' Jim Fox's forthcoming birthday. Jim claims that he does not have birthdays - not because he is remarkably youthful, but because he is remarkably miserable and regards any kind of enjoyment and frivolity as a capital offence. So it will cause him no end of irritation to find a large mound of bright and cheery cards in his porch on the morning of the 18th.

Perhaps we are all misjudging him and he will be in the Ivy House that evening, dressed as a nun or perhaps a cucumber, leading the singing and joyously slapping assorted backs.

I doubt it though.

January 6 Monday

'Twas the Epiphany today, one of the most notable dates in the Christian calendar as it is so difficult to say without teeth.

I took Bethan to the soft play area where she struck up a friendship with a young chap who was also about four years old. Amid the crescendo of giggles that accompanied the two of them throwing an inflatable parrot at one another, I thought it only right that I ask him what his prospects were. He merely gave me a blank stare, but I soon saw for myself how inappropriate he would have been as a possible suitor when it became apparent that he could not even put on his Christmas cardigan without considerable assistance from his grandmother. Rubbish or what?

January 7 Tuesday

An infrequent visitor to the Hut is a flabby black Labrador whose only interests in life are licking people's ears and chocolate. Inappropriately, he is named Tyson after the thoroughly unpleasant heavyweight boxer.

Today he came bounding through the door in a gleeful (and ultimately successful) search for Kit-Kats, dressed as he often is in his Sunderland home shirt. I kid ye not. Not surprisingly, this was to the bemusement of our visitors. One woman gave a loud, disapproving tut then said to her husband, 'You'd think they'd get him a new one,' and she had a point. Tyson's shirt went out of date when we were relegated in 1991 and now looks rather frayed, especially around the collar and front paws.

January 8 Wednesday

Kevin Keegan finally ran away from his job today, so obviously the local media had a rescheduling of programmes usually only reserved for assassinations and declarations of war. The streets of Tyneside are awash with tears.

The problems brought about by his decision are manifold. Most of the pets in Newcastle will only answer to 'Keegan' as is true of a good many of the children. Most of the tattoos are now superseded and the people who make Sugar Puffs will have their work cut out to produce such high quality commercials without their star thespian.

True to form, Kevin was too dignified to storm out of yet another press conference, proving himself to be above all of that by not bothering to have one at all. I shall miss his good grace and gorgeous hair.

January 9 Thursday

Upon arriving at work this morning I saw my friend Dave Irwing trudging unhappily back from the site office. I must stress that he is not a spiv or anything, but he had been to see if he could sell them some turnstiles as he had a job lot on them.

I would have bought one myself, but it would be quite cumbersome in our porch. This is a pity as it would have been invaluable in keeping out undesirables at our Christmas party, although I would have had trouble in paying the little man who operates it.

After what was clearly a most fulfilling day at work, I came home and surprised even myself with how many Hob-Nobs I ate.

January 11 Saturday

The first home game of the year duly arrived this afternoon. Sunderland's mission, which they chose to take, was to give Arsenal a thrashing-and-a-half.

In an enthralling encounter, which can only be described as an advert for football, Sunderland did as expected and slaughtered their ten remaining men 1-0 courtesy of an eye catching own goal. There is nothing like panache, including this.

What was memorable was the PA announcer's goal-scoring proclamation. 'Sunderland's first goal of the afternoon . . . ' he bellowed rather hopefully but gleefully ' . . . was from *TONY ADAMS!!!*' This was more than a little unethical, which of course meant that it was appreciated all the more. Mr. Adams has kept a creditable silence on the incident.

January 12 Sunday

To celebrate yesterday's epoch defining victory over Arsenal, we went for a jolly good night out where I heard a quip that was so feeble and awful that I wish I had made it myself. Shamelessly earwigging this conversation,

I heard about some chap who evidently the chicks would die for. He was a poultry farmer.

January 13 Monday
I read today of a forthcoming film called *Some Mother's Son* which controversially sympathises with the IRA hunger strikers of the early 1980s. But who couldn't sympathise with them. They must have been famished.

I doubt if I could ever have been a hunger striker. Quite apart from having to be a convicted terrorist, they must also possess an iron will, be principled, resilient and prepared to die. And certainly not be the type of person who would sneak over to the biscuit jar in order to guzzle a few custard creams to keep him going. Another drawback to being a hunger striker is that they had absolutely no feel for interior design if that horrible brown wallpaper is anything to go by.

January 14 Tuesday
Days after the event, the media continues to be impressed by the antics of a bloke called Tony Bullimore who was rescued at great expense from a self-inflicted watery grave after failing to sail single-handedly around Australia in a waste paper basket or something. This is about as clever and useful as eating soup through the nostrils and nothing like as much fun.

It has been suggested that it was this type of spirit that drove Columbus, Drake and the like to seek out new lands. But this is not strictly true because as far as I know Australia has already been discovered. Meanwhile, those of us who opt to stay in the pub and not inconvenience anyone are not given the credit we deserve.

And so to bed.

January 15 Wednesday
There came a point at work this afternoon when we had gone for 23 minutes without tea and dunkies, so immediate remedial action was taken.

When the tea arrived, Jackie looked into my cup and turned her nose up then said, 'Urgh! I don't know how you can drink it like that.'

Which was a wholly peculiar comment to make considering that she had made it herself. Not wishing to offend her limited tea-making skills, I drank it anyway, warts and all. Well they looked like warts.

Later it was off to Roker Park to see Sunderland play yet again against Arsenal in the last ever FA Cup game there. The usual tradition of Roker Cup ties was upheld when we lost 2-0. On Saturday, Denis Bergkamp had considerately got himself sent off by macheteing Paul Bracewell. Tonight we saw his darker side as he scored the goal of the month. Bah!

January 16 Thursday

Tonight was set aside for our belated Sunderland AFC staff Christmas party, which is no small ordeal when nobody knows you and vice versa. The trouble was that each department would only talk among themselves and as the department for giving out information on the new stadium consists of me I found myself out on a limb rather.

Only lager could save me.

This meant that my already slim hopes of circulating around the cocktail set and dazzling the bourgeois with urbanity and charm were somewhere between dead and coughing up blood. At least I got to know the bar staff.

January 17 Friday

It was only when I arrived at work this morning that I remembered the hypnotist at last night's party. I was not put under myself, but most of the ticket office staff had been, so I rang them up, ostensibly to ask about the availability of tickets for tomorrow's game with Blackburn, but also to whistle the *Blue Danube* down the telephone to see if they would subsequently become a migrating duck. They didn't. They were no longer in a hypnotic state and their trance-like countenance was attributable to simple boredom.

I wouldn't mind the gift of hypnosis myself, simply to be able to abuse it. I would never be out of Thornton's for a start.

January 18 Saturday

According to studies by the University of Michigan, the universe will cease to exist in 75 trillion years. Cool! This is enough to make most people feel insignificant, but not me. I felt quite hugely important this afternoon when I told three, yes THREE, people that they could not bring bikes into the Hut because their tyres were wet. Admittedly they sneaked back in with them when I went to answer the telephone, but I had made my point.

As if this were not enough heady drama for one day, I then went to watch Sunderland in a heart-stopping 0-0 draw with Blackburn Rovers. I cannot say when our next goal will be sighted, but hopefully it will be some time in the next 75 trillion years.

January 19 Sunday

Tonka and I were sitting in a befittingly dark and cheerless pub tonight when Jim Fox burst unhappily through the door. Being careful not to trip over his face, he stormed over to our table and declared predictably, 'I'm not happy!'

There were three reasons for this latest outburst of gloom. Firstly, he had received a huge pile of birthday cards yesterday, most of which had pictures of fluffy smiley squirrels on them. Then this afternoon Nottingham

Forest had secured an unfavourable home win. But the chief reason for his melancholy is that he is just a miserable git.

I like him.

January 21 Tuesday

An endlessly irritating aspect to being an information officer is that people become rather smug and triumphal if they know something that I don't. 'I know something that you don't!' they say to me triumphantly and smugly at such moments.

And so it was today that a bloke marched up to me in the Hut today, claiming to have superior knowledge of the new pitch. 'Did you know that they put some more fertiliser down this morning?' he asked me, with only the meagrest of effort to suppress his excitement.

When I admitted that I didn't he was delighted and immediately set off outside to inform people that my stadium knowledge was deficient to the tune of 11 tonnes of horse shit.

January 22 Wednesday

I was sitting contentedly in the Ivy House watching (plucky) Stockport take on (star studded) Southampton, when Jim Fox's almost equally saturnine friend Keith declared solemnly to me that people who use the seats in pubs should be shot.

Jim, however, did not agree. Not out of any deference to those who enjoy the mindless thrill of sitting down in a public place, but because this would possibly waste ammunition that should be used on the real enemies of society - people who wear gloves just because it is cold. There is another group that Jim would preserve from being shot, but only because the bullet is too swift a retribution. They are, of course, people who pretentiously say 'lunch' instead of 'dinner'. String 'em up . . .

January 23 Thursday

Sitting in the Red & White Café at lunch time today, trying to wolf down a quite splendid sausage and egg sandwich before any brown sauce could drip out of the sides, I had presumed that I was on my own, so I was somewhat taken aback when I heard someone say, 'Be'ave yourself!' in a menacing Cockney voice.

Then, after a while, the same invisible person urged me to 'Watch that Grant Mitchell!'

The name was not unfamiliar to me, which was why it dawned that I had been listening to the ramblings of the *Eastenders* fruit machine.

They also have a *Popeye* fruit machine which says, 'I'll saves yer Olive!', but the more discerning gambler prefers to lose money on *Eastenders* as it is more gritty and realistic.

January 25 Saturday

Liz and I, among many others, went to Casanova's restaurant to feast upon pizzas and assault the karaoke.

A predictable let down on the singing front was Gerard Callaghan. Undeterred by poor reviews for *Mack The Knife* at Christmas, he proceeded to administer the brutal manslaughter of *To All The Girls I've Loved Before* with his brother Bernie as his accomplice and I could see one woman near the stage shoving away her minestrone soup as they began the second verse.

By the time I got up, my tonsils were lubricated to perfection as I performed a flawless rendition of *Hello Goodbye* to an audibly gasping audience, yet sadly, the Callaghans had by then driven out all of the more reputable agents.

January 29 Wednesday

Leicester City 1 Sunderland 1. The stuff of legends.

January 30 Thursday

In an empty moment at work today, I gazed aimlessly out of the window and had a conversation with myself about the weather as it was such a pleasant day. I concluded that it really was splendid for the time of year, and just as I had done so, my cogitation was spoiled by the sight of some of the biggest snowflakes ever to fall around these parts. Snowflakes which had mystifyingly descended from a clear azure sky.

The mystery was soon cleared up, however, when I saw the words NO FRILLS in bold letters on the side of each snowflake and I realised that the storm had been caused by two steel erectors emptying the rubbish from their pockets after they had spent the morning chomping their way through a family pack of assorted crisps.

January 31 Friday

I was in an excited state for most of today and wanted it to be over with as soon as possible as I begin my holidays tomorrow. I am going to Aston Villa and may even stay there until Sunday.

To irritate the working classes still further, due to my long standing friendship with Sunderland Council's top plumber, Andy Gordon, I shall watch tomorrow's game from an executive box and shall arrive in Birmingham by Ford Fiesta, Tonka's to be precise.

Tomorrow afternoon shall be devoted to football and snobbery. and while I take dainty and gentlemanly nibbles from my chicken-in-a-basket, I shall spare a thought and a glance at those literally and socially beneath me with their cheap seats, pasties and poor vocabulary, i.e. Tonka and Taff.

February 1 Saturday

We arrived in good time to leave our bags at Brummie Mike's house and all was going well until Taff was required in the proceedings as he had Tonka's ticket. Apart from mentioning Warwickshire, he had not really narrowed down his location.

The most serious consequence of this bad planning was that I arrived at the Villa Park Executive-Beautiful-People-Only-And-No-Riff-Raff-Boxes too late for my chicken-in-a-basket. In fact my fellow box members were already on to the rhubarb crumble and custard. Fate is a cruel and fickle mistress.

We lost the game 1-0 too, although I gained some consolation afterwards by annoying the lads with feeble quibbling about the crockery.

February 4 Tuesday

Some time ago, in a vacant moment, I took the trouble to start the rumour that I am a potent literary force. This has now bounced back on me quite regrettably with Lesley Coates asking me to write an update on the new stadium for the internet. The time has therefore come to live up to the lie and so far it is not going well.

Sentences such as, 'Our new ground will make everywhere else look shite' is probably not the kind of subtle marketing angle she had hoped for when she asked me to perform this task, so I amended it to 'Our new ground will make *nearly* everywhere else look shite', but I still couldn't imagine her being completely satisfied with it. Some people are just obsessed with the standard of written English when they would be better served by succinct vulgarity.

February 8 Saturday

Sunderland did not play today as the Premier League is suspended this week. So I spent the afternoon clinging pathetically to the radio, having developed an unhealthy interest in whether Lincoln City had held on against Fulham, or if Ross County could close the gap on Caledonian Thistle at the top of the Scottish Second Division. They didn't.

This sad addiction was reflected in our distinct lack of conversation tonight. We simply do not have enough knowledge of any other subject to form opinions on them. Luckily, someone had been to see Seaham Red Star play Shotton, so he regaled us with a first hand account.

February 9 Sunday

I took the manager of the Ivy House, Bob Fairlie, around our semi-built new stadium and he was by far the most excited person to embark on this tour thus far.

For half-an-hour, all he could do was grin and point and say, 'Look at the seats! Look at the roof! Look at the pitch! Look at the executive upper concourse that will incorporate an array of corporate hospitality facilities!'

Admittedly, this is not an absolutely verbatim account of his comments. He didn't mention the roof for instance, but he was still highly excitable. He used up his camera film in about the first ten minutes in the manner of a Japanese tourist. He did calm down slightly later, but reached fever pitch again as he jumped up and down on the terrace shouting, 'This is my seat! This is my seat!'

February 10 Monday

Over the years I have become quite fanatical about eating my dinner. Today I was so excited by the prospect of this that I began to burst into poetry on the subject;

It's really great to have your dinner
Because it stops you getting thinner
Yes having your dinner is a winner
Even if it was made in Pinner.

If ever a more fitting eulogy was composed in honour of fish fingers and peas, then I know not of it. Then of course, there was cake and custard for dessert;

Afters afters
It fills you to the rafters
If there was any justice
It would win a load of BAFTAs.

I am most pleased with the flawless metre of these stanzas and least pleased at my inability to find a word that rhymes with dessert.

February 11 Tuesday

What better way to commemorate Pancake Day than to scoff a whole pile of them? Reverently of course, it is a religious occasion.

February 12 Wednesday

Ash Wednesday marks the beginning of Lent, which should be 40 days of temperance, abstemiousness and restraint. Unfortunately, Wednesday is an inappropriate day with which to kick off Lent as it is also cheap booze night in Sunderland city centre. As there was also an England match on Sky tonight, the guzzling that was going on really was a slap in the face for temperance, abstemiousness and restraint.

England lost at Wembley to a superior Italian side and our chances of winning the World Cup can be summed up in the two words Batty and David. Still, his inclusion gives all of us hope for a few caps yet.

February 13 Thursday

It is a little known fact that there is a far less well known hut next to mine where three women try to sell hospitality and catering for next season.

They love chocolate with a passion usually only reserved for members of boy bands so it is with a strong feeling of trepidation when I neighbourly ask them if they would like anything from the shops. My back is not what is was and one of them, Jill, can eat a stone of Creme Eggs unaided by oxygen so my fears are not unreasonable.

Still, it is reassuring to know that I can leave women quivering in my wake, even if it was by introducing them to the new limited edition Kit-Kat. Lent is not going terribly well in their hut so far.

February 16 Sunday

Another footyless weekend has passed us by and we are now in an advanced state of cold turkey. In fact we may have to take some drugs just to give ourselves something to do.

February 18 Tuesday

There was the usual smattering of rumours awaiting my arrival at work this morning, all of them absolute piffle.

They emanate from imaginative Care In The Community cases who stand viewing the progress of the new stadium at the end of the fence and gossiping. Today I found out that we have signed Jurgen Klinsman, Peter Reid is now going out with Kylie Minogue, the stadium is two years behind, is sinking into a disused mine shaft and has a poltergeist.

I fervently hope that if I am ever about to be struck on the head with a heavy object, I will not receive a warning from any of these people shouting, 'Look out! You are about to be struck on the head with a heavy object!', because frankly I wouldn't believe them.

February 19 Wednesday

Uncertainty has mounted in the Orient following the death of thousand-year-old Chinese leader, Deng Xiaoping, who fell off his step ladders while changing a light bulb. He must have been important because they put *Watchdog* on a minute late to tell us.

The newsreaders have taken to pronouncing his name as 'Dung' since he officially croaked it. Talk about calling people behind their backs. At least I do it to the living. On the other hand, fancy an otherwise responsible set of parents like Mr. and Mrs. Xiaoping giving their lad a name like Dung.

Still we all went to school with someone who had a funny name - Annette Kurtin, Lance Boyle, Emma Dale and Trevor Arsehole to name but a few.

February 20 Thursday

Intense speculation is now in abundance in the Far East as to who will succeed Deng Xiaoping as leader of China.   Someone with proven leadership qualities would seem to fit the bill.

As all of this coincides with the news that Mick Buxton has vacated the managerial position at Scunthorpe United by mutual consent, who knows what kind of behind the scenes manoeuvrings have taken place? Rumours of a hidden agenda are awash in Scunthorpe, although I tend to think that the Chinese will prefer an appointment of a more internal nature. But you never know he may just go over in a caretaker capacity. I love all of this political intrigue.

February 21 Friday

I stayed in last night, resisting the lure of the bohemian delights of the Ivy House, so that should do me for Lent.

Obviously this entitled me to a good night out and predictably I met Tonka and Taff. On the way to the Dun Cow we were witnesses to a dramatic fire fighting effort at Jackwood Washers, which is likely to be made into a film in years to come. Our local fire brigade stormed in with unshakeable nerve as the flames licked ferociously around their ankles, although it may have been quicker to turn on a tap and leave the plug in the sink.

February 22 Saturday

The City of Sunderland was today reeling from the news of the apocalyptic fire which engulfed Jackwood Washers last night. It was a curious omission from the national news, but still the most talked about incident to occur at the bottom of Hylton Road in the last few weeks, very similar to the *Towering Inferno* but without the tower.

It also gave us an opportunity to talk about something other than football. Our long spell without footy theoretically came to an end this afternoon, but having watched Sunderland's performance against Leeds United (0-1) it is possible to differ.

February 23 Sunday

There comes a time in a chap's life when he sits down and thinks, 'I could murder a Lion Bar'. I personally was struck with this philosophy at precisely a quarter past two this afternoon and I set off from the visitors centre for the shops, battling the elements and bravely facing the wind. I was to regret this, as on the way I saw an even less savoury spitting incident than that of the 11th of August last year.

The blustery conditions made spitting particularly hazardous. One bloke who had obviously made no allowance for the elements ended up with a line of saliva spiralling round the back of his head. This stuck me as odd as he looked like the sort of fellow who would be an experienced hockler, the type who would normally be able to make his phlegm loop-the-loop.

February 25 Tuesday

Bethan may soon be better off by precisely one goldfish. A resplendent young Ivy House barmaid, a filly named Sarah, has moved back to the family nest only to find that her father is resolute on the contentious subject of goldfish. It seems he is perfectly amenable to accommodating dogs, cats, parrots, chimpanzees, wart hogs and the like, but poor old Goldie is out on his ear, if he has an ear.

Sarah's dad has received the official backing of Jim Fox, who applauds the hard line on silent and virtually inanimate pets. 'He's quite right, they're bastards,' he pronounced grimly. Controversial.

February 26 Wednesday

Today saw the funeral of the late Chinese leader, Deng Xiaoping. Plenty of mourners were in attendance so one assumes that there was a lovely spread and a few cans on the go after the burial because he wasn't very popular.

China has had a questionable human rights record under him. He has held the UK to ransom over the repatriation of Hong Kong and was largely responsible for the 1989 Tiananmen Square Massacre. On the other hand they reckon he was a hell of a snooker player.

Furthermore, his judgement was no more fuddled that that referee who gave Chelsea a ridiculous penalty in the Cup against Leicester tonight.

March 1 Saturday

After a dismal defeat to a late goal at Blackburn Rovers this afternoon, Liz and I went to an evening 'do' for the wedding of Keith and Katherine Dunn. To commemorate the occasion of them being welded together they ordered a huge lasagne which guaranteed my presence, invited or not.

March 2 Sunday

Upon opening the Hut this morning, I noticed that the sign giving our opening hours had been vandalised, presumably by a Leeds United supporter as the miscreant had scribbled 'L.U.F.C. ' in permanent marker. I later became convinced that the vandal was indeed a Leeds supporter upon closer examination of the 'F' which looked rather more like an 'E'.

There are not many people who would struggle to spell 'F' properly, but I would imagine that Leeds United supporters are among them.

March 4 Tuesday

Sunderland's last home game against Leeds was not the watershed of awfulness that we all thought it would be. It was easily surpassed in ineptitude by tonight's display against a completely ordinary Tottenham Hotspur.

The crowd booed the pitch, they booed the pies, they booed the programme, they booed the bloke who drew the half-time raffle. They even booed the crowd. Any person or thing vaguely connected with the club was being roundly and routinely abused, extending even to the Hut as I found out after the game. Upon setting literally one foot into the Howard Arms, I was treated to a rousing chorus of 'You can shove your visitors centre up your arse!'

I felt like a real . . . er . . . celebrity.

March 5 Wednesday

Not a good day at work following last night's 4-0 defeat. But doom, gloom, despondency and woe soon gave way to lugubriousness, dismay, mournfulness, cheerlessness, grimness, melancholy and misery. There was not a great deal of joy in the Hut today but plenty of vocabulary.

Today was about the most depressing day at work that I have ever had. The trickle of people who called in did not help my mood either with their frankly crap attempts at cynical black humour. 'It'll be the best ground in the First Division' was the customary jibe, which was nothing short of nauseating as they all presumed that they were the first to say it and they all stood back afterwards waiting for acclaim when a poke in the eye was far more appropriate.

March 7 Friday

Somehow an intellectual was let loose into the Hut this afternoon and given his chance to write his innermost thoughts in the visitor's book, and being by definition abnormal, he paraphrased Howe;

Mine eyes have seen the glory of the building of the ground
Trampling out the vintage where the grapes of wrath are found.

Quite why he could not have written his name and 'Nice job!' or 'Get a striker!' like everyone else will never be known, and I could not bring myself to ask him just in case he told me.

Perhaps he was hoping to impress others with his poetic knowledge. If so he was a miserable failure with the succession of pimply youths who read his comments before squinting and monosyllabically opining that they were 'Shite!'

March 8 Saturday

Having watched Sunderland play on Tuesday and concluding that they would have failed to put a goal past an amputees second eleven, it was a source of some confusion to witness them this afternoon beat Manchester United, double winners, Champions elect, European Cup semi-finalists ad infinitum.

This is quite a silly pattern of behaviour but everyone is most pleased - apart from those who still don't believe that it happened, preferring to think that it was all done by mirrors, a trick of the light or a hologram. I have already given a great deal of thought to the matter and have concluded that it probably did happen, although I am still coming to terms with what went right.

A further anecdote to reach me tonight concerned our mascot Samson The Cat. Standing at the head of both teams as they lined up in the tunnel before kick-off, donned as ever in his black fur, pointy ears and big red nose, he apparently began to point theatrically at his own hooter before turning to the United captain and saying, 'Oi! Look Schmeichel! Same eh?'. This is quite disgraceful.

March 9 Sunday

Jackie has gone for a week-long and completely ill deserved holiday in Tenerife and has been replaced in the meantime by a feisty young local damsel named Natalie.

To use the toilets, she has to go on to the site and therefore wear a safety helmet, but this was to cause her some consternation at the possibility of her hair being flattened. So I had to point out that not wearing a helmet could be counter-productive with regard to keeping her hair in place. In fact her perm could be damaged irreparably if a stainless steel bolt were to be dropped directly on top of her and embedded into her skull. Imagine the split ends. On the other hand it could be a bit of a laugh.

March 10 Monday

Today was Commonwealth Day, but despite the anticipation and excitement usually associated with it, the festive thrill seemed to be missing round here. Perhaps it was the weather, but Commonwealth Day is just not what it was.

March 12 Wednesday

Liz and Bethan were in Sheffield tonight, where Bethan could be spoiled by her grandparents and Liz could watch Sunderland score fewer goals than Sheffield Wednesday.

March 13 Thursday

Today I had an official safety induction, which means that if I go on site and have an accident it is now official, whereas previously I was not entitled to an injury or wound of any description, not even an itch. I contemplated using my newly acquired officialdom to bleed copiously over the East Stand, but in the end decided that this would be abusing the privilege.

The whole induction process took about three minutes with Dave Lennon, although it was an especially rigorous three minutes involving the reading of a sheet of paper. The sheet told me to scrupulously avoid death and disablement as neither are much cop. Then I had to sign my name in my best writing. Otherwise, it was not a particularly challenging exercise.

March 14 Friday

I have often watched the football on television on a Monday evening and heard Nick 'Touchline' Collins say, 'Hi, Nick Collins, Sky Sports, here,' so there was a slightly surreal quality in the Hut today when the very same presenter made me look up from my book by bounding up to me and saying, 'Hi, Nick Collins, Sky Sports, here.'

He wanted some footage of the new stadium to show before Sunday's game at Chelsea, and as I have now been inducted, I was the very man to put on the case.

Nick, as his mates like me call him, was quietly impressed with the place as he ruminated silently whilst picking the remains of a late lunch from his splendid looking moustache, speaking only to tell me not to try so hard to get myself on camera.

March 15 Saturday

Jackie returned to work this morning having completed her holiday in Burma or where ever, and she marked the occasion by presenting me with a duty free Wagon Wheel. It was a while since I had eaten one and frankly I was disappointed. It was titchy.

Worse still, the wrapper misleads one to believe that it has been made beside a camp fire near a giant cactus on the harsh exotic plains of New Mexico, yet a closer examination shows that it came from a factory in Vanwall Road, Maidenhead.

I do not know what the good burghers of Maidenhead suppose a wagon looks like, but their idea differs wildly from mine. A horse drawn skateboard would seem the most likely.

March 16 Sunday

I finished work early and drove off in a barely legal manner to the Ivy House where Sky was showing Sunderland at Chelsea, with touchline comments from Nick 'Personal Friend Of Mine' Collins.

Sunderland blasted two stylish goals past their fashionable (etc) King's Road opponents in a vintage display that sent the fans home happy. The coup-de-grace would have been the prevention of the six goals that were put in at the other end, but you can't have everything.

I missed the television build up to the game including the new stadium footage that Nicky boy (as his closest friends call him) filmed on Friday, but I am assured that I am not featured. Some mate he turned out to be.

March 17 Monday

Today saw a hitherto unseen event when Sunderland signed a player whom people have heard of. Waddle's the name, signing for a knock down fee at the twilight of his career's the game.

Annoyingly, it was also Saint Patrick's Day when everyone celebrates something that has nothing to do with them and they know bugger all about. The Ivy House was packed with people shaking each other's hands to commemorate this most vacuous of occasions. Wearing a plastic leprechaun badge and guzzling a foolish quantity of Guinness does not give anyone honorary citizenship of the Emerald Isle and most of them were about as Irish as Boney M. The top of the morning to them anyway.

March 19 Wednesday

Since Monday, I have become quite childishly excited over the arrival in Sunderland of top footballer, celebrity and all round great bloke, Chris Waddle, so when it was hinted today that I may be called upon to show him around the new stadium, I had to have a Hob-Nob just to remain calm. However, it came down to a toss up between him and a bloke from Chester called Peter who is one of Bernie Callaghan's drinking cronies and guess what . . .

Peter may not be an internationally acclaimed sporting figure for me to boast about meeting, but to his credit he did turn up with a maxi pack of the new chewable variety of Fruit Gums.

March 20 Thursday

One of the women who is to provide the catering at the new stadium failed to mention that she had recently had her photograph taken by the *Sunderland Echo* for a publicity shot. It showed Emma (for 'tis her name) wearing a waitress outfit and a photogenic grin and she was hideously embarrassed at the prospect of being in the paper.

She was hoping to be in an obscure and barely looked at corner somewhere around page 62 and was rewarded with a hardly noticeable seven inches by five colour picture in the diametric centre of the front page. So with any luck no-one will see it. To make her feel better I have stuck the photograph to one of the walls in the Hut. It is not a bad pic really and I like the way her teeth follow you around the room.

March 21 Friday

Halle-Bopp, which sounds like a school disco but is in fact a comet, was in Sunderland tonight. Apparently it is doing the rounds.

It is a magnificent searing mass of celestial matter, a heavenly work of art, a vision of astounding astrological splendour, which will never be seen again in this part of the galaxy during our lifetime, and I missed it because *Play Your Cards Right* was on.

The choice between going outside into the cold and perilously fresh air to see this mound of luminous flying gravel and seeing if two people can name six popular flavours of soup is no choice at all for any self-respecting ignoramus, especially on a Brucie Bonus.

March 22 Saturday

Chris Waddle's Sunderland debut and the game was a one all draw with Nottingham Forest who are even worse than we are. All very disappointing and even I am beginning to concede that our championship hopes are fading.

March 23 Sunday

'Twas Palm Sunday so I washed my hands. Boom! Boom! That, hosanna, was about all that happened today, so please appreciate that I have got my work cut out here.

Probably the most exciting part of the day was raising the flag outside the Hut this morning. This would not have appeared to be a fraught and thrilling activity to the casual observer, what with me only being six rungs up. But given the improbable amount of lager from last night that I was simultaneously trying to keep down, it could be considered as a near death experience. I was certainly rather queasy.

It seemed like such a good idea at the time, such a cheery jape, but I am finished with it now. I will never put that flag up again.

March 24 Monday

Startling news emerged from the end of the fence today when a man came into the Hut and announced that there were no rumours.

I had to sit down to take in this information as I had never known such a thing. I was therefore relieved to discover that the 'no rumours' story was erroneous. It was a mere rumour that there were no rumours. There had been loads of them all along, every one of them stoked with the usual level of veracity. Peter Reid has now dumped Kylie Minogue in favour of the more mature charms of Kate Bush, Andy Melville is on a waiting list for a hip replacement, and the new stadium to be officially opened by Philip Schofield were just for starters.

March 25 Tuesday

The backs of most newspapers have been generous in their praise of Liverpool player, Robbie Fowler, who disputed the awarding of a penalty to his own team in a match at Arsenal last night in what was probably an unprecedented display of honesty for a footballer.

Now I am not one to fish for compliments, but I have on numerous occasions candidly offered my firmest and innermost opinions on the proceedings of a football match and refereeing decisions in particular. Not only that, but I have done so at the top of my voice and with a rich and varied vocabulary without receiving any such eulogies, not even a 'Well said mate'. Sometimes I despair of us strident, foul-mouthed oafs ever being given the credit we deserve.

March 26 Wednesday

I spent too much of the afternoon in a futile argument over the location of west. My interlocutor was insistent that we were building the western section of the stadium in a silly and ill-thought-out area and he was reluctant to acknowledge my argument that we had opted for the tried and trusted arrangement of having west just to the left of east, as is traditional. He did not consider this to be acceptable in a modern sporting arena.

It was reassuring to remember that we were in the Hut and not navigating a ship, otherwise we may have set sail for Seaham Harbour by way of the Cape Of Good Hope.

March 27 Thursday

The racehorse Aldiniti died today so that should stop his gallop.

We were reminded of his famous 1981 Grand National victory and how it was a sporting landmark, a triumph of the human and horse spirit and a highly emotionally charged occasion.

I must confess to feeling a tinge of emotion myself that day, not because I give a toss about horse racing, but because I had placed a hard earned 25 pence on Spartan Missile who finished a heart breaking second. £3.50 I would have had. Still, this is how we gamblers have chosen to live our lives, but I can't help wondering to this day what my life would have been like if the animal had snuffed it 16 years earlier. Kenny Rogers should write a song about me, he really should.

March 28 Friday

Quite cruelly for a bank holiday weekend I shall be working throughout, so the use of the word 'holiday' came in for some stern examination.

This Good Friday was notable only for the laziest ever entry into the visitor's book. The gentleman in question was obviously worn out after writing his name, so faced with the laborious challenge of also putting down his address he eased his mountainous work load by drawing a couple of arrows pointing in the direction of Southwick Road which was where he lived.

I wonder just how much he hates writing his address. That is to say, if I were to face the book in another direction, would he then have to move house?

March 29 Saturday

Part of my duties today included having to answer a stream of inane questions from a vacant looking woman with a protruding bottom lip. For some reason she seemed quite obsessed with the type of clocks that would be visible in the stadium. I told her that we would be reverting to sundials to conserve energy, but my sarcasm was wasted on her. I realised this when she asked me what a sundial was.

When I explained that it was an inanimate device that could display the time during daylight by casting a shadow against the relevant number, she was beside herself with open mouthed admiration. 'Eee! What will they think of next?' she squawked with genuine high regard.

March 30 Sunday

I would not swap the British climate for a seven foot Curly Wurly as it always presents me with an opportunity to moan. Today was warm and dry, with the adverse effect that there was an uncomfortable amount of dust and grit swirling around the site. This in turn meant that unpleasant substances were partially blinding me, being blasted up my nose and creating a filthy and hazardous working environment. Treacherous conditions indeed, but on the plus side, they were conditions that don't half make your Easter egg last longer, albeit more difficult to swallow. The whole of Monkwearmouth really needs a good hoovering.

April 1 Tuesday

After the rigours of sitting around watching Bond movies and scoffing chocolate yesterday, I really could have done with a day off. I thought of staying in bed with the Hut remaining locked up in the fragile hope that my employers would regard it as a jaunty April Fools Day jape. I briefly mused on the possibility of one of the directors ringing me at home to congratulate me on my rib tickling and morale raising tomfoolery, as even the administrators of professional football clubs need their lighter moments.

But it was probably more prudent to ignore the possibility and just go to work as I did in the end. The club has yet to get to grips with the manifold benefits of me staying in bed all day.

April 2 Wednesday

Sunderland's game with Liverpool next week has been put back one day to the Sunday, meaning that we shall have to work a full day on the

Saturday. This was clearly a body blow to Jackie who as a result has had to endure the upheaval and distress that can only be appreciated by others who have known what it is to postpone an appointment at the hairdressers.

She gave an indignant diatribe about the selfishness and lack of consideration that had gone into making this decision. I tried to calm her by pointing out that the switch had been made to accommodate Liverpool's European Cup Winners Cup commitment and not as part of an elaborate conspiracy to sabotage her perm.

April 3 Thursday

Another day, another lot of sighing. The general level of conversation in the Hut today was disappointing to say the least. The most lofty and eloquent plane the banter reached was when the debate reverted to whether cheese was the only flavour of Wotsit available on the market (it isn't).

I'm afraid that shortly after a General Election has been called as well as the discovery of probable life on the Jupiter moon of Europa by an international team of scientists, this was all we could think of by way of discussion.

The atmosphere on Europa has an abundance of nitrogen and carbon, which makes for a distinct likelihood of life out there, so a few jugs of each would not go amiss in the Hut these days.

April 4 Friday

In a less than dramatic career move, I have begun to turn up earlier for work. At the urging of Dave Nicholson, the Project Manager, I have agreed to go into the site offices to do some strutting around. Happily I am adept at appearing important and I spent much of the morning sitting by the window, looking at architects' drawings in the hope that enough passers-by would spot me and recognise me as the vital cog in the industrial machine that I am. This is not a total fallacy as by dinner time I had most of them coloured in. The only difficulty I encountered was in resisting the temptation to hide the plans for the visiting supporters' lavatories, what with me being such a fan of petty vindictiveness.

April 5 Saturday

We played Newcastle United today, so I had to force my breakfast down my neck as I felt so unutterably sick at the very real prospect of being thrashed by them.

Sitting in the pub beforehand drinking and looking at the clock, I felt like Gary Cooper in *High Noon*, only sexier and without a hat and probably a great deal queasier. Watching the game on a screen at Roker Park, thousands of people roared their encouragement, which was really a waste of effort as the lads were actually playing twelve miles away at the Temple of Doom.

Happily, it was not Sunderland who were thumped, quite the opposite as it turned out, with us slaughtering them 1-1, so we shall call it a moral victory. The preposterous ban on visiting supporters continued but not for a man as resourceful as the legendary Davie Dowell who somehow acquired a ticket for the game. He sat silently in his seat, understandably keeping as low a profile as possible. He was succeeding in this until about quarter to three when the teams were warming up. He was let down by his near celebrity status when Sunderland's captain Kevin Ball spotted him in the crowd and gave him a cheery wave and a hearty 'Hello Davie.'

He just about got away with it.

April 9 Wednesday

One of the numerous tasks to fall upon the Project Manager, Mr. Dave Nicholson, was to show Mrs. Molly Gurney around the stadium this afternoon. Her husband, Bobby, was the Robbie Fowler of the 1930s and featured prominently in Sunderland's Championship and FA Cup winning sides of that era.

Dave is a Middlesbrough supporter so I imparted this brief historical outline to him before he set of to meet her so he could pretend not to be ignorant. I could hear him muttering revision on the way out of the office. 'Robbie Fowler of the 1930s and featured prominently in . . .'

He had walked about 30 yards when I remembered with seconds to spare that I had omitted one vital fact, so I bellowed after him, 'Dave! He's dead!', thus saving him from a potentially very embarrassing faux pas.

'How's that rascal Bobby then?' is one pleasantry that under the circumstances should be meticulously avoided.

April 13 Sunday

We lost our rearranged home game with Liverpool this afternoon as was completely expected by all concerned, but is was only 2-1 so we decided to have a bit of a night out on the back of it.

In the Dun Cow tonight we saw a bloke who looked exactly like Swampy the eco-warrior, accompanied by his girlfriend who looked suspiciously like an extra from *The Sullivans*. This was obviously the high point of the weekend and nothing will ever beat it, but on the whole I would rather have beaten Liverpool.

April 16 Wednesday

In the Ivy House tonight I was witness to the less sporting side of our national game. The League Cup final replay between Leicester City and Middlesbrough was on the televisions, although the outcome was of negligible interest to Sunderland supporters. However, we play Middlesbrough on Saturday and Leicester are not yet clear of relegation.

The scenario, therefore, was one of a small cluster of blue shirts at one end of the pub, a handful of red shirts at the other and a huge groundswell of red and white stripes in between, all baying cynically for a half-hour of energy consuming extra time as well as cramp and an horrendous season-ending spate of injuries.

Apparently one of them managed to win the game too, which must have been very nice for them.

April 17 Thursday

I was informed at work today that I would have to accompany a television crew from Grandstand around the stadium. I was positively tingling at the thought of at last meeting Des, the housewives' choice himself, but had to make do with a bloke called Steve Lee who I had honestly never heard of and who has also been overlooked by the housewives.

As retribution for this, I told him that he could stand on the centre spot, which is also the location of one of the water sprinklers. It would have amused me infinitely to see it shoot up his leg in mid spiel. It was not to be though as he finished filming with two minutes to spare, to the lingering regret of myself and Dennis Norden.

April 18 Friday

I had a walk around the new stadium concourse this morning. Being the perspicacious type, I managed to notice two 15 feet by eight feet by five feet black metal boxes after I had banged my knee on one of them. An even closer inspection of them revealed three large stickers saying 'Scoreboards R Us', 'SCOREBOARDS – Prices slashed!' and '£££££££s off all Scoreboards!'

They were scoreboards. I have been assured that they will be even better than the one at Roker Park, which I am old enough to remember working. It would display such priceless epigrams as 'John Kay drives a Mazda', cunning tactical manoeuvres like 'Attack!' (a common prerequisite to scoring), and of course it would report on important developments in the match, such as 'Goal!' in case we hadn't noticed. Those were the days.

April 19 Saturday

Sunderland managed to win away from home this afternoon, so obviously I wasn't there. Our 1-0 victory was at Middlesbrough where we are forever winning, and when success is as certain as this there seemed little point in travelling down just to watch the inevitable. In fact our most recent triumph there was as recent as 1962. Recently recent or what?

Under the circumstances it was essential that I should remove to the Ivy House to illustrate with lager how pleased I am. I was joined my Taff, who would have spent the evening screaming puerile drunken victory songs at umpteen decibels had he not lost his voice at the match, so that was the day's second good result.

It was amusing to watch *Match Of The Day* and see seven million pounds striker, Fabrizio Ravanelli, being made anonymous by Lee Howey, who cost about a tenner. That said, the winning goal was scored by Darren Williams whose fee was easily in the hundreds.

April 20 Sunday

Despite our win yesterday, we still face a horribly fraught three weeks of working out the endless connotations of the remaining games and wishing calamitous misfortune on all the other clubs around us, preferably in the form of hip replacements to key players.

To ease the tension and to take my mind off football for a while, Liz and I went to the cinema to see *Fever Pitch*, which alas, turned out to be about football and not malaria as Tonka had wrongly informed me, probably deliberately.

It was a semi-autobiographical yarn starring the smoulderingly gorgeous Colin Firth. This is whom I shall select to play me when this diary goes to celluloid, as we are virtually identical. Bob Hoskins or Donald Sinden will play Tonka.

April 21 Monday

Four Sunderland players, namely Paul Stewart, Steve Agnew, Allan Johnston and Chris Woods, had the privilege of meeting me this afternoon. I had been roped into giving them a stadium tour.

Standing in the partially built West Stand, it was noted by Mr. Stewart that the pitch seemed to be quite some distance from the nearest seats. I nodded uninterestedly, as this struck me as mere platitude until he leapt to his feet and bawled, 'Stewart, you're fucking *CRAP!*' as loudly as possible. 'Ah, I'll still hear that,' he told his team mates.

As they murmured agreement, I pointed out (in the interest of balance) that the acoustics were such that loud compliments would also reverberate around the ground. This eventuality had not occurred to them.

Later, I finally managed to watch Saturday's *Football Focus* as filmed for *Grandstand* last Thursday. As I watched TV's Steve Lee (a household name in our house) open his report with 'I'm standing on the pitch at Sunderland's new stadium,' I felt strangely smug and powerful as I mused that he had needed to ask my permission to do so. Ha!

I did not warrant a mention on the credits, but they seemed to know who was boss.

I then deemed it necessary to go out and boast to a waiting world about my new capacity as a television executive. This preposterous lie was going very well until I got out of my depth by promising someone that I could use my influence to have *Blake's Seven* repeated.

April 22 Tuesday

All of Saturday's good work at Middlesbrough has been immediately undone by losing at home to Southampton tonight, so don't speak to me. This end of season fretting is worse than waiting for your exam results. By far.

April 23 Wednesday

I am in the Hut increasingly rarely these days and my occupation is now mainly to assist Dave Nicholson who is the Project Manager and the busiest man on Earth too.

Today while he was ordering concrete, preparing for a meeting about car parks, programming a computer, arranging to have his car repaired, organising a site tour for some local dignitaries, negotiating a roof maintenance contract, perfecting his trampoline act and eating chips, the most onerous task put upon me was to decide whether two stirs or three would be the minimum requirement for blending the milk in with the tea.

I suppose this backlog or work was all I deserved for neglecting to put the milk in first. In the end I got Dave to do it. It keeps him active.

April 24 Thursday

Being among the massed ranks of the easily pleased, I was able to spend a pleasurable afternoon looking at the amusing abbreviations that are to be found around the site office. For example, Design Issue Memos are DIM, the Construction Manager is a Con. Man., and best of all, the Female Officials changing area is referred to on the drawing as F. Off. Only a tiny minority of society, say the intelligent and educated, could fail to be amused by this.

On reflection, it can only be a good thing that there is not a Nominal Order Booklet or an Active Regional Service Enquiries file, as the resulting acronyms would render me incapable of work.

April 25 Friday

I was educated in sports psychology this afternoon by none other than a sports psychologist. My idea of covering the visitors changing room in either photographs of Bjork or vomit has been firmly rejected. Instead there will be strategically coloured tiles of gold and blue that are supposed to create a murky effect to hopefully depress the opposition into mental submission. This could be a load of old pig swill, but on the off chance that it isn't we have decided to install them.

More importantly, the continuing debate over the reasons for our precarious league position has now been resolved. It is not due to the lack of a recognised goal scorer or a deficiency of quality in the midfield. It is fairly and squarely due to crap ceramic tiles. Manchester United probably have an official interior designer. Cheats!

April 26 Saturday

The hot show-biz news to emerge from Sunderland today was the appearance of Richard and Judy in the Museum Vaults. This is not some surreal preamble, it really did happen. But the arrival of celebrities was of secondary interest compared to the fact that someone had actually ordered a sherry in there.

They were in town to attend the wedding of TV agony aunt and local girl, Denise Robertson, who has apparently sold the rights of the photographs to *Hello* magazine or such like. Previously they have published pictures of society weddings at Caesar' Palace, The Ritz, Sydney Opera House and so forth, so the editors will be mightily chuffed to capture Denise in wedded bliss outside the Dun Cow to add to this impressive list.

April 28 Monday

Work is going quite well at the moment. Dave Nicholson and I get along well and give each other the benefit of our different and varying experiences.

On Friday he showed me how to fasten my tie in a Windsor knot to impress any potential dignitaries whom I may have to usher around the stadium. Today, in return, I demonstrated to him, in the absence of spoons, how to retrieve the bag from a hot cup of tea using only a paper clip. By the end of the afternoon he had become quite adept at this, although he is not yet ready for the next stage which is the same but equipped with only a used staple.

Little wonder really that coffee drinkers are held in much lower regard. Those arseholes have no finesse. Furthermore, the future of this football club is in safe hands with this sort of expertise on board.

April 29 Tuesday

This afternoon I was called upon to show our goalkeeper Lionel Perez around the stadium. It was a shock to discover that despite being a footballer and a Frenchman to boot, he is actually a nice bloke.

My skills as an interpreter were not called upon, which was fortunate as my French vocabulary, which consists almost entirely of 'Les chiens n'aiment pas les chats' and 'J'aime le picnic avec fromage', is inadequate for even the most cursory explanation of civil engineering.

Lionel has had a tres bien season and a plasterer from Wallsend leapt out from a vomitory to tell him as much. At least I think that is what he said. No one has sufficient linguistic talent to communicate with Wallsend.

April 30 Wednesday

Steve Sutton from BBC *Look North* is the latest media megastar to have had a nosey around the new place. As I have yet to pay my licence fee, I complied with his request to be allowed to film from the pitch. He seemed rather chuffed about this as it allowed the cameraman to pan round from the centre spot, which evidently means a great deal to them.

The BBC visit had immediately followed another from Sky TV, which led Mr. Sutton to ask me if they had also been allowed on to the pitch and he gave gloating clench of the fist when I told him that they hadn't. This revealed an obvious childish streak that does not come over when he is broadcasting.

Why would I do Sky a favour anyway? I don't even subscribe.

May 1 Thursday

Today was General Election day apparently and such was the indifference to this event that people had to remind each other not to vote. Now that is what I call apathy.

The government prayer mat was clearly not used enough and they were annihilated, not least in Sunderland South, which was the first result of the evening to be announced. The count is hastened because the returning officer is simply able to weigh the majority to see how many tons the Labour Party wins by.

The Tories usually finish narrowly ahead of spoiled papers and are rumoured to have resorted to desperate measures this time. The count took place in the Crowtree Leisure Centre, so to disrupt it they booked a five-a-side court for 11pm. A futile move as the count was finished by a quarter to.

May 2 Friday

The North East's media is presently trying to wave the banner for Sunderland boxer, Billy Hardy. He goes into tomorrow's contest with Prince Naseem Hamed as the most defined underdog since Berwick-Upon-Tweed ended their war with the Soviet Union. The local press has rallied to his cause but their optimism is not generally shared.

The Prince is reckoned to be pound for pound the most complete and awesome boxer in the world, has a huge entourage of assorted trainers, advisors and lackeys, receives an income of millions and is likely to be carried into the ring in a sedan chair by half-a-dozen eunuchs. On the face of it this would seem too formidable a challenge for a bloke who recently sold me a set of darts. Good ones mind you, so I hope he wins.

May 3 Saturday

I ended a long and largely unfortunate chapter in my life today when I attended the last ever match at Roker Park.

The usual match day rituals were scrupulously upheld; the singing, the noise, the dubious pies, the missing of the first goal due to being in the toilets at the time. There was a slight departure from tradition when we won the game 3-0, but we did not allow this fact to mar an otherwise momentous occasion, especially when Everton had been magnanimous enough to scale new heights of ineptitude for our benefit. I expect that some of this atmosphere will be lost in the replacement of a 120 Wimpey Homes.

All we have to do now is win at Wimbledon next week and we are saved.

May 4 Sunday

The sporting headlines in Sunderland this weekend have naturally been dominated by the final match at Roker Park. This is good news for Billy Hardy as his fight with Prince Naseem Hamed last night did not go as well as I had hoped.

The bout was shown again this afternoon while I was making popcorn, so I decided to watch it in its entirety between pops. Despite this awful experience, Billy is still an excellent boxer and I felt very sorry for him. But not as sorry as I felt for the people who had forked out for pay-per-view, then organised a social gathering for friends with drinks and nibbles, when the 90 odd seconds could have been put to so much better use.

One week to go.

May 6 Tuesday

I was dispatched to the printers today to have some stadium drawings copied. This happens to be in Hendon, which is where the beautiful people hang out if the Burton House happens to be open.

Upon returning to the car, I noticed a large, bruise faced woman in a light grey t-shirt (the very worst colour for disguising armpit leaks). She was with a child whose t-shirt could have been any colour beneath the Jackson Pollock of ice lolly stains. He had clearly somehow incurred her wrath, as she clattered him around the ears with a *Racing Post* as she screamed, 'Our Barnabus! Pack in splitting your infinitives you little shit!'

Well done madam. In an age where car crime, drug abuse and grammatical errors are a social curse, you have struck a literal blow against one of them.

May 8 Thursday

Today was Ascension Thursday, so I thought I had better get up.

Three days to go.

May 9 Friday

I was playing football this evening, superbly too. I was greeted there by the alarming sight of the absurd Robin Brown with virtually no hair.

He claims to have been drunk at a party, fallen asleep and later woken up to find that unscrupulous friends had coarsely removed his beloved quiff before dumping it as a sorry clump on top of the television. Counter claims say that he was even more drunk than that and actually did it himself with a razor blade.

Either way, it was to provide the basis of an excuse for every piece of ineptitude that he produced on the pitch. 'That would have gone in if I'd had me hair,' 'It was too much for a bald bloke,' and so on.

Two days to go.

May 10 Saturday

Our traumatic and nerve severing weekend began this evening when Liz and I met Redge and Rachel at King's Cross. To take our mind off football for a couple of hours we actually went to a theatre rather than a pub, something I haven't done since I went to see Les Dawson in *Jack And The Beanstalk* a few years ago. I only hope Taff doesn't find out.

Just tomorrow to get out of the way now.

May 11 Sunday

The unbearable tension of the last few weeks has finally been lifted. Admittedly we have been relegated but the uncertainty has gone. Only uncertain events can cause anxiety, just as only certain events can cause pain, misery and despair. Yet despite feeling pained, miserable and desperate, there is also a sense of gloom and despondency. Oh God.

We lost to Wimbledon and I could sense that it would be a depressing day as soon as we left the pub, although this is a common cause of heartache. This was compounded when I was queuing to get in to Selhurst Park and heard that a streaker had been doing her job while I was stuck outside.

At least tomorrow will be better as it is unlikely to bring another relegation. Coventry City stayed up at our expense. We know how but we do not know why.

May 12 Monday

Liz and I did not board our train home until 3pm, which gave us most of the day for the activity of our choosing and there is no shortage of choice in London. However, the delights of the capital were wasted on me in the wake of yesterday's disaster, as the only activity that I was genuinely remotely interested in was sitting with my head between my knees or possibly a trip to Highgate Cemetery.

Under the lachrymose circumstances, there was nothing more likely than a three hour delay, which duly arrived, unlike the train. Bethan was upset at this but any amount of parental absence is easily compensated for by a toy London bus and a Spice Girls album.

And so to bed, in the First Division.

May 13 Tuesday

There was another last ever match at Roker Park tonight, featuring a prize draw, face painting, community singing, a laser show and much more. In fact it featured anything that would take people's minds off football.

I was lurking behind the scenes with some former players who were to take part in a pre-match display of 'Roker Legends', but some of the people we were passing off as 'legends', oh dear, oh dear, oh dear. It crossed my mind to go out on to the pitch and join them, as I was no more obscure than some of them. They had either wildly overrated themselves or were in desperate need of a free buffet.

May 14 Wednesday

I turned up for one of my increasingly rare appearances in the Hut, now in its twilight days. The visitors book is now documentary proof of the unfaltering and mindless optimism of football supporters, which in the case of Sunderland usually proves to be without foundation.

Before Sunday, the entries were all along the lines of 'Staying Up', 'Bring on Man. United. Again' and 'Europe next season'. Since the dreaded drop, they have not even broken their stride and now write 'We'll be back!', 'First Division champs again 1997-98', and 'Pride of the Nationwide'. However, 'Hope the pies are better' is still being used as a virtual punctuation mark. One must never lose one's sense of priority. With the pies in order everything else will fall into place.

May 15 Thursday

Bethan has only owned that Spice Girls album since Monday but has already played it ad infinitum ad nauseam to the point where I can feel a tic developing.

These women are making me feel nervous with their ubiquity so I removed the postcard from the sleeve notes to disable Bethan from sending off for Spice paraphernalia. Instead I wrote down the name and address of fun hater and all-round gloom merchant, Jim Fox, on the back of it. I did not order any of the merchandise for him, but just by sending it he is entitled without question to a free Spice wrist band, a 3D sticker of the girls, and most importantly of all, instant Girl Power.

If this doesn't cheer him up, nothing will.

May 16 Friday

I made a point of watching *Top of the Pops* this evening for the first time since Glen Miller was slugging it out with Mario Lanza to head the hit parade. The reason for my return is that the number one spot is currently occupied by a band named Olive, whose lead singer, one Ruth Anne Boyle, was hitherto better known for her stint behind the bar at the Ivy House where she was famed for the distance and accuracy with which she could flick dry roasted peanuts. There was not a safe ear in the house.

Hopefully her success will continue and she will remember the £1.20 that she owes me from a taxi journey that we took in 1989.

May 17 Saturday

It was the FA Cup final this afternoon which gave Middlesbrough the opportunity to glean some glory from an otherwise miserable season for the North East. They didn't. They lost 2-0 to Chelsea.

They failed to employ what most managers consider to be an essential tactic when trying to win a Cup tie, the time honoured strategy of keeping the opposition at bay for the first 43 seconds. Even Billy Hardy lasted longer than that.

May 18 Sunday

Today was the first of the new stadium open days, which gave the club the first chance to properly show the place off to the public. Meanwhile, the stewards got their first chance to say that you couldn't go down there for any reason, not even to take a quick photograph, and if you do we'll eject you from the ground . . .

However, of all the club officials there, only I had been inducted and it was therefore me that the stewards had to approach for permission to look into the West Stand, presenting me with the opportunity to be magnanimous and unpetty, an opportunity that I failed to take by telling them to sod off. I have waited years for that.

May 19 Monday

I learned today of detailed plans for the football theme bar in the new stadium. The most important and impressive feature in there, at least as far as the hopelessly infantile among us are concerned, will be the entrance.

Turnstiles will be transported from Roker Park and installed so that every tenth person to enter the bar will receive a loud recorded cheer. This will surely soften the blow of relegation.

The only possible pitfall with this brilliant concept is in finding the nine mates who would be considerate enough to walk in before you. My friends are notoriously selfish and likely to want the cheer for themselves. It is at times such as this when you find out who your true friends are.

May 20 Tuesday

I am not normally one to dwell upon dark events that may or may not happen, most of them already have, but I have spent the last week or so worrying about Chris Waddle. Could we persuade him to stay? Can we match his terms? Would we be able to fend off the offers of other interested parties?

Well, we have now dispensed with these gnawing anxieties by sacking him, so all of my worries have been removed in one fell swoop. Conspicuously talented, so out he goes. Not only that, but as he was so famous it gave me a pathetic little buzz to see one of our players on *A Question of Sport* or *The Generation Game* or whatever they call *Swap Shop* these days. All is now gone.

May 23 Friday

Tomorrow sees the Scottish FA Cup final between Kilmarnock and Falkirk, so Liz, Bethan and I have toddled up to Kilmarnock and will pop over to Glasgow tomorrow to watch the game. This is due mainly to my life long affinity with the town and club, but partly because I am ostensibly a Sunderland supporter and am desperate at the moment to associate myself with anything like success. This also explains my prodigious purchases of raffle tickets.

The journey was the usual long and uncomfortable affair, not because of any great distances involved, but due to the dubious quality of the roads. The general standard of road routes in south-west Scotland is usually inferior to the main thoroughfares of Backhouse Park, although there were some richt bonny braes tae see.

May 24 Saturday

Och! The journey tae Ibrox tae watch the fitba did not take long.

We won the Cup, but what a strange afternoon it turned out to be, with particular regard to singing. There was no rendition of the national anthem. Instead, while the dignitaries were being introduced to the teams we had *Cum On Feel The Noize* being blasted around the ground.

More peculiar still is that Kilmarnock have adopted *Paper Roses* as their theme song. They have not even amended it, which is unusual as the common practice is to change the lyrics to incorporate some insults and obscenities to be bawled at the opposition. Not many football supporters get to see their team parading the Cup while dancing in time to the melodious and girlie strains of the lovely Marie Osmond.

May 25 Sunday

By the time we arose this morning, the town of Kilmarnock had been drunk dry and so there seemed little point in staying.

63

It was also reported on BBC Radio Five that hundreds of pairs of knickers had been cleared up from the streets this morning. Clearly, the dinner party is not the medium for celebration in the district. Dinners and parties are two entirely different concepts, although they share an unusually heavy reliance on lager.

May 29 Thursday

It was a mesmerising day at work. After the enchantment that is synonymous with a couple of hours of filing, I was then dispatched with the fascinating task of counting the spaces available for the 'Brick In The Wall' scheme. Obviously there is no way of quantifying just how engrossing this job was, but the figure of 17,991 is embossed on my mind.

I had to stay in tonight, which was a pity, as I was keen to regale the chaps with my brick-counting related adventures and other avenues of tomfoolery. I suppose I still have plenty of years ahead of me for folks to slap me on the back and say, 'Tell us about the time you had to count the brick spaces and there were 17,991 of them.'

It will make my dotage worthwhile.

May 31 Saturday

I was dragged from the Hut this morning to give a guided tour of the stadium to a man called Alan Smith who is the England physiotherapist, no less.

I remembered reading about him saving the life of Paul Warhurst, who had swallowed his tongue during a Sheffield Wednesday match. As a favour, I asked him if the same thing were to happen to Alan Shearer, could he see his way clear to not bothering, or perhaps amputating his foot, just for a laugh.

He gave a little chuckle at what he had mistaken for black humour, but I think he was slightly embarrassed to realise that I had not spoken in jest. I then received a polite 'No', but it was still worth asking.

June 2 Monday

There was quite a hubbub around the new stadium today as Peter Reid ushered in Lee Clark, the club's new record signing, as well as a gaggle of paparazzi. Of course, this gave me a prime opportunity to strut around and appear important.

And why not? After all I played an integral part in the signing. In fact, without my invaluable contribution it could not have gone ahead. Apart from that, no one seemed willing to move the tables and chairs down on to the pitch.

I am not a glutton for publicity, but a small token of recognition would be appreciated, perhaps in the form of a modest 16 page pullout in the Sunderland Echo with pictures of myself in various chair carrying poses.

June 4 Wednesday

Today I met a much respected local journalist called Arthur Appleton. He was polite, courteous, eloquent, warmly enthusiastic about the new stadium and profoundly grateful to be afforded the opportunity of being allowed in to see the project. An absolute gentleman. We could do without his sort around here.

June 7 Saturday

Today there was the buzz around Sunderland that we have come to expect when the Post Office issues a new set of stamps. Is there anything to match the thrill of philately? The theme this time Is World War II bombers, and considering that a first class stamp is all that is required to send a letter to Germany it is in questionable taste and therefore amusing.

June 8 Sunday

Sunderland continues to cry out for a decent cinema and tonight it was crying just a little louder, with the latest bout of spelling mistakes at the apology for a picture house that we have.

(Unfortunately) they are showing *Beavis & Butthead* at present. Only yesterday they had 'Bevis' on the hoarding. A kindly passer-by had presumably gone in to point out that there is an 'a' in 'Beavis' and prompt remedial action was taken. However, they put the required 'a' on the wrong side of the 'v' and it now says 'Bevias'.

It does not take a spectacular imagination to make the likes of us laugh and we launched a string of predictable quips such as Kevin Bell's 'What will they do for the next Sandra Bullock film?'

Her surname is nearly the same as 'Bollocks' you see.

June 10 Tuesday

The latest dignitary to be accompanied around the site by good old me was a High Court judge called Hannah. He had the first name of Justice, which is very popular in the legal profession.

I carried out this task uncomplainingly as you never know when you will need a favour back, even though I was in the midst of a particularly engrossing game of Spot The Ball. Some of the plasterers seemed to recognise him, probably from their insatiable reading of legal manuscripts and not because they are criminals in any way.

He passed judgement on the stadium and in summing up described it as 'Nice' - pending an inquiry and the availability of decent hot dogs.

June 11 Wednesday

I had almost finished my colouring in when Dave Nicholson stuck his head round the door and announced that he had an even more important task than that for me to perform. I immediately recognised the gravity in his tone and asked him how many sugars he wanted in it this time. But it was an even weightier matter than that as this cup of tea was for the Chairman.

Considering the amount of hazardous substances to be found at the site, some supporters will consider this to be a lost opportunity, but I was unwilling to commit regicide. Anyway, he probably has a constitution like Rasputin and the most dangerous compound to hand was a half a packet of Lockets.

June 12 Friday

We have signed another goalkeeper, this time a Dutchman named Edwin Zoetebier. He wanted to be shown around the new stadium and no one was better qualified than me, as I have been to Eindhoven a couple of times and had more than my fair share of frikandels.

He arrived with his equally blonde equally Dutch fiancée, who caught me by surprise when I was trying to find some wellies for her to wear and she said that she would require a pair of size 38s. This is not as remarkable as it sounds, serving only to confirm what a poor European I am, unable to translate shoe sizes, less still a second language.

On the other hand, it serves her right for not being British.

June 13 Friday

Indeed it was a Black Friday. The Hut has been taken away and the sombre mood was encapsulated by the stream of mourners who filed past the patch of weeds where it had once been, reverently raising their headgear as they trudged.

When the Hut first opened back in July 1996, the *Sunderland Echo* marked the occasion with a photograph of my good self at the flag pole, above the caption 'Tony Gillan raises the visitors centre flag for the first time'. The demise did not go unheralded either, even if their commemoration was rather on the cheap side. They used the exact same picture, only this time it was above the caption of 'Tony Gillan lowers the flag for the last time'.

At least it shows me when I was younger and prettier.

June 16 Monday

The site offices were plunged deep into crisis this afternoon. Design changes, inclement weather, late deliveries and so forth, are dealt with urbane resignation, but the whole project grinds to an alarming stand still when the kettle conks out. To put it another way, crises are measured on a scale of one to kettle conking out.

It was I who was laden with the responsibility of swiftly obtaining a new one, leaving the others to look anxiously at their watches while I was out at Parry's Electricals. When I returned with this £15.99 worth of project saving apparatus, it was amid tumultuous appreciation, back slapping et al. It was rather like the end of a George Formby film, as we slurped tea and agreed that it had turned out nice again.

This apart, it was not an eventful day.

June 17 Tuesday

The latest stadium visitor to be left in my charge was the injury ravaged midfielder, Paul Bracewell, who popped in for a hobble early this afternoon.

He was understandably eager for an update on the progress of the physio room. He knows exactly what a physio room should look like and will doubtless become as intimately acquainted with the new one as he has been with all the others. He has been operated on more times than Elizabeth Taylor and surgery to his legs has taken every form except amputation (so far). He has had more accidents than Oliver Hardy. He could make models of the QEII with his scar tissue. You get the general idea.

June 18 Wednesday

It is odd that I should have mentioned Tiananmen Square in the 26th of February 26th because today I was delegated with the surprise task of giving a tour of the stadium to none other than Kate Adie. It was with great pleasure that I told her she would have to wear a safety helmet and tread carefully as she was about to enter a dangerous place.

Anyway, it is not well known, but she is from Sunderland and a big supporter of the football team, and she was filled to the brim with girlish glee when she ran out of the tunnel as well as being animatedly enthusiastic about the whole construction. She was also a great deal more athletic than I would have thought, conquering the steps at a far greater speed than me while expending far less energy, although there really was no need for her to run. Her pace was possibly due to excitement or perhaps because being in an incomplete building for her meant it was being shelled by Serbs.

June 22 Sunday

Over the last few Sundays the club has invited the general public to stick on a hard hat and take a look inside the almost complete stadium - in the hope that we will sell a few more season tickets on the strength of it. My role in this had hitherto been to advise the stewards who were actually conducting the tours. They come to me with a query that the punters might have raised and then go back with some old tosh that I have given them in reply. 'Pitch? Down there. Roof? Up there' etc.

Today, however, the BBC's fly-on-the-wall documentary team asked me to take a more hands-on approach so that they could mike me up and film me taking a tour myself. This was good news as I was most keen to put my mush on television and because most of the stewards do not have what might be described as flawless diction.

It's in the can now. It's a wrap!

June 23 Monday

The most significant development on the site for me today was that the cabins where Dave Nicholson and I work have been sawn off from those of the contractors and dumped on the other side of the road. Charming.

However, this did present me with the opportunity to appear intrepid and buccaneer. This was because we have yet to be connected to an electricity supply, so I had to return to the contractors' cabins to use their kettle and I cut a dashing figure as I staggered through the mud, clinging intently to two cups.

It was all very reminiscent of one of the more exciting chapters of *White Fang* except without any dogs. Despite the inherent danger, I made it back to our new spot complete with two teas with the requisite milk, sugar and rain.

June 25 Wednesday

The stadium's inaugural match will take place in just over a month's time when Sunderland takes on Ajax in a prestigious friendly. There are to be numerous show-biz festivities to accompany the game, all co-ordinated by an agent called Nadia, who has apparently represented the likes of Tina Turner and Rod Stewart, although her influence and wealth did not prevent her from snecking a finger of my Kit-Kat.

Until I met this woman today, I had not realised that the dialogue of *Absolutely Fabulous* was only marginally exaggerated. She was sitting at the opposite side of my desk and chatting into her mobile phone, literally saying things like, 'Okay darling! Yes, wonderful sweetie! TTFN. Ciao!'

She seems to be a most pleasant woman, it's just that living in Sunderland accustoms one to believe that such people do not really exist.

June 26 Thursday

With half of me wanting to allow my bottom lip to tremble theatrically and the other half thinking, 'Good riddance to the old dump', I had a final gander around Roker Park, accompanied by Bethan, Taff and the camcorder.

I have captured for the benefit of future generations the glorious sight and sound of Taff becoming the last ever person to blow his nose in the Fulwell End. The noise level he can achieve with this has been his laudable contribution to the fabled Roker Roar for many years now.

A single blast from his highly audible hooter was enough to rattle what is left of this historic football ground, and impressive though this nasally charged reverberation was, the trembling Fulwell End roof only served to promote the fact that our impending move will not be a day too soon.

June 27 Friday

I met Sunderland's captain Kevin Ball today, which was something of a shock when it happened as the shoddy handwriting on the fax I received had led me to expect Kevin Bell, a friend of mine known around town for his complete lack of celebrity status.

Kevin Ball has a reputation as the most ferocious man on Earth, and unusually for one of my meetings with a player, I was not to be let down as he growled, 'How do you do!' at me whilst rupturing several of my tendons in the course of a hand shake. I had never been so impressed by a footballer since standing behind John Kay in the queue of a kebab shop and marvelling at the amount of salt that he put on his chips.

It is a privilege to occasionally rub shoulders with the cream of British sport.

June 30 Monday

There was a final display of British pomp and ceremony, as they always call it, in Hong Kong today.

However, the cardinal importance of the occasion will have been lost on deaf viewers of *Channel Five News,* who were accidentally given subtitles for the previous programme, a DIY show called *Hot Property*. When Governor Patten was orating on the positive legacy of British rule since 1842, the hard of hearing were left to think that he was commenting that there was plenty of room for a hand basin, even though the toilet is separate from the bathroom.

The deaf might now be extremely badly informed on the future of the colony, but they will probably sleep safely in the erroneous knowledge that it has loft and cavity wall insulation and can easily accommodate a barbecue.

July 1 Tuesday

Willie Watson was in town today. Apart from once owning a sports shop down High Street East and being a dab hand on the spoons, he is probably best known for representing England at cricket as well as football. This has also been achieved by David Gower and Terry Butcher, but as they are quite clearly two different people it is not nearly as impressive.

Obviously, Mr. Watson and his family were all but beside themselves in their eagerness to meet me, but they may have been disguising their desire to see what the new stadium looks like. Yet, how could I refuse? He is the first celebrity I have met to be the subject of a question in Trivial Pursuit.

July 4 Friday

As if wearing a suit to work each day were not a severe enough blow to my once indomitable street cred, the club is now insisting that I should carry a mobile phone. My 'Beautiful Beast' image could be irreparably tarnished by these accoutrements of sophistication.

Embarrassingly, the first call I received was when I was in a crowded bakers as I was nonchalantly ogling some splendid looking pasties. Of course, everyone began to look at me when I began to tell blatant fibs about being at the printers.

July 5 Saturday

Scientists this very day have landed a small lunar type craft on Mars. I do not know why, although people are apt to do all manner of facile things to alleviate the boredom of the close season. I am still massively impressed by this, although I should caveat this by pointing out that I hold the team behind the development of the dunkable biscuit in equal esteem.

The craft on the red planet at the moment can attain a speed of around 16 inches per minute, so it is strangely appropriate that the landing should have taken place on a Saturday night, as this is the top speed for most of us leaving Ku Club at that time.

July 8 Tuesday

I had an appointment this morning with a Mr. Rollin and his lovely daughter Miss Rollin, both of whose first names I have completely forgotten. They are the people responsible for the *Rothman's Football Yearbook*, so I thought I would regale them with some football statistics related banter.

I opened with a spirited, 'I expect you're a topper at footy quizzes then?'

To which he responded with a completely spontaneous and off-the-cuff, 'Not really.'

It was to be a long morning.

At great personal risk of digging a deeper hole, I asked him if he knew that Barry Venison had played 207 times for Sunderland. He didn't, so I suggested that he should write it down sharpish.

July 14 Monday

On a stadium visit today was Mrs. Karen Cram, wife of the athlete Steve. It was ironic that as we entered we were passed by a podgy, sweaty, middle-aged jogger, whose by now scarlet complexion, contrasted strikingly with his Green Flash trainers. 'That wasn't him was it?' I asked flippantly, a question that she rightly chose to ignore.

Until recently her husband was the world mile record holder and is one of the all time great middle distance runners, whereas this bloke would be lucky to get as far as Kershaw's Sea Foods.

July 15 Tuesday

Sunderland winger Michael Gray came to the stadium today. With his bronzed chiselled features, flowing blonde locks and teeth of pearl, he was the unsurprising choice to model the new kit. He and Lee Clark came up to me in full football strips with additional safety helmets and asked how they could get in. How foolish they must have felt at having to walk past several factory units and numerous onlookers dressed like that.

Of course I could have shown them a far shorter and easier route into the stadium - straight down the access tunnel, but where's the fun in that? Besides, I am unlikely to ever be given the opportunity again. It was a chance to strike revenge on behalf of all of us who were rubbish at football but wish otherwise.

July 16 Wednesday

It was with grim irony that we launched our new strip yesterday. The fashion world had just taken delivery of the thunderbolt when news of the murder of Gianni Versace began to filter through. Those in the less chic quarters of Sunderland were relieved to find out that he was only a designer and not an ice cream maker.

We can only hope that he is not the victim of a serial designer killer. Although no life is more valuable than the next, it will be reassuring to know that Mr. C & Mr. A are tucked up similarly in their beds and that Mr. Asda is under armed guard.

July 18 Friday

With a mere 12 days to the stadium's grand opening against Ajax of Amsterdam, things have become rather frenzied on site, or at least they have until Friday afternoon when much of the work force has the option of finishing early.

They began the day with the best of intentions, but by the time the afternoon had arrived the sun was shining, the pubs were open, and, frankly, most of them had guzzled so many chips at lunch time as to render them incapable of even the slightest exertion.

However, one electrician soldiered bravely on, apparently the only one from his cabin who was conscientious enough to do so. He told me as much himself before strolling off like a determined John Wayne to prove it. Very commendable, although I do happen to know that he is also the only one in his cabin to have bought a season ticket.

July 19 Saturday

As a favour to the caterers, I conducted an unusual stadium tour this afternoon, which was comprised entirely of disgruntled wedding guests who had naively expected to be at the reception in a finished Banqueting Suite in a completed stadium. At the point when they should have been polishing off their choice of gateaux, I was guiding them past a pile of bath taps on the spot where the bride's father should have been giving his speech.

I was asked, rather stiffly, how we could expect to finish the job with a mere two weeks to go. Luckily I was able to think on my feet and quickly pointed out that it was not really two weeks and was in fact ten days. That foxed 'em.

July 24 Thursday

As an avid tea drinker, and no stranger to the accompanying biccies, my antagonism to coffee was today extended when my well worn path to the kettle was barred by the delivery of 54 boxes containing coffee percolators, one for each executive box. Another outrage for me to overlook.

July 25 Friday

In a moderately successful attempt at making the stadium appear to be closer to completion than it actually is, a fair amount of signage was put up this afternoon. Among it is a notice above each turnstile listing items that will be prohibited inside the ground including golf umbrellas, cans, bottles, gas canisters, knives and inter-continental ballistic missiles.

All the fun has gone out of football these days.

July 28 Monday

We are now completely beset with Ajax fever, but thankfully this will have gone in 48 hours. Before then we have a pretty grim couple of days ahead of us.

But the game will go ahead which is particularly pleasing for me. Over the past few weeks, every butcher, baker and candlestick maker has been miraculously transformed into a master builder, an architect or a civil engineer with composite knowledge of modern stadia construction. All of them have bleakly assured me that in their expert opinion the match had no chance of ever happening.

Being proved right is something that we smug types anxiously look forward to. By Thursday I will be able to utter those three little words that make the heart sing; 'Told you so.'

July 29 Tuesday

After a long but particularly exciting and frantic day at work, I was invited to the new Sports Bar for a complimentary smattering of drinks and nibbles. I stood out at this privileged gathering as I was the only one to be wearing a hard hat.

The purpose of this occasion was twofold. Firstly it was to indulge in a freebie binge. Beyond that, the Chairman and Chief Executive were to deliver a speech that would reveal the name of the new stadium to a waiting world.

It is to be called The Sunderland Stadium of Light, a controversial decision and one that people immediately decided had undesirable rhyming possibilities. Although I personally think that even the most verbose among us would be pressed to find a word that rhymes with Stadium.

July 30 Wednesday

Despite requiring some frantic last minute clearing up to gain the safety certificate, the Ajax game went ahead and we started as we mean to go on with a goalless draw. Heading was made somewhat difficult by the wearing of hard hats.

Apart from football, there was a bountiful supply of entertainment including Status Quo to appeal to the teenyboppers. The kids just went wild as they disembarked the stage after their last number to do a lap of honour in a Cadillac, the announcer whipping up a frenzy by energetically announcing, 'Let's give it for Quo! This is Rick's first gig since his by-pass!', which brought even more cheering from appreciative teenagers.

I did not have the Quo knocking on my door to ask the way, but people from every other branch of the entertainment industry did. This included singers, dancers, stilt walkers, blokes who look like they are riding ostriches, and someone with rabbits peering from every orifice.

I myself am blessed with an unrivalled talent for balancing a brush vertically on my nose, but I declined to mention this for fear of being roped in.

July 31 Thursday

I had presumed that with the exception of the people who had bought tickets for non-existent seats, everyone was very pleased with last night's proceedings. I found out this morning, however, that there was one further exception.

Following the game there was a fireworks display that followed that illuminated and decorated the North East's sky. This pyrotechnic splendour had been appreciated by all who saw it apart from Tommy the groundsman who marched into our office this morning and angrily announced to me that, 'We need two tons of Mansfield Top! They've burnt the pitch!'

Another complaint came on the telephone from a local woman. She was concerned by the amount of noise generated by the people who had attended the match, some of whom had evidently been shouting at the tops of their voices. I said we would look into it.

August 2 Saturday

Our increasingly desperate desire to watch a game of football took us to Carlisle this afternoon for a pre-season friendly. Ajax or Carlisle United, we treat them all the same so it was another 0-0 draw albeit an emotionally charged one. At one point I almost stopped eating.

August 4 Monday

This afternoon I had to spend an hour or so guarding the new club shop. This was a most welcome task as the shop contains a bed on which is displayed the official club duvet and pillow. I decide that if I was not to

73

guard the place with my life, then the next best option would be to guard the place with total inertia, taking the occasional break from this for a Jaffa Cake to keep me going.

Eventually, a real security guard came along which meant that I could take a well earned rest with a cup of tea and a Curly Wurly. The Curly Wurly was much appreciated after all of that unstinting Jaffa Cake eating.

Otherwise today was quite uneventful.

August 5 Tuesday

Unlike yesterday, described as 'quite uneventful', today was completely uneventful. Not even a Jaffa Cake.

August 6 Wednesday

I had an absolute mountain of colouring in to do today, but was unable to do so without the frequent interruptions of people knocking on the door. All of them had elaborate tales of how they had flown in from Kuala Lumpur solely on the off chance of me allowing them to have a peek at the new stadium, please, I'll be your best mate, I'll die if I can't . . . '

No one ever simply asks, 'Can I have a look please?' which is a far more effective approach.

It would seem that our players are no different. I discovered this when one of them dropped in at the office with his girlfriend who had to go back to London this afternoon so would it be at all possible . . .

He qualified himself by adding 'I'm a player.'

I knew that we had signed a couple of players recently and was trying to match faces to names. I was about to extend my hand and say, 'I know who you are. Jody Craddock isn't it?' when he mercifully beat me to it and said, 'I'm Kevin Phillips,' which gave me a good chance to lie and say that he required no introduction.

Despite my reservations about his story I let them in anyway.

August 7 Thursday

Shock news has reached me from the triathlon world. Serious under-funding means that many of these events are under threat, even the prestigious annual race in Bath. One chap on the radio said that the Bath Triathlon was the biggest event on the calendar, a claim that the organisers of Christmas would vigorously dispute.

With swimming, cycling and running all in the same race, the participants attract much admiration for their physical prowess, but not from me. I find that my morning constitutional of four slices of toast and a bit of scratching has all of the desired (and required) rigour. Anything beyond this is a frivolous and extravagant waste of energy.

August 10 Sunday

The first day of the season at last. For the first time anyone can remember, Sunderland opened on a Sunday, but at least we manage to uphold the tradition of not winning the first one with our customary panache. 2-0 to Sheffield United.

On my previous visit to Bramall Lane, I listened to the most stupid tannoy announcement ever heard at an English football match - 'If you are leaving the ground please use the exits.'

At the time I excused this as a verbal slip, but exactly the same announcement was made today. It would have been fun to hold the request to ridicule by abseiling down the back of the stand to leave. I would have done so too had I not remembered that sarcasm is the lowest form of wit and in this case the most dangerous too.

August 11 Monday

The team photograph was taken in the stadium today. Despite much strategic walking about, I don't think I have managed to be in it.

August 14 Thursday

In common with most football clubs, Sunderland has an inane mascot who indulges in some pointless waving and gyrating before each kick-off. Ours is Samson The Cat and the identity of the person inside the suit is a cautiously guarded secret. This is because all of the genial ambience that follows him would be dispelled if the punters were to find out that he also works in the ticket office where there has been more than a mite of trouble recently. There would be a hefty chance of Samson having his ears and nose removed if word were to spread.

The Sunderland Stadium of Light has its first game tomorrow night and such is the state of ticketing that Samson may not be able to attend. He asked me to stand in, but what do you think my answer was? Furthermore, at the risk of destroying his anonymity and by doing so endangering him, his real name is Tony Davison.

August 15 Friday

Another historically historic day in terms of history for Sunderland Association Football Club today. The first proper game at the new stadium took place tonight and we even managed to beat Manchester City 3-1. This was the real inauguration of the ground as we cannot really count the Ajax friendly. Nor do we consider the game of three-pots-and-in that some electricians had when they sneaked on to the pitch to be a worthy benediction.

For the occasion, a chap called John Mallan and myself were bestowed with the tedious privilege of raising the flags before the match. This is part of my new capacity at work of doing anything that crops up (my official job description now). Upon completion of this, we were met with the alarming sight of the Chief Executive running towards us and waving his arms. Where a 'Magpies Kiss My Arse' flag came from is anyone's guess. It wasn't mine, but we still had to take it back down.

Our opponents were facing their former manager in Peter Reid, and a former player in Niall Quinn who scored an extremely fortuitous goal after 17 minutes. They also had a player become the first to be sent off in the new stadium, but with 15 minutes to go they thought they had earned a point when they equalised with a penalty. But Sunderland went straight back down the other end and cruelly scored not one but two more goals.

This type of misery represents an average day out for Manchester City supporters.

August 18 Monday

I took some time to fully admire our plush new lifts. With their wood panelling, brass hand rails and marble floors, they are certainly there to be admired, although aesthetic splendour did not prevent them from conking out this morning.

They even have their own vocabulary, which is pretty clever stuff, even if 'Going up', 'Doors closing', 'Third floor' and 'Going down' is about all you get. I have yet to meet the woman who provides the voice for this, but she already has my sympathy and admiration. I expect she really goes for it when she is out on the razzle with the woman who does the Speaking Clock. 'Work? Don't talk to me about work . . . '

August 19 Tuesday

There was a startling item of postage waiting for me at work this morning. A few days ago I showed an elderly gentleman around the stadium and today I received a card from him that profusely thanked me for the visit.

The headline writers could have a field day (whatever that is) with this one. 'SAFC In Satisfied Punter Shock' and '"Yes I REALLY Am Pleased" Says Old Bloke' spring to mind. In the meantime, I have suggested that we have his card laminated and the gentleman in question be stuffed and mounted on a pedestal then positioned in the foyer for all to see. Otherwise he will descend into mythology along with the Team of All Talents, the Lambton Worm, and the man who liked the pasties at Roker Park.

August 20 Wednesday

People had often been known to grumble about the old ticket office at Roker Park, with all of the inherent problems of it being too small and too old. The same people now hark back to these days as a halcyon era of ticketing to be cherished in the memory. Things have become that fraught. These days we have supporters still waiting for season tickets months after paying for them, double, treble and quadruple bookings, lost mail, enormous queues of angry punters and general all-round mayhem.

Peter Reid has said that he wants the stadium to become a fortress, but the ticket office has taken this rather too literally and has managed to prevent more people from entering than a row of archers could. The good news is that they may have a *Watchdog Special* all to themselves.

August 21 Thursday

I was ambling around the changing rooms this afternoon when I stumbled across the magnetic board on which team tactics are planned. There is a little badge for each player and it is achingly tempting to mess about with them, or to perhaps even swap them for the ones on my fridge at home.

Happily I shall be present at Port Vale on Saturday to behold the sight of Niall Quinn playing in goal. And twin strikers up front according to the tactics board will be one of the Mr. Men and a banana so we are in with a chance.

August 22 Friday

Today I read of a fiendish plot by devious City types to make a quick profit in the shares in Chelsea FC. They had intended to spark off the entirely specious rumour that Ruud Gullit had bled to death in a tragic baking accident and before the news could be conclusively proved to have been false, they would have steamed in to buy shares at their lowest ever price.

Mr. Gullit contacted the media to strenuously deny that he was dead, although I suppose that just contacting them would have done. He is said to be understandably very angry about the whole affair, but it is not known if he contacted his broker first.

August 23 Saturday

Rrrrr! Us men!

Bernie Callaghan's big stag weekend began with the match at Port Vale where I stood on my seat at the end of the game to applaud the team as they left the pitch, but this was just to be different because they were crap and lost 3-1.

Then it was back on board the mini-bus for a cultural tour of Blackpool. One blight so far on a terrifically butch and masculine weekend was that best man Gerard Callaghan's organisational shortcomings meant that we had to choose a fellow bloke to share a bed with. I chose Kevin Bell, mainly because he is the skinniest member of our entourage and therefore the least likely to spend his hours of slumber in a drunken, gape-mouthed sweaty snore.

And so to bed, tentatively.

August 24 Sunday

We awoke to find that there are not a great deal of activities to participate in on a Sunday afternoon in Blackpool, save the mindless acquisition of bouncy balls at the fair.

In my capacity as connoisseur of fake novelty dog poo, I had a mooch around some tawdry joke shops and noticed what I thought were some pink pointy ones. But it seems that this particular shop was not entirely preoccupied with jokes. Nor were these devices for dispensing vinegar, which was my second inaccurate guess. They were for something altogether more horrid.

August 25 Monday

I decided to make the most of the exotic climes of Blackpool this morning by wandering down to the sea front with Davie Dowell to buy some lavish gifts. Who could resist an unofficial Spice Girls key ring and mug, as well as a cigarette lighter in the shape of a hand grenade?

There was high drama on the way back to the guest house. As we reached the summit of a hump back bridge, a woman in a Caravette pulled up next to us and got out to knock on the door of a nearby house. As she did so, the vehicle began to roll forward, so I bolted into action, whirling round to Davie so he could keep hold of my Spicy paraphernalia while I sprinted heroically after it, shouting, 'Missus! Missus!' as I went.

My gallantry came to an embarrassing halt when I noticed that it was a left-hand drive and under the comfortable control of a bloke who was no doubt wondering why I was trying to catch up with him on foot.

August 26 Tuesday

Today was not a good day.

As things stand it seems that I have only a few weeks left to work at the club. I should soon be on my way with severance pay of about eight quid and a bottle of Merrydown Cider. Now I know how Chris Waddle felt, although it is probably worse for me as I am far less likely than he to be offered the manager's position at Burnley. For one thing he already has it.

My mood has been compounded by the news that Birdseye are to discontinue the production of Arctic Rolls. As I said, today was not a good day.

August 28 Thursday

Tomorrow is Bernie and Lesley's wedding and I have decided that it would be something of an affront to wear the same tie that I have used virtually every day for a year, so I decided to borrow one from Taff's sizeable collection. 'A sensible one!' commanded Liz before I set off to his house, which for those of us with a childishly contrary nature is a green light to choose the most garish and annoying neckwear available.

I selected a suave little number depicting Scooby Doo, with drool cascading from his elongated tongue as he daydreams about bones. It is indeed a corker, so much so that Taff began to regret saying that I could borrow any one that I pleased as it is bound to eclipse the Wily Coyote effort that he will be sporting.

Bernie's last night as a bachelor was spent in the Ivy House. Is that worth noting?

August 29 Friday

After the wedding ceremony which Bernie and Lesley Callaghan (as they are now called) insisted was necessary (a point on which I was forced to concede), it was time to knuckle down to the serious business of indulging in about ten hours of solid gluttony.

Gerard's best man's speech was very well received. In the course of it, he read out a card from Bob Murray, which supposedly said 'May your love shine out like a beacon in this, the Marriage of Light.'

John Fickling, our Chief Executive, was sitting behind me at this point, but I did not want to turn round to see if he was laughing in case he wasn't.

A splendid evening was had by all with the exceptions of the barman and Taff who found it difficult to come to terms with the amount of compliments that were being directed at my tie.

August 30 Saturday

Today saw the second proper game at the new stadium and those of us who had hoped to witness another historically historic day in terms of history were not to be disappointed as it was to be the first time we lost there.

The 1-0 defeat to Norwich City was enhanced by a large gate, which was fortunate as there were over 33,000 people present and they needed a large gate to get in and out.

By the time I arrived at the Ivy House a pensive gloom had descended upon the place, and we gamely tried to find things to be cheerful about. It was a nice day, we had been to a lovely wedding the day before, we might win on Tuesday, we were in the pub, and at least no public figures have been killed in a car crash so far this weekend.

August 31 Sunday

I woke up to the shock news that Princess Diana had been killed in a car accident in Paris. Inconsiderately, she died after the Sunday newspapers had gone to print, which was a pity as they missed out on some fine headline opportunities such as, 'IT'S A RIGHT ROYAL PILE UP', 'DI CROAKS IT IN FROG LAND' or simply 'OOPS MA'AM'.

It seems that the process of canonisation is already well underway. Tributes have gushed in to say what a warm, wonderful, vibrant, caring, wonderful, fabulous, beautiful, wonderful, lovely, generous, wonderful, kind, perceptive, gorgeous, wonderful and totally brill individual she was. Good at pop quizes too apparently.

I personally never met the woman so I wouldn't like to comment on how considerate, charitable, tender, loving and scrummy she was.

September 1 Monday

The blanket coverage of Princess Diana's demise continued today and a well tucked in blanket it is too, with reporters at various locations giving us the latest update on how dead she still is.

Sporting fixtures have been postponed in the flimsy hope of achieving something by this, but not so Sunderland's game with Oxford United tomorrow night. The club had to work out a statement to announce that the match would be played, something along the lines of 'Despite the tragic and untimely death of Her Royal Highness . . . ' or 'Although the club naturally grieves for the Princess . . . '

Anything long winded or pompous was the order of the day. Concise, snappy suggestions such as 'Di dead, match goes ahead!' were thought to be inappropriate.

September 2 Tuesday

Sunderland played Oxford tonight and we won too. I was always confident of this as we have an unblemished record against college teams. Even the likes of St. Andrew's, Brunel and Monkwearmouth Sixth Form College would have struggled against us in this kind of form.

As happens at every game now, John Mallan and I were put upon to raise and lower the flags. This is quite an irksome task, but one which is jollied along by wearing the Union Jack like a cape, a la Sally Gunnell, something that John was not prepared to copy with the Vaux Lambton's flag.

Better news still was that because of Princess Di going, we could whip them up and down much more quickly as they were not as high up as normal.

September 4 Thursday

I was back in a suit today as I was called upon to give a tour to Hilary Armstrong MP who, according to the card she gave me, is the Minister for Housing and Local Government. So simpering and sycophancy were the order of the day.

This afternoon was testimony to the variation that now occurs within my job. For about an hour I was engaged in some strenuous grinning, whilst discussing the rigours of a late night division when you have also been invited back to Number Ten for sherry and nibbles.

After a passable impersonation of someone who fully understood what a chore this must be, I bade my farewell to the minister then went to empty the bins.

September 5 Friday

I had a significant break with tradition tonight when I went to see Sunderland win away from home and a right old walkover it was too.

Happily trekking back to the car after a thoroughly one sided victory over Bradford City, we encountered a home supporter who was a football hooligan of the lowest order. His attempts to spark off crowd trouble consisted completely of standing on a street corner reciting the (presumably) self-penned poem, *Red And White, Load Of Shite.* The title was actually the whole of the poem too. Standing there waiting for someone to assail him on the strength of it was poor quality hooliganism indeed.

It should be noted that when attempting to instigate a fracas, people who have just watched their team win 4-0 are notoriously difficult to provoke.

September 6 Saturday

There was not an awful lot to do today. Not a single shop was open, nor a cinema, nor a video rental shop, not even a cupboard. Worse still, there was no football and nothing on television except a funeral. What a tragic waste of a Saturday.

For some reason, everyone seems to have bought flowers using money that could have been better spent on virtually anything else, and flowers, it should be noted, that were sent to the deceased rather than the bereaved (?). Many of these flowers were strewn at the hearse as it made its journey, which could have been dangerous as they were impairing the driver's vision to the point where he had to switch on the windscreen wipers. Good thing too, otherwise there could have been a dreadful car crash.

September 8 Monday

To obviate the possibility that I may not do every possible job at the club before they finally give me the boot, I was actually put on reception today, a short yet ill advised appointment as the company's public face.

At a time when protocol features prominently in the news, it seemed fitting that I should learn the correct verbal procedure for answering the telephone. My diction was beyond reproach when speaking to customers and associates, but it was not my choice of words that was called into question as much as the fact that they had to negotiate a gargantuan quantity of barbecue beef Wotsits before vacating my mouth. This is apparently to the detriment of public relations.

September 9 Tuesday

As the owner of a car that deserves an appreciative pat on the chassis and a cup of oil with a biscuit just for getting me to work, it gives me a perverse inverted pleasure to park it right next to the vehicles of the directors, all of which look to have cost considerably more than the five hundred quid that I paid for mine.

I was informed today by someone who knows about these things that the car of Financial Director, David Stonehouse, a machine called a Mercedes Kompressor, is priced at around £34,000. At this price I would expect certain features to be included that have been omitted, such as having more seats than the allotted two and having the word 'Compressor' spelled correctly.

Actually, for £34,000 I would expect a decent sized bungalow with a well kept garden.

September 10 Wednesday

The ever expanding variety of work that our department undertakes went one further today. Catherine Melvin from Commercial informed me that there was a problem with the bins in the women's toilets, so I offered to swap them with the ones in the men's because we're not bothered are we?

But she insisted that a special type of 'ladies' bin' was required and that there was more to it than just slapping on a couple of transfers featuring wild flowers. No. It is all rather gruesome and involves the moon. It is hardly a fitting subject to dwell upon in this noble publication. Still, you live and learn.

September 14 Sunday

Sunderland were live on television at Birmingham this afternoon and we won 1-0. Evidently we have discovered a loophole in the law that says we are prohibited from winning on television.

September 16 Tuesday

There was a less than gripping Coca-Cola Cup tie with Bury in a half empty stadium this evening, but it was enlivened by the walky-talkies. I wanted to use them to say 'Get down to the corner of Third and Atlantic. We have a suspected homicide at the Long Beach Motel,' but was not allowed to do so.

The dialogue over the airwaves was not quite as snappy and chic as this, the most memorable exchange concerned a pile of vomit that had been deposited adjacent to Exit 24. This was low priority puke as Exit 24 serves the visiting supporters. But the radios still give you a real sense of being at the very heart of our national sport.

September 17 Wednesday
The first named 'Bricks in the Wall' went up today. Ooooh!

September 20 Saturday
We drew 1-1 at home to Wolverhampton Wanderers. Our goal was a magnificent diving header from Martin Smith. Their equaliser was an own goal by Andy Melville, sliced in at an angle that Pythagoras would have difficulty explaining

September 23 Tuesday
John Mallan and I had been working flat out for literally 20 minutes this morning and so felt justified in taking time to have a game of head tennis in the warm-up area. He beat me quite heavily too, although I felt it was quite unsporting of him not to point out beforehand that he was a regular for Spelter Works Road College throughout the 1962-63 season. I had to sulk for the remainder of the day.

His sledge hammer had cracked my nut and I was far from happy with this.

September 26 Friday
When walking through reception this afternoon I was informed that someone was on the telephone for me. It was a chap from our opponents on Sunday, Middlesbrough, who wears their mascot costume on a match day.

As it turned out, he had been given the wrong Tony. He actually wanted to speak to Tony Davison who is his opposite number at Sunderland. Realising this, I began to make my way to Tony's desk to pass on the message, which led me to ponder the downward spiral that my career is on. Surely running errands between Roary the Lion and Samson The Cat is about as low as it gets.

At least we aren't playing West Ham. I could not bring myself to do a favour for someone called Harry the Hammer.

September 27 Saturday
Alas, it was my birthday today. Among the glittering array of prezzies accumulated were a Broons book, a toothbrush and a St. Michael's crispy aromatic duck, so from this we can probably deduce that I am a difficult person to buy for. It also proved that my hints for a medium sized semi close to the beach have fallen on conveniently deaf ears.

Matters are made worse by me having to go to work in the morning, which has postponed the traditional, self-presented birthday gift of an evening boozing my head clean off. Maybe next year.

September 28 Sunday

Off to work, where we had quite an unfortunate defeat against Middlesbrough. But what I shall remember most about the match is the dumbfounding rigidity with which dress restrictions are enforced in the Banqueting Suite.

An electrician was asked for over the radio to investigate some flickering lights. A sparky was promptly dispatched there, but upon arrival was equally promptly chucked out for wearing jeans. This soon to be famous tale could have had an even worse outcome for the lad if he had been wearing trainers too, in which case he would have been disembowelled.

Samson The Cat and Roary the Lion had a half-time nose-to-nose confrontation, much to the delight of the partisan crowd, each set of supporters chanting 'Samson! Samson!' or 'Roary! Roary!' to encourage their respective champion. Sadly, the two gladiators might be in some trouble because of this. It was a most distressing incident and the powers that be should not be deterred from implementing a draconian punishment just because yobbos like me were doubled with laughter.

September 29 Monday

I write this entry at the outset of British Fashion Week. Much is being made of the 'fact' that this country lags behind others when it comes to style.

Who decided this? *I* have decided that we as a nation are at the forefront of chic and that it is the others who need to sort out their wardrobes. British Fashion Week is the perfect opportunity to state unequivocally that from now on, gentlemen wearing khaki shorts in warm weather must complement them with sandals, beige knee length socks and a fawn tank-top, a rig-out that only the British seem to be able to pull off with any aplomb. Any deviation from this simply fails as haute couture.

October 3 Friday

We are at Redge's house in London at the moment! Boooaaaghhh! Not in a fit condition to write any more than this at prusunt.

October 4 Saturday

A right miserable trek we made to Reading today. To lose 4-0 to this lot and deserve to requires something over and above incompetence. It needs satanic intervention. Our lot must have led some evil past lives.

Before the humiliation, we gathered at a pub by a canal where we tried to prevail upon Taff to organise some taxis to the ground. He stared at us with genuine incredulity, as though we had asked him to move Berkshire four inches to the left and blurted out, 'How can I order taxis? I'm completely pissed!'

84

Didn't we feel the daft ones, although a rather posh middle-aged couple sitting on a nearby low wall that Taff subsequently fell over were most amused. He is probably being discussed at a dinner party as I write.

October 5 Sunday

As usual, the highlight of my weekend away was completely disassociated from football. We had a stroll around the Natural History Museum this afternoon and it was truly fascinating.

I found out that Britain only became separated from mainland Europe at the last ice age ten thousand years ago, most of the dinosaurs were not carnivorous and that I weigh twelve hundred times less than a blue whale.

However, the most useful piece of knowledge that I acquired today was that when visiting a London museum in the future I should bring my own dinner. Not enough scientific evidence has yet been collated to justify charging a quid for a cup of tea.

October 7 Tuesday

The gossip around the club at present is that the stadium is to be officially opened by some old sailor. This turned out to be Prince Andrew. I thought that the stadium had already been officially opened by Ajax, but I wish it had been Prince Andrew instead of the Dutch ones, as we would have beaten him easily.

Extensive preparations are already underway and we have even mooted plans to buy a tin of Mr. Sheen, subject to majority approval at a board meeting of course.

October 10 Friday

Today I saw Steve Agnew's arse!

This hugely impressive claim to fame came about when I was showing two people around the stadium who will be setting up official tours at a later date. When we arrived at the changing rooms, I made a joke about checking them first for naked footballers, as one of the party was female. As my inspection was just a precaution and I was not really expecting to see one, it was quite a shock to turn the corner and see the said arse winking at me. Naturally I took backward steps, mainly through surprise, but also because there was a naked man standing in front of me.

It was immediately decided not to feature this on the tours.

October 11 Saturday

Liz and I were invited to Bernie and Lesley's house to watch some Italian police spend their evening indiscriminately, but sociably, bludgeoning football supporters, interspersed with Italy and England's goalless draw.

The evening was well complemented by an appropriate meal of pasta and pizza. This put me in mind of the gimmick used by the Jacobean Club during the 1994 World Cup. They would have hamburgers for the USA matches, pumpernickel for Germany, chilli for Mexico and so on. There was some disappointment at the final, won by Brazil, when a bowl of nuts was unceremoniously dumped on the bar.

People should not grumble. If Chad had qualified they would have got nothing.

October 13 Monday

Tragically, it would seem that the Country and Western singer, Mr. John Denver, has had his last hit, *Monterey Bay*, where he crashed his light aircraft earlier today.

As has already been pointed out by unamusing people everywhere, this was an ironic end for the man who wrote a song called *Leaving On A Jet Plane*. Yet, putting the predictability of this comment to one side for the moment, as he sits strumming his guitar on his little cloud, he must be ruing the fact that he did not compose a song entitled *Dying Peacefully In Your Sleep At A Ripe Old Age*. At least he got to follow in the footsteps of Jim Reeves and Buddy Holly.

It is strange to think that he will no longer be there to be taken home on his country road, or just hanging around, waiting to have his senses filled up like a night in the forest, like a mountain in spring time, like a walk in the . . .

October 15 Wednesday

We lost again to Middlesbrough, this time in the Coca-Cola Cup third round. The good news is that Edwin Zoetebier was playing in goal. This means that if we can sign someone called Xavier we will have completed the alphabet.

October 16 Thursday

No doubt they were all wetting themselves at the *Guinness Book Of Records* today as somebody broke the land speed record. Nobody knows why. This is simply an extravagant and ostentatious waste of petrol, although if they buy it from Mobil and collect the Premier Points they should easily have enough for an ironing board.

I am advised against such cynicism by those who feel that this is an advancement in speed generally, and that this will help to pave the way for me to arrive at work in about 14 seconds. This is of course cobblers. Donald Campbell drove a car at 430 miles an hour in 1964, but 33 years later I have yet to own a vehicle that will do much over 60, although a two hundred quid budget contributes to this.

October 18 Saturday

Home attendances are dwindling alarmingly, but we began to arrest that slide today by actually beating Huddersfield Town. Deliberately.

October 21 Tuesday

Another home game, this time a goalless draw with Swindon Town. I am afraid that a better writer than me is required to think of anything further to report on the matter, apart from Peter Reid making disparaging comments from the dugout about Steve MacMahon's legs.

Never mind, it will soon be May.

October 25 Saturday

Despite letting the now departed Paul Stewart score a goal past us, Sunderland still managed to beat a Stoke City side that was otherwise about as impressive as a pile of old toe nail clippings. A roaring fire can be made with a bulging mound of old toe nail clippings.

I am afraid I was not there. In fact, I was in Hills the bookshop at half-time with a radio stuck to my ear. It was in there that a well to do, retired colonel type asked me how Newcastle were also faring. When I informed him that they were losing again, he grinned and opined with eloquence and unmistakable sarcasm that it was a 'very great pity'.

It is gratifying to know that posh people hate the Mags too.

October 28 Tuesday

It was Bethan's fifth birthday today, so she had the mandatory party in the Stadium Sports Bar which she and her friends attended with the express intention of making as much noise as possible. I got ten per cent off as a member of staff and I also got to miss the first hour, which isn't bad. When I arrived the party goers were belting each other around the head with balloons, so I surmised that things were going well.

To make the party more fulfilling, for me anyway, I actively assisted the guests with the guzzling of sausage rolls and, with the utmost respect to my gluttony, there was a sound agenda behind this. I had paid for the food. Next year there will be a 'Who can eat the least?' competition which should save a few quid.

October 30 Thursday

I was sitting in the kitchen at work today (the Kitchen Of Light), minding other people's business with that quiet yet deeply attractive demeanour of mine, when Christine from Marketing came in and abruptly asked this fellow what he was doing.

This was rather curious as the lad was standing at the time with a pumpkin in one hand, a knife in the other and on the day before Hallowe'en. Some appreciative applause rippled around the room in recognition of the daftest question to be raised in 1997 so far, and one which is unlikely to be beaten with only two months left.

He was of course making a lantern to repel any witches from the Admin. Building, although he has not exactly been one hundred per cent successful in this so far.

November 1 Saturday

It was all aboard for Stockport County, where we smuggled out a totally undeserved point when Lee Clark equalised with the last kick of the game. We overcame our guilt by guffawing uncontrollably.

On the way down, Bernie, me and Taff were discussing some fairly inconsequential matters when Taff struggled to remember a particular word. Ironically, the word was 'memorise' and as Bernie and I began to titter, Taff indignantly defended his ignorance by declaring that 'Words are shite!' - except for the word 'shite' which he rather likes.

This means that we can now file away words alongside literature, opera, real ale, France and just about anything that isn't football.

Why play 'let's see how many red cars we can spot' when Taff is there for entertainment?

November 4 Tuesday

We preserved our position among a select band of mediocre Fist Division teams by securing another goalless draw with Charlton Athletic.

November 8 Saturday

It is beginning to look among the current despondency as though Sunderland have signed a very good centre forward in Kevin Phillips. He scored yet another goal today in yet another draw, this time with Nottingham Forest, and dabbled in a little celebration of a Klinsman type dive on his chest.

This was much to the appreciation of the crowd, but I suspect to the chagrin of Brenda and Christine in the laundry, who frown upon stubborn grass stains being acquired from such unnecessary horseplay.

He'll have to go.

November 9 Sunday

Annoyingly, I had to be at work today to prepare for tomorrow's visit of fourth in line to the throne and fat sailor Prince Andrew, the Duke of York, or Porky Yorky as inferior satirists call him.

I had a sneaky look at the guest list for luncheon (as we will call it for the next two days) and felt slightly wounded at not being invited. This is probably just as well for two reasons, the first being the conspicuous absence of Cheesy Wotsits from the menu, the second being that the head of the Tyne & Wear Development Corporation, Mr. Alistair Balls, is to attend with his wife Beryl.

It would be of mountainous difficulty to display any decorum in the company of someone called Beryl Balls, the best comedy ailment that I have heard for a while.

November 10 Monday

As expected, the Duke of York arrived in time for his lunch and then officially opened the stadium, which could mean that I have been trespassing until now!

In a way, it is no bad thing that this visit has taken place, as it has resulted in many jobs that would normally have been overlooked now being completed. Areas that were previously as grubby as a sailor's duvet are now in pristine condition. Things that were already clean were cleaned again anyway. Things that do not need to ever be cleaned were cleaned nonetheless. For example, I would question the necessity of cleaning the cleaning utensils. All of this effort just for one podgy matelot to have his dinner.

November 11 Tuesday

Things were pretty much back to normal today after yesterday's royal visit. The place is still gleamingly clean, but we have signed an off-hire note for the Hubble Telescope which we have used to locate any fag ends that would have otherwise been missed and it can now concentrate on Jupiter which is much easier to find.

The resumption of normality was much appreciated by those of us whose visits to the lav were punctuated by fear of being interrupted and forcibly ejected from the stadium by men descending ropes in black polo neck jumpers and matching balaclavas. Others are content with the deluded memories of HRH actually being interested in us.

November 15 Saturday

Our win at Portsmouth this afternoon was nothing less than historic. We came from a goal behind to win for the first time since 1990. A great deal has happened since then, Prime Ministers have come and gone, Bethan was born, Terry Scott passed away, the Gulf War was fought and Marathons changed to Snickers. Although, apart from that it has been quite dull around the place.

Local statisticians have been enjoying themselves in the light of this momentous event. Did you know, for instance, that if another seven years elapses before this happens again, people will be really pissed off?

November 18 Tuesday

John Mallan and I spent the morning rounding up unused television stands and making a fortune by selling them to the scrap yard. We gathered a good mound of iron which should get the construction of the Ark Royal off to a good start.

However, going to Monte Carlo was crossed off my itinerary for another year when we got off the weigh bridge and found that we stood to make precisely 16 pounds and 50 pence between us. We though of asking the club's coach to lie in the back of the van to bolster the weight and obtain money by deception. But Bobby Saxton, who is not dissimilar to the old priest in *Father Ted,* would be likely to regard this as a cheap jibe about his physique.

November 19 Wednesday

The players trained in the stadium today for some reason. As I strolled through reception, I chanced to walk past Kevin Ball who, ever courteous, said hello and politely enquired if I would mind awfully taking the keys to the physio's car and hiding it.

I was not too sure about this, so he assured me that I could have a lift back, as though this was the only consideration before taking a vehicle without the owner's consent. We soon established that this was childish, petty and mean spirited, then did it. As club captain he has responsibility for general frivolity and arsing about and will clearly not shirk from this.

November 22 Saturday

We went down to Bury in our customary droves and we drew 1-1, but to me the football was almost incidental to the days proceedings.

The first sight to greet us as we joined the traffic jam in the centre of Bury was that of Taff, bounding towards us, carrying a crook lock and asking people for lifts. 'Aye aye,' said Liz, 'looks like he's written off another car.'

Educated conjecture at that stage, yet completely accurate.

The moral here is don't read and drive. He blamed Tonka, who had been in the passenger seat when he drew attention to an article in the *Mirror,* which featured a cloud that looked like Princess Diana and was obviously of far more interest than the road.

One of the other passengers, Gerard Callaghan, came back with us and must have begun to suspect that it was not his day when my car conked out temporarily on the A1 and a tyre blew out on the A19. When we finally arrived back at the Ivy House, we reflected that it had indeed been a hard-earned point.

November 24 Monday

Tony Davison aka Samson The Cat sauntered up to me in the kitchen at work and invited me to a party on Wednesday night. It is to be a proper man's affair with football videos, food fights, projectile vomiting and a competition to see who can consume the most brandy through a straw nasally. Rrrrr!

What a night it will be, so I beat my chest, shook his hand (with all my strength obviously) and told him I would be there, where men are men.

Of course, this was total male bravado on my part as I have no intention of attending, but I could not very well tell him that this was because I had to take Bethan to see *Snow White On Ice.*

November 26 Wednesday

Snow White on Ice was a joy to behold, if not a little predictable.

November 29 Saturday

Another home game today and I stood for it in what is now my customary position between the two dugouts, anonymously prying the goings on between the benches.

I have justified me being there by allotting myself with the pivotal task of pulling the retractable tunnel in and out. If you think of this as a very menial task that any able bodied person would be able to do, then you would be quite wrong because I wouldn't let any other able bodied person do it.

We beat Tranmere Rovers 3-0 and because the BBC's fly-on-the-wall documentary team was having a final snoop around the place, I was virtually horizontal in the course of trying to get on camera.

December 2 Tuesday

72 hours without watching a football match is no effortless feat, so we went to Hartlepool to see *the* United put on a sterling show of footballing prowess. Only a team of the calibre of Hull City could stop them and so it proved in a beguiling two-two draw.

Suddenly being a Sunderland supporter does not seem like such a bad lot after all. However, the pies at the Victoria Ground actually do live up to their good reputation. Believe the hype!

December 5 Friday

I was up at the training this afternoon to carry out the mundane task of measuring up for yet another broken window. I was in a great hurry as I was extremely busy and the chip shop was about to close.

I was therefore not pleased to arrive there and see so many people littering the place and generally getting in the way. I needed access to the head tennis area and was further hindered in this by Alex Rae, the self-appointed Minister for Tomfoolery and Arsing About, who would not allow me to enter on the grounds that it was 'Couples only'. With the last cod being plopped into the fryer as he spoke, this was no time for high jinks, and it was crisps again for dinner.

91

December 6 Saturday
We went to Queen's Park Rangers and won 1-0 as wrongly predicted by me last night.

December 9 Tuesday
The BSE crisis has swung into yet another avenue of farce today, with the news that a lorry load of imported meat had arrived at Holyhead much to the annoyance of local farmers, who, when word got round, arrived en masse at the port and besieged the vehicle with angry rural chants of 'Now look here!' and 'This just won't do!' and other passionate cantations.

The slogan on the side of the lorry, 'One Hundred Per Cent Irish Beef', was seen as an inflammatory Gaelic gloat. But, there were some acutely embarrassed farmers when they found out that it referred to a troupe of male strippers called Celtic Nights.

I just thought I would mention it.

December 12 Friday
The club's latest gimmick is to have two Twentieth Century Fox type searchlights to draw attention to the stadium in a spectacular and eye catching manner. The idea came from the directors, who might not have ushered in the scheme with such urbane alacrity if it was they and not us who had to lug the things up to the roof through the plant room with John Mallan's washing line.

At least I got the chance to keep Tonka awake at night by aiming one of them at his bedroom window, and the shadow puppet of a dog that I had looming over the Wearside night sky was simply spellbinding.

December 13 Saturday
Another home game and another win, 2-0 over West Bromwich Albion this time. This is beginning to look quite sexy.

December 16 Tuesday
We had another excursion to the training ground where we had further confirmation that meeting footballers does not always live up to expectations.

Niall Quinn, an otherwise lovely chap, staggered past me on his way back to the changing rooms, perspiration seeping from every part of his body except for his left nostril which was being occupied by a rather drippy and unpleasant looking snot. It was trying to vacate his body but probably didn't fancy the long journey ahead of it to the ground.

Little wonder then that so much is written about them, even the Bard would be inspired. 'Shall I compare thee to a summer's day,' I mused.

Indeed, Niall does invite the comparison as both are rather long and sweaty, although only one of them has played for Ireland.

December 17 Wednesday
After damaging virtually every muscle, tissue, sinew, bone and blood cell in the course of positioning those two searchlights on Friday, it has been decided that they are not quite positioned correctly and that we shall have to move them accordingly. I think Tonka has phoned up and complained.

December 20 Saturday
The mighty shall not stand in our way, nor will Crewe Alexandra. We won 3-0 at (unfashionable) Gresty Road.

December 22 Monday
I had harboured hopes of idling away the last couple of working days before Christmas, a hope that was dispersed when I was sent to the training ground to drag some furniture across a muddy field. What larks.

Most of the players were there, hanging around and being sweaty. In a room full of affluent and celebrated men, it is easy for some people to feel insignificant and anonymous, but not me. There are two objects that can lend the owner immediate attention and respect, assuming that no one else present has them. One is a gun, the other is a bag of chips. Guess which one I had.

The snivelling manner in which they appealed for chips was exactly as they would have told the referee that it was an accident really.

December 24 Wednesday
Christmas Eve in Sunderland city centre involves a good deal of drink, the wearing of tinsel in the hair and mistletoe on the button of your jeans, spraying shaving foam at each other and singing *Happy Christmas, War Is Over* in the bus station. Obviously it is difficult to resist the lure of this and stay in, but somehow I pulled it off.

December 25 Thursday
We had a good few people round for Christmas dinner, so I nipped over to the stadium to borrow a foldable table. The players were in there training. Ha!

December 26 Friday
We had a full house for our victory over Boxing Day Bradford City today. Flouncing down the tunnel at half-time, I bumped into rock goddess Ruth Anne 'You're Not Alone' Boyle (see the 16th of May), who was pulling out the winners in the prize draw in her new capacity as best-celebrity-we-could-get.

As a group of nearby youths became visibly excited by the mere sight of her and began to shout for autographs, all I could think was, 'It's only Ruth,' remembering her nicking my crisps in years gone by.

However, our disco diva let herself down rather by tugging at my sleeve and squealing, 'It's Peter Reid!' as she looked over at the home dugout. Fame is indeed a fickle mistress. Still, I was much the same when I saw Bill Maynard buying a cream slice in Littlewood's.

December 28 Sunday

Oxford United 1 Sunderland 1. Does anyone want me to elaborate on this?

December 30 Tuesday

The ticket office has ended the year with the traditional fiasco, this time over the allocation of tickets for the forthcoming FA Cup game at Rotherham. It was therefore not a good day to bump into Taff who is well capable of mounting any horse, no matter what height it has attained, and his latest steed is of many hands high.

His latest bout of indignation has led to him arranging a meeting for himself and Davie Dowell with the club secretary. Tickets could be sold for this meeting if we could rely upon the ticket office to allocate them.

Taff's proposed opening gambit of 'Why are you so crap?' is a strategically bold move, although Mr. Blackbourne may consider it to be something of a loaded question.

December 31 Wednesday

Well, 1997 was mainly rubbish.

1998

January 1 Thursday

The year kicked off with a spooky coincidence. With nothing better to do today, I looked back on my diary entry for New Year's Day last year and was intrigued to discover that I spent it lying around the house, complaining about the telly, eating anything within arm's reach to avoid a trek to the kitchen, avoiding fresh air at all costs until it was time to venture outdoors (in a taxi of course), and down to the Ivy House.

A quick browse through a few other diaries reveals that this sequence of events happens on this date with a regularity that almost defied mathematical probability. It made me think. It made me think last year too. I went down to the Ivy House in a taxi to ponder this.

January 2 Friday

The white knuckle ride that is 1998 continued with event upon exhilarating event. No sooner had I been to the shops for the paper, than it was off to the garage to have a couple of drive shafts put into the car, then back to the shops for some batteries and a tin of ravioli (which I always find lends an exotic touch to toast).

After this roller coaster of an afternoon, it seemed prudent that I should take things easy from there on and have a night in. There was also the fact that I had almost boozed my head off during the proceeding week.

The pace will quicken still further tomorrow. We are off to Rotherham.

January 3 Saturday

Our FA Cup tie with Rotherham United was a possible upset, a potential banana skin, perhaps they could throw a spanner in the works sort of game. All wrong as it turned out because they were crap and we beat them 5-1 in the least surprising result of the day.

Kevin Phillips scored four goals which smacks of showing off to me, but everyone seemed to enjoy it as he swaggered before a crowd that was singing his name. After a while I became rather bored with this and wanted to start a different song and what could be more different than 'Kevin Phillips is hopelessly inadequate!' But it never really got going, partly because I could not think of a tune that would fit the words properly.

January 4 Sunday

There was even more David and Goliath stuff in the FA Cup today when Wimbledon played Wrexham. Wimbledon are still in the Cup too which is no surprise to those of us who know our Old Testament.

Actually the analogy is not a very good one as it is fairly obvious that David would win. This is for three very valid reasons. The first reason is that as top Philistine, Goliath was a baddie and therefore fated to lose. Secondly is that David's biggest fan was God which can only be a boost. Finally and most importantly, David had a whacking great sling and half a brick for ammunition, with which he could hit a canary, let alone a large Philistine, on the bonce from two hundred paces. Goliath, on the other hand, had no such weaponry or skill.

Where is David's disadvantage there?

January 5 Monday

The papers today carried a list of the supposed hundred most influential artists of the Twentieth Century. They are so influential that I had heard of exactly 53 of them. Controversial omissions include Simone de Bouvoir, P.G. Wodehouse, Francis Bacon and Tony Hart.

One notable inclusion is Jackson Pollock and having seen some of his paintings I can only assume that this accolade is in recognition of him providing mankind with the most appropriate rhyming slang possible.

My personal choices for inclusion would have included Harry Carpenter, Rustie Lee, whoever wrote the song *Baggy Trousers* and anyone who will mend our shower. Credit where it is due and lots more fun.

January 6 Tuesday

For many people, the Epiphany signifies that the festivities have ended and that the decorations should be taken down. For us poor souls it means that we take down the enormous searchlights from the stadium roof.

This is the second pair we have used, having put them up a couple of weeks ago with the stated intention of making Bob Murray say 'Oooooh!', but he only said 'Ooh!' so we have taken them down again. The first set only managed an 'Mmm' and were therefore something of a non-starter.

They are not bright and powerful enough, so with this in mind I expect the next set to be capable of char-grilling the moon. Incidentally, the Great Wall of China and our lights are the only man made objects that are visible from the moon.

January 7 Wednesday

I sat vegetating on the settee this evening and soon became bored. Then I became super deluxe bored and then economy sized bored with extra tedium. God I was BORED!

It got to the point where I began to read Liz's magazines having been mildly intrigued by the promise on the cover of *Marie Claire* of telling me where I would be in six months time. I expected to see a picture of either the settee or the Ivy House, but it seems that all manner of strange and wonderful things will have happened to me by then. This is due to Venus packing in Neptune to go out with hunky Jupiter or something.

The difficulties of keeping a diary on a day as dull as this have to be experienced to be appreciated.

January 8 Thursday

I was late for work this morning. I had told myself that I would just have another five minutes in bed and lapsed back into a marvellous but time consuming dream about soup and that was that.

The first thing that I did when I arrived was to say sorry to a cleaner for my tardiness. But this was more of an expression of regret than remorse, the reason being that she was hopping around with more energy than I had previously given her credit for as a result of having dropped a cumbersome Morphy Richard vacuum cleaner on her foot. In other words, had I been a mere 90 seconds earlier I would have been able to witness this rather amusing accident taking place.

What might have been.

January 9 Friday

I was in the board room today under the pretence of inspecting the furniture, but I was really just watching the television. The news was mainly concerned with the destructive forces of nature that have inflicted a trail of devastation around the country, endangering lives and property, not to mention the irreparable damage to trees, flora and fauna.

In a trailer for one of their imminent features, *This Morning*, which came on immediately afterwards, really captured the gravity of the situation. A peremptory voice abruptly announced, 'Blizzards! Storms! Hurricanes! Home threatening cyclones! We have Nicky Clarke to tell you what to do with YOUR hair in this weather . . . '

So finger on the pulse as usual then. Only day time television can accurately recreate the trauma of losing the front of your house and then discovering split ends as well.

January 10 Saturday

There was a very good game at home to Sheffield United today that we won 4-2. While working / posing at the match, there is a code of professional ethics which dictates that a certain amount of detachment be used regarding events on the pitch. I patently failed to adhere to this code this afternoon. Upon seeing the decisive fourth goal being scored, I raced forward a full three yards and leapt to a height that was a personal best, hands above my head and walkie-talkie in mid air a yard higher still. Get in! What a goal!

I was in the tunnel at the time and a sideways glance from a member of the Sheffield United bench was enough to suggest that he doubted my impartiality.

January 11 Sunday

It was a perfect day today, dedicated entirely to gluttony, sloth and football. Having virtually boozed my head off last night on the back of yesterday's win, I cleverly spent half of the day in bed, getting up at about one o'clock to watch the video of the match whilst steadily transferring the contents of a lengthy shopping list from the fridge and into me.

After a lie down to recuperate, it was time to go to the Ivy House to continue research into just how much more booze would be required to actually decapitate myself. By the time I left for home I felt justifiably proud of myself, as for today at least, I have been a great bloke.

January 12 Monday

A glorious weekend came to an horrific end this morning. The mere fact that it was Monday was a harsh enough fact to deal with in itself. It was then compounded by having to conduct the post match toilet inspection.

For the record, there were two blockages, both of them in the female areas as is often the case, which always amazes me. To look at these blockages, it seems unlikely that they could be caused by a mere woman unless she had bowels like Dr. Who's Tardis. Indeed the sheer volume of it would put many a larger mammal to shame.

Physically, I suppose this is quite an achievement, but not one that any woman is likely to own up to, so it is with some temerity that they complain about childbirth.

January 14 Wednesday

I looked into my pigeon hole as soon as I arrived at work and immediately felt the cold steely grip of dejection upon seeing that there was no post for me. This feeling lasted for about an hour, which was how long it took me to remember that Saint Valentine's Day is on the 14th of February and not January. Phew!

January 16 Friday

With Sunderland already established as the cultural capital of the entire world, that reputation has been further cemented by the publication of today's local album charts. At Number One is Prokofiev with his *Dance Of The Knights* from the second act of his ballet, *Romeo and Juliet*. The popularity of this piece stems from the fact that it is played at the stadium before the teams take to the pitch. Showaddywaddy are Number Two.

The new found popularity of this bit of classical has left the record shops with some difficulty in understanding what is required when confronted with a request for 'that tune from the match.' Most of them have gone home with the theme from *Z Cars* by accident.

However, we must not be snobs on this one, not least because one of the directors suggested *Raiders Of The Lost Ark* for our signature tune. Mind you, *Bonanza* would have been fun.

January 17 Saturday

We set off for Manchester and were therefore happenin', mad for it our kid. We beat City 1-0 in a non-event of a game, before embarking upon the serious business of seeing how much we could impair our speech and balance with Boddingtons.

While we were out and about, Davie Smith made a hopeful attempt at seducing an androgynous boiler with the sympathy method, claiming to have a fibre glass foot as a result of a car crash. 16 stone Gerard Callaghan helpfully loaned some plausibility to this lie by stamping on the said foot with all his might and saying, 'See. That doesn't hurt him.'

Gratitude was not as evident as it might have been.

January 19 Monday

I had a popular modern music radio station playing in the van today. One of the songs that they played was *Always On My Mind* by the late Elvis Presley. This song always puts a shudder down my spine when I hear the line, 'Maybe I didn't treat you, quite as good as I should have'. In fact, the dreadful grammar employed in this line would send a shudder down the spine of anyone who values good English.

Furthermore, if we are to be magnanimous enough to allow him the sloppy colloquialism 'ain't', then he could at least afford us the courtesy of singing, 'You ain't anything like a hound dog', otherwise this type of beat combo music will never catch on among the young people.

January 20 Tuesday

There are plans afoot at the club to build a new 'Training Academy' complete with 19 football pitches. The expected furore about it being a green belt area took about ten minutes to occur.

'This is a green belt area you know,' said a bloke with glasses on the local news. He also had green braces to add weight to his argument, although this might just have been our cheap telly.

The ignorant amongst us are left to wonder why this would jeopardise a green belt, unless I have been significantly misled as to the colour of football pitches. What we need is a beige belt, then we could build what we like, unless it was green.

99

January 21 Wednesday

I was returning from the switch room, where I had been playing at *Close Encounters* by turning the floodlights on and off, when who should I see but the eponymous hero of *John Craven's Newsround*. He now presents an agricultural and environmental programme called *Country File* and was therefore looking for the pitch. It was all to do with this green belt business.

It has been a few years now, but I'll bet he still knows a thing or two about pandas and breakthroughs in school dinners. I would have asked him too had he not said, 'Bye for now,' then sodded off with his camera crew. Still, it was another climatic moment in my career and one that I intend to boast about for at least a month. I even made him a cup of tea at the training ground later on. Oh yes.

January 22 Thursday

The atmosphere at work was rather mundane, which was surely inevitable given the glory-soaked events of yesterday. Having been within touching distance of the stars, the descent back to Earth was a hard one and completely John Cravenless.

Worse than that, I have even been deprived of the pleasure of telling people about meeting him, having already run out of people to tell. Strangely, the hordes of folk that I have informed have been somewhere between polite and indifferent.

The one exception was Bob Fairley and he got him confused with someone else. 'John Craven eh?' he repeated excitedly, 'Brilliant! Custy! GET DOWN SHEP!'

Oh well.

January 23 Friday

The latest L'Oreal commercial is nothing other than a severe let-down with regards to its star. Not sexy at all. For a start it is a bloke, secondly it is a footballer and thirdly it is David Ginola.

With a scrupulous regard to fair play to the wildly overrated ex-Mag and whinging French ponce, his hair is in first rate condition. The style on the other hand is about as appealing as looking at it. The same shiny, bouncing effect could have been achieved in quadruple if they had got the Guildford Four to do the ad.

January 24 Saturday

The road to Wembley proved to be a rather truncated one. In fact it ended at Tranmere, which is some way short to tell the truth.

I had our victory all planned out. What with us being unbeaten in 17 games, having the most prolific goal scorer in the country at present and Tranmere on something of a slippery slope, only a win could be assured. Alas, one should always be aware of potential flaws in even the most masterly of strategies and in this case the flaw was that we always lose at Prenton Park.

Perhaps I should switch sports. I was in Ashbrooke rugby club this evening for Andy Wayman's engagement party. They bite each other's ears off but they always go for a drink afterwards. Bloody great blokes!

January 25 Sunday

I was up with the larks this morning and was even in time for lunch. The reason for this unseemly early rise was to catch the great John Craven in *Country File*. But the programme was an overall disappointment. Despite my assiduous efforts on Wednesday, walking back and forth, jumping up and down, arm waving, etc., I did not appear on screen in any way shape or form. Not a digit.

What an extravagant waste of effort.

January 26 Monday

I sneaked out of our office this afternoon in order to fill the kettle for a sly cup of tea, but I was caught out quite spectacularly. I had just opened the door of the players lounge to use the tap when the door opposite swung open too and I was faced with the manager, the club secretary, the chief executive and a throng of photographers and reporters.

This seemed to be an excessively severe, not to say swift retribution for an illicit tea break. So I was glad to see them all ignore me and file past. It transpired that they were gathering to witness and record the signing of a new player called Daniel Dichio and were therefore too distracted to be aware of any corruption that might surround me concerning tea.

January 27 Tuesday

I was chatting with John Cooke the kit manager this morning. I found him in felicitous mood at the prospect of returning to his native Salford for a drunken weekend in 'God's Country'. He seemed intent upon convincing me of its urban charms and would have succeeded had I not been there and seen it for myself.

John actually used to play for Sunderland. The embarrassment that would ensue if he ever found out that I still have his autograph somewhere is something that I try not to think about.

January 28 Wednesday

Sunderland finally lost a league game this evening, at Norwich. Before the game, the good people in the Ivy House were magnanimous enough to suggest that it was inconceivable that we could continue indefinitely without a defeat and, this being so, it may as well be to an affable, family-orientated club like Norwich City. They have a long tradition of mutual friendship with Sunderland.

Strangely then, the same people were quite saturated with bitterness and odium, which seems reasonable to the ungracious and amazingly small-minded amongst us. This bigotry was apparently fed by the fact that the citizens of Norwich are in-bred country bumpkins whose city is almost impenetrable because of their sub-standard roads being clogged up with slow moving tractors and ploughs. The Ivy House stands for nothing if not enlightenment.

January 29 Thursday
I spent much of today up at the training ground, setting up the fax machine in Peter Reid's office. It had been repeatedly stressed to me that this was of paramount importance. Were I not to perform this task soon the consequences could have been catastrophic. We would be unable to buy or sell players or pass on information to the media, and as such our share price would plummet and the whole club would stagger into disaster.

Happily I was able to avert any possible cataclysmic outcome by bravely following the instructions in the manual, although I was unable to do this immediately, as he wouldn't let me in because he wanted to watch the cricket. A close run thing then.

January 30 Friday
I was out tonight with an old friend called Steve Martin (no not that one). Our conversation was rather stunted at first as we had not seen each other for a while and he is one of those strange, shallow people who is not very interested in football.

After we had covered Byzantine art and the evolution of man, we moved on to this acquaintance of ours who has recently had surgery on an in-growing hair on his arse. This made Steve wonder out loud (and a little too graphically for my liking) what it would be like if all of his chest hairs began to do the same. 'Urgh!' he opined, 'can you imagine it? Eventually they'd get so far down that they'd start to scratch your lungs. Yak! Ha! Ha! Ha! Ha!"

I then moved on from lager to what Steve was drinking.

January 31 Saturday
Before our sexy 4-2 victory over Port Vale this afternoon, Dave Nicholson and I put the finishing touches to the boardroom toilets, signs above the male and female that say 'Heroes' and 'Heroines' respectively. All of the other toilets in the building have the usual man symbol for the gents and the same man with a skirt on for the ladies, but THIS was the boardroom.

Admiration for the might and majesty of the imperial bogs could be tempered were it to be discovered that we had stuck Heroes and Heroines on to the Swiss pear surrounds with Blu Tak. The Chairman's suspicions have already been aroused, what with him being less than two yards behind us while we were doing it.

February 2 Monday

I decided that it would be wise to make a cursory check of the boardroom toilets this morning, which was a good thing too, as the signs that we had put up so methodically on Saturday had not been the geometric success we had hoped for. 'Heroines' looked decidedly wonky, whereas 'Heroes' was not on the wall at all.

I am at pains to point out that these deficiencies are in no way due to any questionable adhesive qualities of Blu Tak, rather than my own shortcomings as an artisan.

Things began to get worse when we could not find the 'Heroes' sign at all, but at least this gave me the chance to ask, 'Whatever happened to the Heroes?'

February 4 Wednesday

Today we had to set up a podium for a press conference that is being staged tomorrow. The BBC is launching its fly-on-the-wall documentary, the subject this time being, Lord preserve us, Sunderland Association Football Club.

Later I was discussing this forthcoming televisual feast with Tommy the groundsman who is set to feature prominently on the programme. He was wondering whether he had succeeded in getting his face on the goggle box, and having spoken to the crew I could assure him that he had. Apparently, whenever the cameras appeared he would find a way to make himself noticed, stopping short only at conjuring, palm reading and doing the can-can - each of which I wish I had thought of as I am less likely to be featured than him.

February 5 Thursday

The gentlemen of the press all gathered at the appointed time with the dual purpose of previewing the documentary and in the hope of seeing a Director or two fall through our hastily constructed podium.

Having seen a 20 minute trailer of *Premier Passions*, for 'tis the title, the only aspect in which the viewing hacks seemed to be interested in was the Anglo-Saxon nature of Peter Reid's vocabulary. He is absolutely brilliant at swearing, so much so that his diction would fail to make any sense if the obscenities were removed.

Premier Profanity, as it will be known, is due for transmission from the 24th of February and will not feature me.

February 6 Friday

The headline in one newspaper, referring to *Premier Passions*, was 'BLUE PETER', but Mr Reid did not feature in the the main photograph. Just after yesterday's press conference, Tommy the groundsman was posing for pictures in front of the West Stand and this morning he was for some reason surprised to see himself in print, above a caption which read something like 'Tommy is great and everyone must love him'.

He sat back to wallow in his new found high profile praise, and while reclining he rolled his eyes and said, 'Eee! Embarrassing!', without managing to convince anyone else present that he meant this.

February 7 Saturday

Sunderland were playing away to Wolverhampton Wanderers today. Such is our poor recent record at Molineux that the *Football Echo* will have had any number of snappy headlines on standby such as, 'Thrown To The Wolves', 'Wolves Savage Sunderland' or 'Sunderland Lose To Wolves With The Leftovers Made In To A Very Nice Casserole'.

However, all of this journalistic artistry will have been wasted as we somehow contrived to win the game, in the last minute too, which gave them less time to think of an alternative. Hence, the insipid and long-winded 'Sunderland Manage To Score A Goal Whereas Wolves Do Not'. It doesn't exactly roll off the tongue, but full marks for smugness.

February 9 Monday

Tommy the groundsman mania is in its infancy at the moment, but those of us in the know can see it coming. It shouldn't be long before *Hello Magazine* pop along with their cameras, hoping to capture him in the garage with his vintage lawnmowers and state-of-the-art fertiliser. Then, perhaps a browse through his wardrobe of club anoraks. There is surely a place for him on *Celebrity Squares*, possibly on the bottom row where Arthur Mullard used to sit glowering at Nookie Bear.

February 10 Tuesday

It is nice to know that some footballers are just like the rest of us. At the training ground today, I overheard Kevin Ball describing to someone at length the goal he scored at Wolves on Saturday, much as I would do in the Ivy House after a game of five-a-side.

February 11 Wednesday

I was presented with a splendid task today when I was asked to check on the wellbeing of the televisions in the executive boxes. This was great news as I flipped them all on to Cartoon Network and managed to see an entire episode of the *Hair Bear Bunch* for the first time in years, albeit on 54 different sets.

February 12 Thursday

With fame beckoning, Tommy the groundsman has something of a spring in his step at the moment and was especially chirpy today. I know this because I heard him whistling the theme tune from *Hawaii Five-O*.

With the sole intention of puncturing his good mood, I went over to inform him that the star of that programme, Jack Lord, had died several weeks ago, and it seemed to do the trick. However, I did not manage to exacerbate this by further notifying him that TV's Denver Pyle, Uncle Jessie from *The Dukes Of Hazzard*, had also recently passed away. But this still shows the value of being an avid obituary reader.

February 13 Friday

I became needlessly excited today when I was asked if I could give a tour of the stadium to a representative of a club from outside the Football League. The prospect of sucking up to the president of Real Madrid or Ajax was quite appealing, considerably more so than the reality which was the club doctor of Rushden and Diamonds FC and a few of his mates. They are playing Gateshead tomorrow in the Conference and were keen to have a squint around our place like everyone else.

Yet I should not carp. They were very nice people and they presented me with a Rushden and Diamonds FC club tie for my trouble that I shall wear with pride. I just don't know when or why.

February 14 Saturday

What could be more romantic on St. Valentine's day than going to the match? However, these tenderly felt plans were cruelly side tracked by Birmingham City who have qualified for the fifth round of the FA Cup rather than play us. Quite what this entails, I am not qualified to say.

February 15 Sunday

To prove that it is still feasible for me to competently perform two tasks at once, I lay on the settee and listened to the *Shipping Forecast*. When that was over I tuned into Sunderland's very own Sun City 103.4 FM. Their DJ claimed that if one were to lay out all of their records side to side, then they would go around the world 103.4 times. The cynic in me almost made me stand up.

I have chosen not to believe this statistic because I doubt whether their collection would go out of the studio and as far as Food Giant. One possible explanation is that they may own a couple of million copies of *The Living Years*, which from what I have heard is not out of the question.

February 16 Monday

We have let it be known that we are available for work at the Charlie Hurley Training Ground at any time, with the small proviso that the canteen is open. The food is really rather good up there and free, as it is for the players who can hardly be expected to pay for it on their measly stipend. Our developing problem is that we are running out of spurious reasons to go there (cleaning door knobs, rearranging coat hangers, etc).

The question arising from all this is how many people does it take to change a light bulb at the training ground? The answer depends heavily on how much spaghetti they have left. If there is custard for afters the answer could be as many as six.

February 17 Tuesday

An awfully long day at work today as there was a game this evening. There was a full house so it was quite a touching gesture on the part of Reading to be slightly worse than woeful and allow us to win easily.

One blight on the night was a problem that we had with the hot water. Labouring under the erroneous assumption that it had been sorted, I cheerfully approached Kevin Ball after the game and asked if the showers had been okay. The answer was a joyless, 'No. It was cold and it was yellow.'

I only asked him because I was expecting a cheery affirmative and was therefore quite taken aback and slightly embarrassed. I am also frightened of him, so it was a good thing that we had won.

February 18 Wednesday

I heard this morning that Manchester City have sacked their manager, Frank Clark. This is hardly newsworthy for the same reason that someone boiling an egg or scratching their navel is of minimal public interest.

He was actually at our game last night, making notes on Reading, as they are City's next opponents. All a complete waste of time as things turned out, unless he was on overtime.

February 20 Friday

We are on the verge of war with Iraq again and not without good reason, one of those good reasons being that we will win.   Accusation, counter-accusation, demands, threats and brinkmanship, it's all there and really quite exciting.

Attempts at arbitration are being made, so to understand what it must feel like to act as a mediator during an international crisis, Radio Five invited a bloke called Julian Gibson to give us an insight. Julian works for ACAS and was thought to have been a fitting choice as he has resolved a dispute involving some particularly militant dinner ladies in Spennymoor. Some cynics may think of this as trivialising the issue.

February 21 Saturday

Our stadium was half full today, the reason being that we had hired huge screens to plonk on the pitch for people to watch a beamback of our game at Middlesbrough. I wish we hadn't bothered. After an encouraging opening 12 seconds, we went off the boil for the remaining 5388 and deserved to lose 3-1.

Crowd behaviour under these circumstances is really quite peculiar. I do not know of anyone who would sit at home and vociferously boo the television then join in loudly with the chanting (apart from Taff), so why this happened today is beyond me.

Sunderland's overall record on television is hardly enviable. For that matter, we haven't fared too well on the radio down the years either. Bring back *Pathe News*, that's what I say. We were good then.

February 23 Monday

The Museum Vaults has a new sticker on its front window. This, I'm afraid, was the main news of today. It has the bold instruction 'Louts Keep Out', which I immediately became sceptical about, assuming it to be as futile as one of those 'Baby On Board' efforts.

No sooner had I began to scoff at the efficacy of the sticker, than I noticed a gang of burly tattooed vulgar ne'erdo-wells, louts in other words, at the window. They were about to enter the pub and cause unwanted fractiousness, when their leader notices the message and said, 'Well, I'm not staying where I'm not wanted, come on louts, let's go elsewhere.'

It shows what I know.

February 24 Tuesday

We travelled down to Huddersfield tonight to watch Sunderland make heavy weather of beating them 3-2. Inept but exciting.

Among our ensemble was Lisa Shepherd who is one of those weird individuals who made it to adulthood without having attended a football match. Urgh! In fact tonight was her first game. I had expected her to be asking who the man in the black was and about the offside rule (of course), as well as pointing out which player had the nicest legs. In the event she was more perspicacious on the finer points of the game than I had given her credit for, mainly through watching it on television, although she did harbour a curious misapprehension that key moments would be immediately followed by an action replay.

February 25 Wednesday

The first episode of *Premier Passions* was transmitted last night, complete with the promised deluge of bad language. It was reminiscent of *Quadrophenia*, but with football instead of scooters and without anyone going to Brighton and certainly no soundtrack by The Who. Actually, it wasn't very much like *Quadrophenia* at all apart from the abundance of swearing.

A negative side to this temporary fame that has been thrust upon the staff is that we shall spend the next six weeks or so saying, 'Ooh. TV star!' to each other.

February 26 Thursday

It was blustery this morning when I was outside repairing the lower hinges of the door to the production kitchen lift. It was a delicate operation requiring patience, a steady hand, considerable artisanship and an enormous hammer.

While I was there on my knees, a car pulled up and out of it appeared Clair Cogdon from commercial who was unfortunately greeted by a huge gust of wind that apparently raised her skirt. 'Eee! Did you see me knickers there?' she asked loudly, giving away her local origins into the bargain.

I assured her that as a gentleman I was bound by honour to avert my eyes under such circumstances, and therefore I could not possibly have seen her pale blue with white lace trim pants, monogrammed with her initials. When I described them to all the lads in the Ivy House later, they were to a man impressed by my chivalry in the matter.

February 28 Saturday

We dropped two important points by drawing at home to Ipswich Town. But more irritating than this is the accumulating celebrity of Tommy the groundsman who seems to have began to replace the divots in the pitch rather closer to the crowd than previously. 'Look! It's him!' was the murmur at half-time.

Tonight's *Football Echo* described our very own seed king as 'modest Tommy' which I suppose is 50 per cent accurate being as Tommy is his name, but he is actually about as modest as Cassius Clay. Admiration for him is garnered unabated and it is truly amazing how popular he is amongst people who have never met him.

March 4 Wednesday

Sunderland went crazy, ape, bonkers, mad, silly sausage tonight. We went to Nottingham Forest with the hope of leaving with a draw, yet the outcome was that we kicked their East Midlands arses to the tune of 3-0 in B flat! Hurrah!

March 5 Thursday

Being well known as the sort of bloke who is more cultured than a novelist talking to an architect about paintings during an opera, I tend to watch *Late Review* on Thursdays. One of the regular panelists is a bloke called Tom Paulin, who likes virtually no book, play, exhibition or painting ever produced. He does have a soft spot for any Augustan poet who may have died of malnutrition in about 1708, but that's about it. It is fervently hoped that he never gets his teeth into anything as hopelessly lightweight as this diary.

Added to this, he seems to have a burning antipathy to football, soap operas and pop music and probably despises booze, so I hope he never comes for a night out on the razzle with me. Perhaps I am wrong and he enthrals the company with his loud shirts, jokes and card tricks. After all, I have never met him.

March 7 Saturday

Things got better still this afternoon when we conclusively proved that we are superior to even Stockport County. The people we have to deal with at work on a match day though!

Today we had a visit from Tony Banks MP, the Minister for Sport, and he gave me the dubious distinction of being directly involved with the breaking of one of New Labour's political pledges. When he was appointed to office, he promised not to tread on the toes of anyone in football, but when he took a step back to look at the picture in reception his heel went plumb into my left foot as was walking past.

In his defence, he gave an immediate apology and assured me that it would have hurt considerably more under the previous administration.

March 9 Monday

Only 19 days to the Varsity Boat race now. Surely some sort of advent calendar is in order.

March 10 Tuesday

The latest gimmick to be unveiled, literally, by the club is an impressive four metre high ornamental Davy lamp next to the ticket office. It was to be lit for the public before tonight's one-all draw with Birmingham City by Bob Murray and I sincerely hope that he did not conclude his speech with 'Let there be light' as this is one of God's lines. He might be the Chairman, but there is a limit.

Apart from that, there was no light, not for a couple of hours anyway. When Dave Nicholson said 'Gibraltar!' over the radio, it should have lit up, but after the 18th 'Gibraltar!' without a switch-on we began to suspect a fault. Some component or other had conked out in its infancy, leaving an acutely embarrassed Bob to grin uneasily at the gathered crowd. To compound matters there was a heavy downpour too.

Although this is nothing to laugh about, ha! ha! ha! ha! ha! ha!

March 11 Wednesday

The new Davy lamp is clearly the latest source of pride and paranoia at the moment. John Mallan and I received an 'urgent' message concerning the lamp, which apparently had an unsightly item at the apex this morning. We were never to find out what.

Having traipsed round with a ladder, we climbed up it to inspect and found precisely nothing. The emergency could have been caused by anything. Alarming possibilities such as a carrier bag or a crisp packet flashed across our minds. My own feeling it that the offending item flew back to its nest after a passer-by had shouted 'Shoo!' at it. Happily, interest in it will soon wane.

March 13 Friday

It seems that we are to be struck by an asteroid. At first this seemed like a spectacular Friday the 13th mishap, but it is not due until the year 2028 by which time I could well be dead so it hardly matters. I have no real preference as to where it lands so long as it is not on the Ivy House or me, although an asteroid the exact shape and size of North Tyneside could provide interesting if remote possibilities.

Asteroids are worse than meteorites if you ask me and I shall tell you why. Some of them are capable of dislodging the Earth from its axis and quite honestly that is the type of thing that gets right on my wick. I fully intend to write a letter.

March 15 Sunday

I had to go into work this afternoon mainly because we were playing at Charlton Athletic (1-1) on Sky Television and I don't have a dish. The other reason was that I was required to drag a large banner onto the centre circle for a publicity shoot, no doubt giving the girls a Diet Coke break while I was at it.

While I was there, it became quite apparent that the other staff based in the Administration Building have no idea how to find their way around the stadium. One such person named Helen Smith asked me where there was a telephone with which she could contact reception, an odd request seeing as she was standing in it at the time. Interestingly, she has a degree in geography so I assume that the syllabus did not cover receptions.

March 17 Tuesday

This evening's latest instalment of *Premier Passions* contained the by now expected abundance of fruity jargon. At one point in a half-time team talk, Peter Reid turned to his players and snarled, 'I don't mind losing, but I don't like losing shite!'

Of course, one can do nothing but squirm when listening to such scandalously coarse language. In this instance, all he had to do to make the sentence grammatically acceptable was to employ the adverb 'shitely'. However, it may be that I have misinterpreted him entirely and that he had actually misplaced some faeces.

March 21 Saturday

I had my usual culinary prelude to today's home game, a pre-match meal of a cheese sandwich and a chicken pie. Kerry, who has the central task of ordering these meals, urged me to make a more exotic and adventurous choice and I was willing to dabble in pheasant, swan, escargot, quail's eggs, shallots in a white wine sauce, or indeed any old rubbish. Yet the menu at the Roker Pie Shop is not that extensive, so a cheese sandwich and a chicken pie it was then.

This afternoon we simply put Portsmouth to the sword. Keeping the form book well away from the window to prevent any dangerous mishaps, we set about our task with cruel gusto and administered a metaphorical birching. We annihilated them 2-1.

March 23 Monday

Top of the agenda today, the novelty of the Davy lamp having worn thin, was the acquisition of suitably sumptuous lavatory paper for the 'Heroes' and 'Heroines' in the boardroom. Clearly they are unable to use the single ply mass produced stuff that ordinary mortals use, less still the hard hitting, hard-to-bear-when-used *Daily Mirror.* The executive backside is clearly unused to this type of punishment.

No, they have to use quadruple ply material, air woven by angels, which most importantly have pictures of flamingos or a paisley pattern imprinted, otherwise the directorial arse would be in danger of dropping off. Happily, there is a nearby branch of Kwik Save.

March 26 Thursday

We were called to the players lounge to put pictures of the squad up on the wall. Typically, the task was made more difficult by the addendum that they should be placed in alphabetical order.

The problem was exacerbated by the fact that it was transfer deadline day. As soon as we had put up the last picture, some smart-arse sashayed into the room and told us that John Mullin had been sold to Burnley which meant that we had to adjust the position of everyone after 'M'. That done, an even smarter-arse told us that he was only on loan, so we had to go back to where we had put them in the first place.

This was all very annoying, but at least he is called John Mullin and not John Aaaah, otherwise we would have had to move the lot.

111

March 28 Saturday

The government decided some time ago that certain sporting events should be preserved for the nation's pleasure by retaining them for terrestrial television. These 'jewels in the crown' as they are known do not include any of Sunderland's epoch making home games with Bury, including today's 2-1 win, as it does not have the required level of fashion.

This is curiously not supposed to be the case with today's Boat Race, which has been retained along with events that are actually popular. This particular jewel is probably still on the BBC because Sky find it as dull as the rest of us, although finding 18 students who are out of bed before noon on a Saturday is still something of a scoop.

April 1 Wednesday

It was announced on the radio in Lisbon today that Iran had withdrawn from the World Cup for political reasons and that their place in Group F was to be taken by Portugal. The result was impromptu street parties, people riding around in the tops of cars singing and waving the national flag amid general national euphoria. Now that's what I call an April Fool.

It is certainly a vast improvement on the mundane drivel that passes for a practical joke in this country. As ever on this date, we had the usual unconvincing and fatuous efforts of the newspapers - Cheddar Gorge to be turned into a night club, left handed Mars Bars, spectacles for pigs . . . zzzzz . . .

April 3 Friday

Sunderland played at Tranmere again tonight and I put myself in a proper quandary over whether to go or not.

The argument against going was that we have only ever played there six times, and on the three occasions that I have been we have lost all of them. However, we also lost the other three games too. So basically we always lose there.

Faced with the paradox of being damned if I did and damned if I didn't, I didn't to save money. Despite my absence we won 2-0. I have decided to take full credit for this result. Although I am not superstitious, I still ate the right tea, washed the various parts of my anatomy in the correct order, washed my underpants and everything.

April 8 Wednesday

Dave Nicholson says he will recommend that I be trained in the use of the stadium's electronic scoreboards and I am keen to learn. I suppose it could be useful for mundane things such as ticket availability, emergency procedures and team news, but absolutely worth its weight in gold when it comes to rude and petty abuse.

Imagine 40,000 people going home, taking with them vital subliminal information like 'The Mags are shite and they're getting beat' and 'Tonka is a puff'. But when I mentioned these possibilities to Dave his enthusiasm became rather more tempered.

April 10 Friday

I have always thought that to describe today as Good Friday is odd. I mean, Our Lord died today which can't be good now can it? On the other hand, I was working at double time and a lieu day, which can't be bad.

15 minutes into our extremely disappointing draw with Queen's Park Rangers tonight, we received a call saying that the Cable & Wireless match sponsors poster had not been put up. Mr. Cable and Mr. Wireless were apparently doing their nut, but were mollified slightly when it was put up at half-time with the finest Sellotape that money could buy.

However, when the continuing rain storm brought it back down and it ended up as a soggy limp mound next to the pitch, nuts were done further. Oops.

April 13 Monday

Liz and I went to West Bromwich Albion with some really duff advice on how to get there. We took an obscure route through some obscure places, often getting stuck behind some agricultural vehicle or other. We almost missed the kick-off of a very entertaining three all draw and a visit to a pub became out of the question.

The fact that we managed to take in the scenic splendour of Trumpton, Chigley as well as Camberwick Green instead of the undeniably dull M1 was still more irritation than consolation. We had no choice but to travel back on the motorway as our ball of string had run out before we had even got down as far as Lichfield.

April 16 Thursday

Owing to a complete absence of any strange turn of events, a dearth of intriguing occurrences and an abundance of predictable behaviour, I was in the Ivy House tonight.

Some trendy young fellow-me-lad inserted ten shillings into the jukebox and played a song called *Dirty Old Town*, which contains the line 'I kissed my girl by the factory wall'. This struck me as unnecessarily vulgar until someone explained to me that a factory wall is just the wall of a factory and not some revolting euphemism.

Good news for Dr. Hook then who retain the mantle of most obscene line ever written for 'When you're in love with a beautiful woman, it's hard'.

April 17 Friday

We dared to hope that Middlesbrough would lose at home to tonight, but as they were playing Manchester City, we could not say why. There was more chance of me staying in tonight.

April 18 Saturday

We had what will hopefully be our anti-penultimate home game of the season with Crewe Alexandra today and we won 2-1. It is now touch and go for automatic promotion, with two places available for Middlesbrough Nottingham Forest and ourselves. I have not been this excited since the time I saw Frank Carson in the Dun Cow.

April 23 Thursday

It has been decided that we should install another 740 seats in time for Saturday's home game with Stoke City. We were assured by the company carrying out the work that this would not be a problem, but we began to suspect that this might not be true when we noticed that they had only installed 15 by this morning.

So like Clark Kent, I changed from my suit and lowered myself to do some grubby manual labour with some other fellows more suited to these tasks. To make this dull and strenuous job even more arduous, we had to contend with the legend 'Hurry up you lazy shites!' in six feet letters at each end of the stadium which, if you ask me, is an inappropriate use of the scoreboards by the stadium manager.

April 25 Saturday

Today we played Stoke City in the last scheduled home game of the season and won 3-0. Of course, all of the talk in the stadium was concerned with the snazzy and newly installed seats. Oh yes.

I was asked by a steward why these new seats were white when all of the others are red. I offered him the aesthetic explanation about the post-modern, minimalist, abstract, visual counterpoint effect, confident that if I did not know what I was talking about than he would be in no position to query me. I had no intention of telling him the simple truth that there were no red ones left, although this particular steward would have struggled with even this more straightforward account.

April 27 Monday

After an illicit bit of nosing around this afternoon, I acquired the rumour of a pre-season friendly with Barcelona. This immediately rendered me excited at the prospect of meeting the great Ronaldo, the sublimely gifted Brazilian World Player Of The Year. I could shake his hand, get his autograph, invite him back to ours for tea and dunkies, then take him to the

Willow Pond where we could perhaps secure a lock-in on the back of his fame.

Oh yes. I had any amount of chumming up to the great man all neatly planned when I was struck by the realisation that he had been transferred to Inter Milan about a year ago. Never mind, the match would be on a Tuesday which is a dull night out and anyway he's crap.

April 28 Tuesday

We lost a vital game at Ipswich tonight, thereby almost certainly consigning and confining ourselves to the play-offs.

There is nothing like a defeat to bring out the bigotry in the likes of me and so it proved. As I watched the game, it occurred to me that only a football match could tear the people of Ipswich away from the maypole that they had undoubtedly been prancing around in their smocks as they wave their pitchforks, pausing only to swig cider from a clay jug, not too much though as they have to drive the combine harvester back to the potatoes.

Still, the main thing for me is not to become bitter. One day I will actually go to Ipswich.

April 30 Thursday

Alan Shearer has been in the news as usual. The England forward, family man, ambassador for the nation, and every year's Mr. Wonderful, has proved this week that he is not quite worthy of the mantle of Hardest Shot In Football. This title would go to the person who actually succeeds in removing Neil Lennon's head from his shoulders with just the one kick. Shearer came close.

Alan claims that it was an accident when he booted Lennon in the mush at the speed of sound. The fact that he will get away with it does not prevent his excuse from being the worst since Tonka missed PE at school after claiming to have ruptured his Fallopian tube.

May 2 Saturday

Liz and I boarded a train to embark upon a weekend of variety and excitement in London where there are any number of new and mind broadening experiences to be had. We were greeted on the platform at King's Cross by Redge and Rachel, whereupon the women immediately hit the shops while Redge and I went to some pub near Brixton tube station. These types of opportunities do not arise very often so one must grasp them with both hands when they do.

Tomorrow we intend to continue with our wildly avant-garde and experimentalist behaviour. We are going to a football match where I believe Sunderland will be playing.

115

May 3 Sunday

We made the short-ish trip to Swindon. They used to make Spitfires there and now have a very intricate roundabout. That's all there is to know about Swindon.

Anyway we beat them, took over their town, drowned out their efforts to have their manager sacked and ate all the hot dogs. But valiant though all of this was, we must still compete in the play-offs if we are to be promoted.

This was all rather disappointing, but the day out was not completely without success, as by the end of it we had discovered a way to make Swindon look like the swinging metropolis that it isn't by having a night on the tiles in Surbiton.

May 6 Wednesday

I had to show some German students round the stadium. I am really bored with such chores by now and the sooner we employ some tour guides the better for all concerned. At least they would be unlikely to make up facts to amuse themselves and confuse their guests. The Germans were happy to return to Hamburg with tales of an underground zoo beneath the pitch, but it isn't true. A tour guide would not have mentioned the war either . . .

May 7 Thursday

Our play-off opponents are to be Sheffield United and they have selfishly demanded 3,000 tickets for our home leg, which meant that John Mallan and I had to move the segregation when there were televisions to be watched.

We had some difficulty in removing the very first bolt, having neglected to put a washer with the nut when inserting it previously. My suggestion to this was to leave the capacity at a thousand, incur the wrath of the opposing club, provoke the hostility of the media, aggravate the Football Association into punitive measures, possibly be given a hefty fine, but above all, not to have to remove the bolt. However, John said that we should just get some pliers instead.

He was probably right to do this.

May 10 Sunday

We arrived in Sheffield for the first leg, 15 minutes too early for this pub called the Half Moon to open, and while we were clicking our heels and waiting we were offered the chance to make an early start in a wine bar round the corner. Having gratefully accepted the offer, we went in and began to make ourselves comfortable.

Then after about ten minutes of chin wagging and glass clinking, the manager of this establishment asked us to drink up and leave. We enquired as to whether there was some sort of problem, to which he replied that there was no problem, he just wanted to close so that he could go out for a drink?!?!?

We lost 2-1.

May 13 Wednesday

According to large sections of tonight's crowd when we played Sheffield United yet again, we are by FAR the greatest team the world has ever seen, which is probably magnifying our accomplishments a tad, although we did win 2-0.

So we will therefore be at Wembley Stadium on the 25th of May, but I have already decided not to make the trip, having made three disastrous trips to the old dump in the past. The trek home is an awfully long one. My Wembley record reads, played three, lost three, goals for zilch, goals against four (two of which were own goals), extortionately priced and foul tasting hot dogs several, misery skip loads. Although it did only rain twice.

Que sera sera, we're going to the Ivy House to watch it on the telly in all probability.

May 16 Saturday

This afternoon I watched what was easily the funniest FA Cup final since 1974. Newcastle managed to get to Wembley, but were narrowly humiliated by Arsenal. There is nothing quite like football for Schadenfreude, with the possible exceptions of disease and financial ruination.

We watched the game in the caravan in Hexham, where many of the other caravan dwellers are Newcastle supporters. Beforehand we went round saying how good it would be for the North East if they were to pull it off, but we gave ourselves away when Arsenal's first goal went in by screaming our approval as the caravan and all of its accoutrements rattled with joy.

Later, I thought it would be good sport to drive home through Newcastle city centre wearing a Sunderland shirt for purposes of annoyance. It wasn't. It was about the most stupid thing I could have done. I had dangerously underestimated the number of red lights I would have to wait at outside of pubs that were crowded with Mags who are well-known for being at their most dangerous when bitter.

I lived to tell the tale and returned to the Ivy House where I heard an account of Taff's Cup Final viewing habits. The cheers that greeted Arsenal's second goal were followed by sharp gasps as the shelf that Taff was standing on gave up the good fight and parted company with the wall. The sound of breath being drawn was then interrupted by that of Taff's hips ricocheting around the pub furniture as he descended gracelessly to the floor. Icing on the cake or what?

117

May 17 Sunday

My increasingly faint hopes of turning Bethan into a child prodigy involved us watching a history programme on BBC2 today. This was as unsuccessful as my previous attempts. The programme showed the famous black and white photograph of Winston Churchill making the victory sign on the steps of 10 Downing Street. But all this immortal gesture managed to inspire in Bethan was the excited observation of 'Look! Girl power!' before she lost interest and sloped off to play with a bucket. How depressing

May 19 Tuesday

Usually I would rather drink a bucket of dust than go to a supermarket, but we were out of Toffee Crisps so the die was cast. Asda seemed like as good a place as any (super value, friendly service).

Washing up liquid was also required, although obviously not with the same urgency. Being a flash type who values his labels I plumped for fairy liquid, which seemed like a bargain at only seventy-nine pence. But no sooner had I chucked it in the trolley than I remembered that with Fairy, a few more pence makes a lot more sense, so I put it back on the shelf and went to the newsagent to get some for a pound.

May 20 Wednesday

Tickets for the play-off final went on general sale today and what a queue there was. At the head of it were people who had been there for a couple of days, sitting on deck chairs in their track suit with dogs on ropes. A policeman friend of mine told me that the crime rate in Southwick has been unusually low since Monday and would have liked us to delay the sale.

May 21 Thursday

Unbeknown to us, the players came down to the stadium to train today, which is unusual. This meant that we had to postpone a scattering of ashes that was due to take place at eleven o'clock. We had to put the mourners in an executive box with a cup of tea each while they waited. Dave Nicholson went in to apologise to them for the inconvenience, but an elderly lady who appeared to be the head of the family said that she didn't mind as she was having a good look around as it was the first time she had been to the stadium. 'And his,' she added, rather alarmingly we thought, pointing at the urn.

May 22 Friday

Tempting Fate or what? This afternoon our time was consumed by the making of arrangements for a public address system, scaffolding, a master of ceremonies, parking measures and crowd control. Yes, Tuesday's victory parade will be a precisely run as well as joyous occasion. Of course, our labours have been carried out under the hopeful assumption that we are going to win on Monday.

The sublime misery that will abound on Tuesday should we fail to gain promotion will only be minimally assuaged by the fact that we will have a damn easy day. The lack of any need for a public address system, scaffolding, a master of ceremonies, parking measures and crowd control should obviate the need for much work, and will enable us to concentrate of tea and self-pity.

May 25 Monday

Friday's work activities could not have tempted Fate any more than they did if they had handed over a tenner, their favourite records and a Twix.

We lost on penalties to Charlton Athletic after a 4-4 draw. The game was a classic, but at this precise moment in time this does not provide a flicker of consolation.

This probably sounds ungracious, but Charlton are exactly the type of club to do this to us. Whereas Sunderland can count Steve Cram, Dave Stewart and Peter O'Toole among our ranks of supporters, the best that Sky TV could manage to wheel out as a celebrity Charlton fan was the bloke from the Flash advert who lets it do all the hard work. At this point we should have known what to expect.

Having steadfastly refused to travel to Wembley because of absurd superstition, I watched the game in the Sunderland AFC Sports Bar and afterwards went down to the home team dugout to sit with my head between my legs for a couple of hours. This is becoming something of an end of season tradition with me.

May 26 Tuesday

A combination of depression and hangovers meant that a good number of staff did not turn up for work today. Two exceptions were Ronnie and Mark, a plumber and electrician respectively, who started with the club today.

I had decided when I got out of bed this morning to be resilient, sanguine and amiable, despite the tragedy that unfolded yesterday, but when I met Ronnie he came out with the inflammatory comment of 'Hello. I'm Ronnie. You must be Tony,' so in reply I told him to piss off and die. So I did not fare too well in the resilient sanguine and amiable stakes, although there was no need for him to go round saying things like that.

I am by now beginning to come to terms with defeat, rising with knightly good grace above the ravages of despair, but might just go out and smash some bastard's face in anyway.

May 27 Wednesday

Today was slightly less depressing than yesterday, but only slightly. I have been known to lay awake at night, pondering upon where God might live, or gravity, or infinity, but nothing has ever disrupted my sleep like putting the ball in the net ten times at Wembley and still being beaten.

It was pointed out to me this evening that this will make Sunderland the subject of a really smashing quiz question, but even the possibility of being in Trivial Pursuit has failed to provide succour. If it ever crops up I would not have the heart to answer it correctly.

I have not been this miserable since the episode of Stan Ogden's funeral in *Coronation Street.*

May 30 Saturday

Now that the football season has been over for about ten minutes, attention has turned to the World Cup. Debate in the pubs has become preoccupied with team selection. Should we play Owen or Sheringham? Neville or Southgate? Batty or a footballer? Using my skill and judgement, I have selected a team capable of winning the competition. Argentina.

Such is my belief in them that I strode purposefully into a bookies and slammed down two, yes TWO, quid that said they would do so. It was an act of bravado that drew gasps as the cashier rang head office to see if they would accept the bet. They did, despite the 14 quid that I could fleece them for.

June 1 Monday

My future is now a great deal more secure and I am back to working in a suit and for more money. But I would still rather have beaten Charlton a week ago.

June 2 Tuesday

Kerry, who I will now be working with closely, scampered back from lunch with a packet of wine gums and a grin, the latter as a result of having just booked a week's holiday in Corfu. Apparently her boyfriend had given her an ultimatum that it was all over if she was to go there. She elaborated, 'He told me that if I went to Corfu without him then we were finished, so I got down to Thomas Cook before he could change his mind. Would you like a wine gum?'

She was clearly nursing a broken heart, so I though it best to leave her on her own for a while, although I still had a wine gum, albeit a green one, as she bravely disguised her misery by singing *Zip-A Dee-Doo-Dah.*

June 6 Saturday

It was decided with quite outlandish optimism that we should have a barbecue this afternoon. Obviously the Equatorial downpour prevented us from actually eating outside, but we took turns at standing over the barbie with an umbrella while the rest sat in the dining room with the back door open for that authentic at one with nature feel to the proceedings. It wasn't so bad as eventually the rain eased off and we had managed to convince ourselves that it was quite a warm day. Certainly, there seemed to be a definite upturn in the temperature once we had put our coats on.

It was a lovely meal too. The right sauce is one thing, but the vital ingredient to a successful spare rib is clearly drizzle.

June 9 Tuesday

Today I was bestowed with the dreary task of accompanying the health and safety people around on their close season inspection of the kiosks. Mercifully they moved with increasing speed as they went round and I wondered why this was, until one of them said, 'We had better make this the last one, I've got to be back by eleven to see those stool samples.'

This cherished image that she had presented us with inspired me to make a lame pun about kitchen furniture, but she did not even reply with a polite smile. She must attach a great deal of gravitas to her job. As they say, it may just be pooh to you and I, but it is her bread and butter.

June 10 Wednesday

The World Cup opening fixture took place today with (plucky) Scotland taking on (mighty) Brazil. The expected South American victory was thanks in no small part to the Scotland defence who managed to contrive an own goal that would have taken Busby Berkeley about six months to choreograph.

Matters are compounded as they are accompanied on their travels by a turgid World Cup song called *Don't Come Home Too Soon*. This seems like a strange fear for them to express anyway. I have studied their fixtures and can say with quite some certainty that they will not make an early return. Their final group match against Morocco kicks off at eight in the evening in St. Etienne, so even if they were too board their plane immediately afterwards it would still be gone midnight when they touched down in Prestwick. This should be late enough for anyone.

June 11 Thursday

It was a day for plumping up the cushions and preparing to be enthralled in your own living room. Cameroon's 1-1 draw with Austria is as much as a young man in his prime could ask for on a balmy midsummer's evening.

June 12 Friday

Nigeria 3 the United States of America 0. I still think this is great.

June 13 Saturday

Saudi Arabia 1 Demark 1. I must say my interest is beginning to wane slightly.

June 14 Sunday

I did not watch Paraguay's goalless draw with Bulgaria.

June 15 Monday

Everyone but everyone was working indoors today. This was possibly a quirk of fate or possibly due to inclement weather, but it would be unprofessional to assume that this was because England were playing Tunisia and there are umpteen televisions in the stadium

June 16 Tuesday

Our usual work van was out for a pedicure or something this morning so I went to snivel around Wayne Walls from Football In The Community to see if I could borrow theirs and he agreed. Despite this good will, I was still put out to see what a deplorably grubby condition it was in, complete with the usual aphorisms 'Wash me!' and 'Cleaned by Stevie Wonder' inscribed in the dirt. What if my friends had seen me driving this? What if I'd had an accident?

I did not want to respond to this hospitality with ingratitude so I went about my business in it as quickly as possible before returning the keys, pausing only to write 'Wayne is a puff' on the passenger door.

June 18 Thursday

Ronnie the plumber arrived at work with some new artwork on his upper arm. He is now decorated with a tattoo of the club crest, so I for one will be lobbying for another change in design just to annoy him.

Ronnie feels that all of the club's employees should have this done to them, especially the maintenance who should also have a crossed hammer and screwdriver on the other arm. Personally, I am against the idea as I do not like tattoos at all, unless of course it is a really classy affair, such as a snake wrapping itself around a dagger, or a nude woman in front of some playing cards as often modelled by bus drivers.

June 22 Monday

I entered a busy Ivy House tonight to watch England play plucky minnows Romania. It really is worthy of admiration how these little countries have a sufficiently positive attitude to keep telling themselves that they can beat the likes of England.

I was pondering this notion for longer than most people as I was in the toilets when Romania scored their winning goal.

June 24 Wednesday

The World Cup is now two weeks old and I am afraid that even football bores like me are becoming slightly tired of it. Even tonight's encounter between South Africa and Saudi Arabia failed to exude the magic of earlier clashes, such as the never to be forgotten game between South Korea and either Mexico or Norway, I forget which.

However, rather than fall behind in the facile unspoken male contest that is taking place in the Ivy House to see who can garner the most obscure and trivial France '98 facts, I watched and memorised it. This enabled me to turn round to Kevin Bell and remark upon how well Al-Jaber had tucked away his penalty.

June 26 Friday

England played Colombia tonight which brought forth a barrage of weak jokes about drugs. 'Get down the line!', 'Have a crack!', etc.

The only other feature I can really recall from an otherwise featureless 2-0 win was the presence of the ageing Colombian centre forward, Carlos Valderama, and his continued use of a spectacularly silly hair cut. I would have thought that the joke was wearing a bit thin by now, but no, he plods on resembling nothing other than a picture of the sun by an extremely untalented child.

Bethan, on the other hand, was heartily amused by his outlandish coiffure, but then she can not remember most of the last 14 years.

June 30 Tuesday

England were dumped in the second round of the World Cup tonight. Failure to beat a mediocre Argentina side confirms our treasured international status as total nobodies in the world pecking order. But, for about two days, the papers will harp on about how brave, gallant, virtuous, hard-done by and generally lovely our lads are.

As usual, we lost on penalties. The principal duffer on this occasion was the great David Batty whose effort was commendable even if it was not successful. Those of us who have followed David's career closely were not aware of an ability to kick a ball forward. The man has an endless repertoire.

July 1 Wednesday

Having just endured the wettest June since 12 million BC, save a few that we had during the last ice age, hopes have been elevated that we may witness a glimmer of sky at some point in July. Indeed, the early signs were encouraging when the mist evaporated in order to make way for the drizzle, which in turn moved on to allow a downpour to take place, but only for a while as it was soon time for the heavy showers to take over. After all this, the weather began to take a turn for the worse.

In short, a real disappointment thus far, but as July will surely continue tomorrow it may get better. I had a quick look at the forecast that the club has faxed from the Met. Office. Snow.

July 7 Tuesday

The players are now back from six weeks of sunbathing and floozying. Some of them have been seen loitering around the admin. building. Among them was Martin Scott who I bumped into on the ground floor as I entered the lift and he began to walk up the stairs.

Of course, he beat me to the second floor, which led to his smug comment of 'See. It's quicker and it's better for you.'

He missed the point on two counts. One was that I am never in a hurry to return to my desk. The other was that if I were in any way concerned with my health then I would not have my renowned devotion to chips. My preference for lifts could also partly explain why I am also less injury prone than him.

July 10 Friday

Sunday's World Cup final between France and Brazil is certainly of interest, but it is a mere aside compared to real football. I read the fixture list for the 1998-99 season and saw that Sunderland open the season by playing Queen's Park Rangers at home. Anyone who is not tingling with anticipation at this is obviously weird.

July 12 Sunday

France cantered to a three-nil victory are Brazil in the World Cup final. They truly are a fine team with the exception of one Stephane Guivarc'h and I am not only saying this because he has recently signed for Newcastle.

When we first heard that they had lured a French international midfielder into their grubby homestead we became agitated and envious. But having now watched him play on several occasions, these fears have been allayed. I had never seen him in action prior to the tournament and neither, I suspect, had Newcastle United

July 13 Monday

With the World Cup now over for another four years, it seems obvious to some people that England would have won it had David Beckham not been sent off against Argentina. This extraordinary cobblers was what I had to put up with in the Ivy House this evening. The fact that we lost to Argentina, who then lost to Holland, who then lost to Brazil, who then lost to France, is being treated as nothing more than a statistical quirk. A detail rather than a flaw.

'They all had the rub of the green on the day,' was one straw being frantically clutched at, which presumably applied to Romania who also beat us. Happily 2002 is just around the corner.

July 15 Wednesday

It was St. Swithin's Day today. Apparently, Swithin was being laughed at and verbally abused by some tough looking yokels for transporting his mother around in a wheelbarrow for which he cursed them with 40 days and 40 nights of rain. As a result, their crops were drowned.

I have no idea where St. Swithin lived, but if it was Sunderland his prediction was hardly a rash one. Saying that August and half of July will be a washout is not really sticking your neck out round our way, considering that it has been pissing down since Christmas.

July 16 Thursday

Dave Nicholson is on holiday and in his absence I came dangerously close to having to make a decision. There are problems afoot with underground gases at the stadium and we have been urged to install a new vent at a cost of around 15 grand. The bloke from the International Mining Company said that failure to install the vent could lead to danger, licences being revoked, explosions, deaths and disaster, but the decision was entirely ours. I still went running to a director to make it.

July 17 Friday

It was Liz's birthday, and me being the smooth romantic type, I had already purchased her gift some weeks ago. In fact I had already given it to her to ensure that she would not spoil it by getting a season ticket herself. I also presented her with a World Cup birthday card before whisking her off for a dreamy evening at some of the mores seductive hostelries that the bottom of Hylton Road has to offer.

So another year is chalked up for Liz, which makes one wonder; why is a year a year? It is only because that is how long it takes the Earth to orbit the sun. It is curious to consider that if we lived on Pluto, neither of us would be old enough to go to the pubs yet.

July 22 Wednesday

I had a day off work today so that we could make the secular pilgrimage to Granada Studios in Manchester and the inner sanctum that is Coronation Street. £15 admission fee may seem rather stiff to some, but it is only a fraction of the air fare to Mecca and you are unlikely to see a life-size cardboard cut-out of Albert Tatlock there.

After a day of reverential sightseeing, we returned home with a Hilda Ogden t-shirt, some Percy Sugden boiled sweets, a Gail Platt fridge magnet and numerous key fobs. Bethan, on the other hand, preferred to spend her money in the Sooty shop so I am afraid that she has come home with some right old tat.

July 23 Thursday

I was talking to the Chief Executive about our lovely new gas vents which are a positive boon for any passer-by with step ladders who might fancy a good lung full of methane to take home.

He was commending the Commercial Director for utilising a bamboo tree to disguise one of the stacks, commenting on what a top stroke he had pulled. I do not agree. Previously it blended in as another lamp post, but he has now drawn attention to it with this tree clambering around it and it may engender a swarm of marauding pandas. Of course, being gutless and having a malleable mind when it comes to lying to protect my career, I expressed ready agreement with him and said that I wished I had thought of it.

July 24 Friday

I ordered 90 bins for the concourse from a place in Portsmouth and today they arrived. The press have not been informed yet so you have an exclusive.

July 26 Sunday

Holidays. We welded some important looking things back on to the car, and then putting a small crucifix on the dashboard, we hoped that it would get us to London.

I made the mistake of telling Bethan that it wasn't far really, which resulted in the first 'Are we nearly there yet?' somewhere in the vicinity of Darlington. She was rather bored for most of the time and games of 'I spy', 'How many red cars can you see?' and 'See who can name the most components to the four stroke internal combustion engine' did precious little to lift her tedium, especially that last one.

Anyway, the car made it and after discussing the multitude of things to do in the capital, we decided to watch the telly.

July 27 Monday

We took Bethan to London Zoo today, as she has been keen to visit one for some time. We had an amble round Regent's Park first, during which I attempted to save a few quid by pretending that we were already in the zoo. I thought there was enough wildlife to be going on with - dogs, sparrows, pigeons, a few wasps and even the odd bluebottle all in evidence. Sadly though, even five year olds aren't that thick so it was another £8.50 down the nick.

When we got inside, we found that the animals were nearly all bored dopey looking creatures, with the exception of one particularly excitable

126

stick insect. No great thrills there then, although Bethan was pleased to see a giraffe having a wee.

July 28 Tuesday

Bethan proved her worth today by providing the rest of us with a legitimate excuse to visit Legoland.

Some of the structures created with Lego are very impressive and life-like too. Several major British landmarks such as Edinburgh Castle, Buckingham Palace and the Penshaw Monument are featured, but I was most impressed with the authenticity of Stonehenge, coming as it did with models of the Wiltshire Constabulary chasing hippies around Salisbury Plain (and this is not a joke, this is completely true).

Back in Brixton, Redge and I had a convivial evening of boozing and coarse language and we even managed a lock-in somewhere, for which we felt justifiably proud of ourselves. Liz and Rachel were less impressed with our achievement.

July 29 Wednesday

We pushed our luck with the car still further by scraping it along the M40 to Oxford. My mind is now at rest, as the next time we shall need the car will be to return to Sunderland on Friday. The AA can do the work for me then.

Oxford is a small, but very interesting city, due to it being an historic seat of learning with a long and rich heritage, but none of this is much cop as far as Bethan is concerned. For example, I tried to summon some enthusiasm from her when we were standing outside a house once lived in by Cecil Rhodes (imperialist 1853-1902), but as Cecil had never appeared in *Fraggle Rock* and had never bothered to live in Pizza Hut, she gave me a look which told me where I could stick it.

July 30 Thursday

This afternoon we sauntered down to the world famous Bodleian Library. I was interested to see if they had the 1978 *Beezer* annual on their shelves as it contains both *Mr. Licko* and *Our Sheriff's An Ape*. Unfortunately, it transpired that only students can be admitted. Apparently they get a lot of them round here and cheesy holiday makers in football shirts are particularly frowned upon.

Therefore, their claim that they house a copy of every book that was ever published in Great Britain is thrown into some dubiety. Why should we believe them when they won't even let us in? For all we know it might only contain a few fruit machines and a pool table.

July 31 Friday

Today we made the thankless trip home. Again, we spiritedly tried for Bethan's sake to remove some of the drudgery of travel by playing games. Seeing how many blue cars we could spot soon fell by the wayside in favour of spotting the most preposterous name for a clapped out old caravan.

No sooner had we overtaken 'Spirit Of Destiny' than we were hard on the axels of 'Night Zephyr' and 'Sirocco Of The Road', then on to the refreshingly honest 'Old Crappy'. Yet even this travel game became dull after a while, so we moved on to 'Spot the field' and 'Count the trees'. It was a long journey.

August 2 Sunday

Away with this holiday malarkey. Only six days to the new football season. Tally ho!

August 6 Thursday

I made a grim return to work this morning and immediately became involved with the traditional pre-match panic.

On this occasion it was to do with the installation of white seats which have been positioned in such a way as to spell out the cheesy colloquialism 'HA' WAY THE LADS'. Delay was caused by arguments over whether to have some black seats placed to the side of the lettering to create a shadow effect, but eventually it was decided not to have them.

Then we had to contend with a rowdy demonstration from the eight people who are disgruntled at the prospect of having to sit on an apostrophe next season.

The last bolt went in about ten minutes before the press arrived to take photographs of these new seats. I only hope that no one wants to sit on them.

August 7 Friday

I am bubbling with excitement as this is the eve of a new football season. Tomorrow is the first day of the rest of our lives and I haven't even got a clean shirt.

August 8 Saturday

The football season finally began today and, apart from our 1-0 victory over Queen's Park Rangers, the day was notable for two events. The first was that Lee Clark broke his fibula. As he writhed past me on a stretcher, I did all that I could to help him, although gawping at his ankle and saying 'Ooh!' was of limited assistance.

The other significant incident, as far as I was concerned anyway, was that I was designated as bus driver for a couple of dozen cheerleaders, who after a hard afternoon of leading cheers had to catch a train back to London. The Crown Jewels (for 'twas they) were grateful to the point of saying 'Thank you', although the story was longer and far more detailed by the time I got down the Ivy House to relate it.

August 9 Sunday
A sedulous examination of the league table has revealed that we are joint top.

August 11 Tuesday
The novelty of the new football season, uncharacteristically warm weather and simply being unable to think of anything better to do on a Tuesday evening, all conspired to take us down to York for the first round first leg of the Worthington Cup.

It was a tedious 2-0 win, but it was worth the trip to see our first goal, a clearance from the goalkeeper which cannoned into the net via the arse of Danny Dichio, who then had the audacity to accept praise for this as though some assiduously worked training ground move had paid off. Nevertheless, he scored both goals.

On the way home we were vetted by some highly suspicious policemen before being allowed into the village of Easingwold. We finally persuaded them that we were after some fish suppers rather than an insurrection, although four people eating chips in the street could well be construed as a riot in Easingwold.

August 12 Wednesday
I popped down to the physio room this morning to sniff some Ralgex and I saw Martin Scott in there in the middle of what looked like a pedicure. He enlightened me by saying that his foot had been stamped on during the match at Bootham Crescent last night and consequently his toes had swollen to 15 times their normal size. So to drain them of any superfluous blood, water, tissue, snot, etc., the club physiotherapist had put holes in his toes with a drill. Yak!

Personally, I would have preferred to have kept the enormous toes rather than have them bored into and I now have to seriously reconsider whether to be a footballer when I grow up. All rather horrid, but the good news is that the physio has agreed to lend us his drill to put some pictures up.

August 15 Saturday
For the first time in quite a while, we had to listen to the football on the radio which is excruciating because it usually leaves you with not the slightest notion of what is going on. Commentators provide little help.

When they are describing a promising move, the crowd has often already said 'Ooooh!' so we know in advance that a goal was not forthcoming.

I could have gone to Swindon if I had really wanted to, but I was there on the 3rd of May when I used all of the facilities in the hour before the game.

The result this time was a one-all draw and not a good one by all accounts, so credit where it is due. One week into the football season and we have already racked up three boring games.

August 16 Sunday

I took Bethan to Crowtree Leisure Centre this morning so I could boot her on to the soft play while I read the Sunday papers. Any devoted parent would do the same.

August 18 Tuesday

Bravado, kudos and sheer swashbuckling were all visible in abundant quantities tonight, in the Worthington Cup first round second leg. Sunderland 2 York City 1. Ha!

August 22 Saturday

Today we were at home to Tranmere Rovers and their forward line was led by Craig Russell who was received very favourably by the crowd. This was mainly because he did so well during his time as a Sunderland player, but also because he was decent enough to turn up accompanied by ten colleagues who looked so lethargic that we presume that they would rather have gone to the pictures.

We won 5-0. This is more like it. Yet Tranmere contrived to make matters worse for themselves by wearing a hideous orange and green strip which was a mite too raffish for people to watch the game and eat at the same time.

After the game, Craig trudged dejectedly up the stairs to the players' lounge and was asked, in a comforting sort of way, if he was 'As sick as a parrot'. To his eternal credit, he responded to this cliché by saying that he had certainly looked like one.

August 25 Tuesday

I bumped into some Watford supporters outside the north tunnel this afternoon. I acceded to their request for a quick look inside, thanked them for selling us Kevin Phillips for about 40p, then let them get back for their teas so they would be in good time to witness this evening's 4-1 stuffing of their team. Gloat while you can, you may not get another chance.

August 27 Thursday

The only news that seemed to be allowed round these parts today was the departure of Kenny Dalglish from Newcastle United, which has facilitated the speedy arrival of Ruud Gullit to Tyneside, who has promised 'sexy football'.

Local media coverage is already tiresome, with numerous features on whether there are enough clothes shops in the area to meet fashion conscious Ruud's demand for designer labels. Clearly, we also need to know about ascending sales in unamusing dreadlock wigs. The main description of him, which even at this early stage has been bandied about ad nauseam, is that he is a 'cosmopolitan' man, although he has also leafed through *Marie Claire* on occasions (geddit?).

Tomorrow we may have a 90 minute documentary on how he takes his tea, if we are lucky.

August 29 Saturday

We went to Ipswich Town and avenged our defeat of the 28th of April by cuffing them by the same score, 2-0. If this was not sexy football, then it was certainly on the acceptable side of tarty. The victory also removed the necessity of combining punitive measures with insane preconceptions about Suffolk.

Had we lost again, it would have been scythe down their maypole! Pluck out the seams on their smocks! Stab their combine harvesters with their pitchforks! Wee in the clay jug they drink their cider from! Or is that Devon?

This behaviour is not for me anyway. Apart from being too nice for that sort of thing, I watched the game on television. I have still never been to Ipswich.

August 30 Sunday

'Ruud Awakening' will be the almost compulsory headline in tomorrow's newspapers. Mr. Gullit's first game in charge at Newcastle saw a lavish display of arse kicking and a 4-1 defeat at home to Liverpool. They were promised sexy football at St. James' Park and they got it, but not in the way that was hoped. However, it is fair to say, as did one undeniably crude fellow of my acquaint called Ian, that they were certainly fucked.

Sales analysts are now predicting a slump in the sales of those unamusing dreadlock wigs, but better times ahead for the manufacturers of 'Ruud Out!' t-shirts.

August 31 Monday

While out and about this evening, a few of us were crowing about the latest debacle at Newcastle and how St. Michael Owen had put in a sneaky hat-trick for our amusement, when something occurred to me. I do not

131

know what the converse cliché of rubbing salt in the wounds is, but if I did I would employ it here as I remembered that he was in my Ivy House dream team, where a weekly winner can scoop anything up to four pints of Heineken with lime.

I am fairly confident of victory because although a couple of my rivals have also bought Owen, at least one of them also has Shay Given.

September 1 Tuesday

At work I bumped into John Fickling in the kitchen where we discussed the heart warming series of football results that had taken place over the weekend. He then expressed further delight that Damon Hill had won the Belgian Grand Prix on Sunday. Although I would prefer to watch paint than a car race (it doesn't even necessarily have to be drying), I could not pass up this opportunity for sycophancy and replied that my weekend had been rendered complete by this motorised boredom.

Nevertheless, it seemed to make him happy and he left me with a smile on his face and, metaphorically at least, an arse that was considerably cleaner.

September 2 Wednesday

Hopes have been expressed along the lines of having an Indian summer. Yet we are now into September and these hopes have so far been unrealised. The only way that our summer can be anything like the one in India is if it starts bucketing down over there too.

Our summer finally began this afternoon at around half past two when there was what may or may not have been a break in the clouds, but it had ended by tea time. This is quite possibly the worst summer we have had since the last one. As ever, there is always next year, something of a stock phrase for a Sunderland supporter.

September 4 Friday

Those of us ordained with the task of maintaining the stadium were recently issued with a t-shirt for each day of the working week. Most of mine are surplus to requirements as I now only indulge in vulgar manual labour on a match day. Still, these stylish garments are about the cut of my jib, so I paraded myself in one of them whilst out on the razzle this evening and a resplendent and eye-catching figure I was too.

I was standing in the queue for the bank in a busy High Street West, easily eclipsing my fellow queuers fashion wise, when I heard a fearsome cackle behind me followed by, 'Hey! You want to stop wearing your work clothes to go out! Ha! Ha!'.

How enchanting it was to meet Leanne and Claire, two winsome and genteel young ladies from the administration building.

September 8 Tuesday

We were at home to Bristol City and chucked it away rather by letting in a late equaliser in a 1-1 draw. The game was also on television so we had some difficulty in getting rid of the visiting supporters as they were keen to watch the 44 replays of their goal. It was I who had to go round to the South Stand with the remote control and then run away as fast as the sandwiches I had scoffed would allow.

September 11 Friday

We almost damaged the club's dull-ometer this morning. It was the shareholders' Annual General Meeting.

September 12 Saturday

Sunderland came perilously close to losing this season's unbeaten record. We were 1-0 behind at Wolves this afternoon when we won a corner and Kevin Phillips asked the referee how much time was left. He was told ten seconds, so there must have been about six seconds remaining when he nudged in the equaliser.

This type of story represents why I still harbour hopes of becoming a professional footballer, and let's face it, there is only my abject lack of talent that is preventing this from happening.

September 15 Tuesday

Roaring was ripped, swash was buckled and barn was stormed. Sunderland 3 Chester City 0 in the second round first leg of the Worthington Cup. Kevin Phillips was injured, which will please some people who would prefer a centre forward that can be vociferously slagged off for turning up.

September 16 Wednesday

I was in the print room this morning indulging in the type of frivolous arsing about that gets people through the day. I was impressing upon Rob the printer that you put your left leg in, your left leg out, your left leg in and you shake it all about, you do the hokey-cokey and you turn around, THAT'S what its all about! as I thumped on the table to make my point even more forcibly.

I did the hokey-cokey, but when I turned around it was something of a shock to see the Chairman standing there and smiling curiously at me. He and two other important looking blokes (they had briefcases) were evidently amused, but this failed to stop me from feeling like a prize nob.

September 17 Thursday

Sunderland supporters have a new song about Niall Quinn wearing disco pants(?). It seems that the best possible rhyme for 'pants' is 'Adam And The Ants'. Poet Laureate beware.

September 19 Saturday

I got a bloke called Mickey Johnson a ticket to this afternoon's game with Oxford United. We were leading after two minutes and went on to win the game 7-0, a record defeat for Oxford. This was actually Mickey's first visit to the stadium. I have assured him that it is like this every week.

September 22 Tuesday

There was a bewildering absence of blanket media coverage for Sunderland's 1-0 second round second leg Worthington Cup win at Chester City. This can only be a conspiracy.

September 25 Friday

Me and Andy Wind, a renowned fun bloke to be with, took the train down to London where we made our way to Knightsbridge to meet Davie Smith who works there. It is notoriously difficult to enter a bar in this neck of the woods wearing a football shirt, so we employed the old Trojan trick of entering a pub at three o'clock, about five hours before the bouncers arrived, and staying in there until chucking out time. Clever what? Who says that football supporters are drunken no-users.

Later, at Davie's house in Surbiton, we saw that he has recently acquired three ready made children, who were not there but had left plenty evidence of their existence. This is something that is too daunting to contemplate, but at least I got to sleep on the top bunk.

September 26 Saturday

We made the mistake of travelling down to Portsmouth without jackets to look tough, but this only meant that a local grocer did a brisk trade in bin liners before kick-off.

After a 1-1 draw in incessant rain, we returned to Surbiton for an evening of quaffing and scoffing, culminating in a trip to an Indian restaurant. I was just negotiating the vestiges of a vindaloo when Taff nipped over the road to return with a bag, which turned out to be a Kentucky Fried Chicken bargain bucket. This was a spectacular display of gluttony even for Taff. Our fellow diners, although queasy at the very thought of chomping into this lot after an Indian meal, gave an appreciative little ripple of applause. After all, Taff is currently the greediest man in Surrey. Surely.

September 27 Sunday

The high drama of Fratton Park now firmly behind us, we boarded the train home. I had my shoes off, newspaper in one hand, Curly Wurly in the other, when my equilibrium was disturbed by the realisation that today is my birthday. This happened just as we were entering Peterborough station, so when we left it I felt as though I was a year older, although this is apparently quite common.

When I returned home, I found that Bethan was considerably more excited about my birthday than I was. Copious amounts of cake and sausage rolls had seen to that. But there were thrills-a-plenty for me too when I opened that gift voucher for Boots.

September 29 Tuesday

Sunderland gained a useful 2-2 draw at Norwich City. Our equaliser was an own goal, punched into the net by their keeper. This is not as satisfying as a box to box seven man move with defenders floundering in its wake, but it is certainly a lot funnier.

October 1 Thursday

I was sent on a vital mission in connection with ceiling tiles, which meant that I could nip into the bakers for another fix of corned beef pasties. As I cruised along in the van with the window down, my shades on and some hot sounds loudly accompanying me, it occurred to be that I was freezing, could barely see the road in front of me and was having to put up with some fairly awful music.

Nevertheless, I had achieved the main aim of the exercise, which was to look brill. In terms of style, I was easily the most accomplished person in Greggs, and also the youngest by a good 40 years.

October 3 Saturday

It was a frustrating afternoon as we drew 0-0 at home to Bradford City. Michael Bridges was on the bench but did not play, much to the annoyance of some. They should be pleased, because even if we end the season having won the league by a squillion points, they can still cling to this for a whinge.

October 5 Monday

As far as I can see, the club is now really striving for Premier League status and I like to think of myself as playing a major part in this effort, even if it isn't true. Most of my day was devoted to compiling a register for the stadium's fire extinguishers, a task not overly imbued with incident and human interest.

I was saying as much to a chap called Joe in the Ivy House tonight. But he was dismissive, saying that I had only carried out a dull task whereas he

135

had a dull job. It seems he fixes metal sheets together with steel bolts. Now that must be riveting.

October 9 Friday

At the insistence of Dave Nicholson, who says it will be beneficial to the club and myself, I am to be further educated and enrolled today.

It was a classical student setting, dreaming spires, punting along the canals, people out on picnics reading poetry beneath the shade of a willow tree. It was strikingly reminiscent of the chapter in *Brideshead Revisited* when Sebastian Flyte has the first day of his occupational health and safety course at South Tyneside College, while on day release from his welding job.

October 12 Monday

Celebrity slob Paul Gascoigne has finally bitten the bullet and gone to a clinic for people who can't stop boozing. Among those offering support was Malcolm MacDonald, a fellow recovering plonky. He explained to us, with what he thought was a simple analogy, that inside Gazza was a mass of spaghetti and on the end of each strand of spaghetti was a demon, so the end of each of these strands had to be located in order to exorcise each demon.

This leaves us with three possibilities concerning Malcolm. Either he is plain bonkers, or he has moved on from grog to LSD, or he has genuinely identified a serious satanic and pasta related social illness.

October 13 Tuesday

Back to school this afternoon where they will groom me to be a health and safety guru. They were off to a fine start when they told me that the four main considerations for manual handling are load, individual, task and environment, making the neat acronym LITE. Manual handling is LITE work.

This semed like a useful method of leaning to me, so I applied it to the manual handling steps, which are identify, evaluate, avoid, assess, reduce, inform, train, implement, monitor and reassess. Unfortunately, the initials to these words make the far clumsier acronym of IEAARITIMR, which is unlikely to be as easy to remember and nigh on impossible to slip into a conversation.

Further bad news is that my intentions of keeping a low profile in class were immediately scuppered when it became known that I work at Sunderland Football Club. This announcement was met with roughly equal amounts of commendation and derision, as well as making me at once the most conspicuous member of the group, with the exception of the bloke who brought in the x-ray of his shattered forearm to impress upon us the importance of health and safety. What a weirdo!

October 18 Sunday

This season has so far gone extremely well. By half-time at the Hawthorns we were 2-0 down, but we ended the game as 3-2 winners. Probably more remarkable than this is the fact that we are now even winning games on live television, when previously there had been more live coronations than Sunderland wins.

October 19 Monday

At work, we are equipped with two-way radios and until today I had not realised how impressive a reception radius they had. I had a call from Dave Nicholson asking me what my location was, to which I replied that I was in a kitchen to the south of the stadium. This was a misleading rather than totally specious reply as I was having a quick glass of pop and a Wagon Wheel in my own kitchen, about two miles to the south of the stadium and as far as I could get without being out of range.

These radios really come into their own when one of us gets to the chip shop and forgets what someone has ordered.

October 21 Wednesday

The lure of Huddersfield proved irresistible for the second time this year and we gained a 1-1 draw. Far more remarkable than that was my car managing the journey there and back again.

October 22 Thursday

I passed last night's goal scorer Kevin Ball on the stairs. He said hello then asked me if I drove a blue Vauxhall Astra. Despite my embarrassment at still owning this heap, I confirmed that I did, before defensively adding, 'It's better than it looks.'

It seems that he went home in a car rather than the team bus, and as he overtook me, he slowed down just to have a look at who would be seen dead or otherwise in such a vehicle. I informed him that it had got us home safely, which he was pleased about as he had therefore won a small wager with one of his fellow travellers.

October 24 Saturday

Normal people just want to see their team win. A freaky and eldritch minority insist that we be given entertainment too. It was the majority who went home happy. Sunderland 1 Bury 0. Good old Danny Dichio.

October 27 Tuesday

In another evening of glamour and excitement, we took on Grimsby Town in the Worthington Cup fourth round. Such is the lure of the competition these days, the adult portion of the crowd were keenest on any result that would see them back in the pub quicker, rather than one which would keep us in the cold as well as this daft Cup (as we call it until we get to the final).

It was all-square after 90 minutes, and when the final whistle blew an audible murmur of, 'Shit. Extra time,' went round the stadium as the number of pints to swill down after the game was reduced by two. A late goal from Niall Quinn preserved us from a penalty shoot-out, whatever one of those might be.

And so to bed.

October 28 Wednesday

Bethan's birthday. She was six and received loads of boxed games with thousands of bit in and a pile of confectionery. SHE gets everything HER!

October 29 Thursday

I wish I hadn't made that rather flippant entry about the Poet Laureate on the 17th of September. Ted Hughes has died. Oops.

November 1 Sunday

To the Ivy House to watch Sky Television. It was a spiffing production featuring Bolton Wanderers 1 Sunderland 3. The number of Sunderland victories that have been televised live now surpasses that of coronations and is rapidly nearing the total of royal funerals.

November 2 Monday

Birmingham City Council, in an act of cheerlessness worthy of Jim Fox himself, has nominally banned Christmas. To cross the city's cultural and religious differences, the festive period is to become known as 'Wintermas', which is bound to catch on. Critics have been quick to point out that this is all a bit silly as they seem to think that absolutely no one will call it this. Kevin Bell and I have generously stepped into the fray by faxing them with helpful alternative suggestions, such as Prezziemas and Wherestheradiotimesmas. They have not thus far responded, but give them a chance. In the meantime, merry Boozemas and a happy new lager.

November 3 Tuesday

We would have beaten Manchester United, Real Madrid or Juventus tonight, but we opted for Crewe Alexandra instead as it is much easier. 4-1.

November 7 Saturday

We would have beaten Inter Milan, Bayern Munich or Ajax this afternoon, but we opted for Grimsby Town instead as it is much easier. 3-1.

November 11 Wednesday
Today was Veterans Day in the United States Of America; so with the play-offs still fresh in the mind, it was richly appropriate that tonight's Worthington Cup tie should end in another penalty shoot out. We won at Everton, which is a far happier outcome, but somehow not such a good story.

Even in the midst of this jubilant occasion, one will always find someone who can heap jaundiced negativity on the event. 'I would fine the lot of them!' piped up one whinging sourpuss amid the cheery chatter in the pub. Pray why? For not doing it on the 25th of May of course.

November 13 Friday
One of the less desirable facets to my job is the scatterings of ashes that I have to accompany every couple of weeks or so. Some people will go to any lengths to get on the pitch. Today's lot arrived, in a surprisingly upbeat mood with a big tub full of Dad. When they had rang to arrange the scattering, Kerry asked if they were at all superstitious as the only available date was Friday the 13th. It did not concern them and they insisted that Dad would not have minded on the very reasonable premise that things could not get any worse for him. Save for an unlikely hoovering mishap, this was quite true.

November 14 Saturday
To Port Vale where we won 2-0. We are having difficulty in coming to terms with what is going right at the moment.

November 15 Sunday
It would be gratifying to report that I had something better to do than read about Prince Charles' 50th birthday, but apart from finding some Kraft Dairylea Cheese Triangles that I didn't know we had, this was not the case.

Geri Halliwell moved a step further away from the Laureate job with her ditty composed in honour of His Royal Highness which contained a line that expressed hopes that he would become king in the near future. Other stars at this bash managed to pass on more becoming messages than 'I hope your mother dies soon,' and hasn't this woman ever heard of iambic pentameter?

November 17 Tuesday
Apparently there was a most impressive meteor shower tonight. I am not certain as to exactly where, but somewhere in the sky. The Earth passed through the tail of Comet Tempel-Tuttle, which could aggravate my hay fever. Scientists are expected to glean information from it on the origins of the universe when it is established which gases it is comprised of. It may also in its course cause significant damage to various satellites that

139

orbit the planet, which could in turn prevent Eurosport from showing the Big Truck Mega-Derby from downtown Antwerp, so as far as I can see, only intergalactic granules and good news are emerging from the heavens at the moment.

November 18 Wednesday

I had a choice at work today of ringing around for some vital supplies of road salt and related implements, which could in theory save a home game from postponement this winter, or reading the obituaries page in the paper. It was while carrying out one of these tasks that I noticed that Paddy Clancy has died, and as a result legendary folk group the Clancy Brothers are a man short. All of their fierce internecine rivalry must seem rather trivial now.

November 21 Saturday

We allowed Barnsley into our majestic stadium this afternoon. Having shown them the best ground in the country, we then came back from a two goal deficit and watched them miss a penalty. They then had Ashley Ward sent off. He had scored earlier, so when he fumed his way past me down the tunnel, I thought smugly that he who laughs last laughs longest. How correct this proved to be as they went down the other end of the pitch to score the winner with ten men. Damn cheek if you ask me!

As ever, certain sections of the crowd were extremely disgruntled at this from Sunderland and made their feelings known. Why not? They had paid their money and to lose for the second time in eight months is simply not acceptable.

November 24 Tuesday

My collegiate efforts to save Sunderland AFC from all manner of grim hazards continued this afternoon with a lecture on electricity, which was rather a struggle for those of us who don't know our ohms from our electrodes.

We were asked to suggest reasons why a person might be electrocuted and I suggested that having lots of amps put into the body could be a reason. Also being convicted of a homicide in the state of Texas could provide such a danger. I was a trifle bored if the truth were known. But being factually indisputable did not protect me from accusations of levity, particularly from a grey curly haired woman with a long face. I had no riposte, but only because pointing out her resemblance to a Bedlington terrier would have been a bit too brutal.

November 27 Friday

I have acquired a £150 jacket and all thanks to my own incompetence. The 'Ha'way the lads' seats that I mentioned at the beginning of August did not have proper numbers on them at first, so I whizzed round with a permanent marker and scribbled them on. This resulted in one chap with a light coloured jacket complaining that 'we' had made an indelible mark on the back of it. He sent it in and it was agreed that we should reimburse him, but as he did not want the jacket and I am less fussy than him, I wore it to go out tonight. I have also memorised the seat number and might see if I can score some trousers off him too.

November 28 Saturday
To Sheffield United in my splendid new jacket, where my prediction of doing well to draw was happily endowed with my usual dose of accuracy. United seemed to have decided upon a tactic of studiously avoiding the ball, not a successful ploy and we won 4-0. But there must always be a dissenting voice.

This voice was today provided by someone sitting three along from me, wearing a cap, scarf and a hugely impressive moustache. He was vehemently ordering the Sunderland players to put their backs into it, which would not have attracted much notice had it not been 15 minutes before kick-off. He wasn't kidding either. Liz pointed out that just as the players were stretching and loosening, so he was warming up his abuse.

December 1 Tuesday
We had a home tie in the quarter-finals of the Worthington Cup. We could have drawn Wimbledon, Chelsea, Tottenham, Leicester, Blackburn or Manchester United, but where would the thrill of achievement be in beating any of that lot? Sunderland 3 Luton Town 0.

December 5 Saturday
Sunderland won an absolutely dire game of football this afternoon when we scraped past Stockport County by one goal to nil. But the main talking point was the condition of the pitch. Owing to a fault with the under-soil heating early this morning, there was a scattering of snow on the pitch, which the referee advised against clearing. It was good news, particularly for our department, that no one was injured.

At least we are now aware that we only had to go into the crowd to ask for advice, because the city's pubs were this evening stuffed to the beams with experts who had identified what had gone wrong. 'The boiler exploded!', 'The hot water tank was full of dead pigeons!', 'The Mags got in and pissed on the pilot light!', etc.

December 6 Sunday
The boiler that serves the under-soil heating is an understandably sensitive issue at present, which is why I had a telephone call at about three o'clock this morning to say that the pilot light had gone out and would I attend to it?

The taxi driver who took me across was far too chatty for my liking at that time of the morning and he cheerily asked me why I was off to the stadium at that time of the day. Everyone is now aware of yesterday's problems, so when I told him I was going to switch on the pitch heating, he took it the wrong way and said, 'Well if that's your attitude!' and drove on in a silent huff. I was not being sarcastic, but at least it shut his trap for the remainder of the journey.

December 9 Wednesday

The repercussions of Saturday's technical difficulties continued into this afternoon. I had a call from reception saying that there was a bloke down there who was demanding to speak to someone from our department about the pitch. He had bought tickets for the next three home games and was seeking a promise that they would all go ahead.

I gave him an explicit, cast-iron, unequivocal, unambiguous, definite, indubitable, copper-bottomed guarantee that there was no danger whatsoever of any of these games being postponed or abandoned. But as I also told him that my name was Dave Nicholson, he would be advised to take these pie-crusts with a dollop of salt.

December 10 Thursday

Having heroically returned from a mission to remove rusty padlocks from traffic barriers, this conquering hero returned to the office with the warm glow of pride within. When I alighted the lift on the second floor, I was passed by Leanne, who wobbled her snout appreciatively and said, 'Ooh! You smell nice, what is it?'.

I was about to lie to her and say that it was some exclusive cologne. But the only after-shave names I could remember were Brut, Blue Stratos and J.R. Ewing (limited edition some years ago). I therefore opted to tell her the truth that it was WD40.

As she walked away from me down the corridor, cackling, I contemplated that one day she would make someone a lovely cheap date.

December 12 Saturday

Sunderland were the beneficiaries of yet another walkover today when Port Vale were contemptuously beaten 2-0. The only point at which I was in any way nervous throughout the afternoon was before the game.

Samson The Cat was limbering up for yet another untrying afternoon of paid tomfoolery when he sliced a ball over to me at the touchline near the tunnel. My return pass was really no better as I scudded the Port Vale mascot on the side of the ear. Boomer the Bloodhound, for 'twas he, was not best pleased and gave me a menacing stare as I stood behind Sergeant Harris, rather intimidated. You should have seen the shoulders on him!

December 15 Tuesday

Are we tough or what? We beat Crystal Palace 2-0 even though it was quite cold.

December 16 Wednesday

One of my lesser-known aptitudes is that of disc jockeying and this evening I was reeled in to the Ivy House to display this gift. I spent a pleasant few hours a-mixing-and-a-scratching, a-whirling-and-a-twirling and generally impressing the laymen with my technical wizardry, although I had to politely ask Bob if he could put the stylus on for me.

I used this temporary power to provide a musical education for the young people, although tonight's American cruise missile attack on Baghdad that people wanted to watch proved to be a crude interruption of a fine but rarely played track by Rocky Sharpe And The Replays. That's showbiz.

December 17 Thursday

There was a reserve match at the stadium tonight. The venue was switched from Durham because a larger than usual crowd was expected as Manchester United provided the opposition. However, the attendance was way in excess of any prediction that I had heard, even that of the taxi driver who took me home last night. So the start of the game was delayed by half an hour and even then a couple of thousand people missed the kick-off.

Remarkably, the only people with prior knowledge of the huge turnout left home after everyone else, with the sole intention of standing at the back of the queue in smug martyrdom, saying, 'This is ridiculous. I knew there would be 20,583 people here.'

December 19 Saturday

There was a beam back today. Sunderland's goalless draw at Birmingham City was relayed back to the stadium. Most people there were reasonably happy with the result, but later dismayed that it did not receive anything like the national coverage that Middlesbrough did. The less diehard Sunderland supporters conceded that Boro's win at Manchester United was probably a more newsworthy encounter, but the more biased among us were insisting that this was no big deal. Sunderland are always winning at Old Trafford, our last win there was as recent as 1968.

Middlesbrough's victory was bad news for their former player Bernie Slaven who, in a shameful display of little faith, said that if they pulled it off he would show his arse in Binn's window. Binn's have apparently agreed to this, so this should provide an extra festive thrill for Christmas shoppers on Teesside.

December 20 Sunday

I picked the long straw and therefore it was Liz who had to accompany Bethan to the theatre to see *Snow White And The Seven Dwarves*, which, in a disagreeable quirk of fate, starred Ant and Dec. Despite this palpable handicap, there were plenty of happy little faces emerging from the exits when I went to pick them up (I mean Liz and Bethan, not Ant and Dec).

The magic may have been eroded somewhat for the kiddiewinks who spotted Sleepy and Dopey, hurtling towards the Dun Cow rather than lose any more valuable lager time. They must have barely finished bowing when they made the journey from stage to pub in a very impressive time for such little legs.

December 21 Monday

This evening saw the Sunderland AFC staff party, with the option of crazy 1970s outfits for those wacky enough to wear them. It was worth attending to see John Fickling in yellow satin tight-arsed flares. Being a notoriously stiff-limbed-stick-in-the-mud I did not participate in this, but I did make a concession to the festivities by taking along a mouth organ.

Alas, I am incapable of playing a note, yet undaunted, I gave backing to a particularly heart felt rendition of *Wind Beneath My Wings* by some woman from the warehouse on the karaoke. She spent the remainder of the evening trying to find out who it was, which seems a mite touchy. There's just no pleasing some divas.

December 25 Friday

I had a day off today.

December 26 Saturday

Sunderland have now played 32 league and Cup games this season and lost only two of them. One of these defeats came today at Tranmere. We always lose at Tranmere. I don't know why this fixture has to be played. We should just give them the three points and save a great deal of time and effort.

The evening was far more felicitous. Liz and I rounded it off with a convivial bout of boozing and coarse language at Bernie and Lesley's house. We returned home to guzzle further, but our chomping and slurping was interrupted by a loud crash as a good section of the gable end found its way into the bedroom. I can only think of this as a negative development, although in fairness we are not dead.

December 27 Sunday

I found myself going into work today in the aftermath of some wind damage to the stadium. Dave Nicholson was shaking his head ruefully at the scene of the damage and said, 'This shouldn't have happened. My

144

house was built in the 1940s and it doesn't get damaged in the wind.' Our house was also built around that time, but as half of it was removed last night I kept quiet so as not to spoil an otherwise reasonable point.

Tomorrow's game will go ahead as we wouldn't dare postpone the big one with Crewe Alexandra.

December 28 Monday

An excellent day. We beat Crewe Alexandra 2-0, with the added dividend of no one having their block knocked off by any part of the stadium that the wind might not have liked.

December 31 Thursday

This morning the administration building was littered with hangovers. There was a girls night out last night, as for some reason they thought it a sound plan to get absolutely blitzed the day before New Year's Eve and they were now paying the price for all of this boozying and floozying. Being a helpful sort of mug, I agreed to go to McDonald's to buy them a huge box of greasy fodder which they hoped would dispel their self-inflicted illness, but I only went after giving in to dreadful incessant snivelling.

It was an heroic return to the admin. by me, which also reinforced sexual stereotypes, as they sat at their desks whining, while it was man the hunter who was out garnering the food.

1999

January 1 Friday

The year is now 1999 which I find difficult to believe, having been led to understand that by now I would be flying to work in a silver space suit, perhaps stopping on the way for a fried breakfast capsule.

According to Prince, to party like it's 1999 entails a tumultuous soiree and unbounded pleasure. So it was with a distinct lack of foresight that he wrote this song, as all that I have done so far this year is take Bethan to feed the ducks and talk about footy with Tonka and Taff in the Ivy House. What a disappointingly misleading song.

January 2 Saturday

Football wise it has been a rip-roaring inception to the year. Sunderland laughed in the face of fear, before contemptuously tickling it on the chin, then marching into the fourth round of the FA Cup by majestically sweeping aside the valiant Lincoln City 1-0 with a ricochet off Gavin McCann's knee. Although others thought it was all a bit crap.

I had never previously been to Lincoln and found it to be remarkably flat. They do have one substantial hill, but have squandered it by plonking an eleventh century Gothic cathedral at its summit. What a waste.

January 3 Sunday

After a pleasant stagger around some of the more salubrious hostelries in our second to none city centre, I returned to the Ivy House in a state of high spirits. However, I was accused in there by someone cleverer than me (and everyone was cleverer than me by this stage) of being hedonic.

I responded with a dignified silence, as I did not know what this word meant and tried to find it in the dictionary when I got home. It was quite a shock to find myself denounced as an insectivorous quadruped with a pig-like snout armed with many spines, but equally relieving to realise that I was so pissed that I had looked up 'hedgehog' instead.

January 4 Monday

Rumour has it that the world will end in 1999, which would render the writing of this diary a useless exercise. There is much fear based on crackpot theories, but no need to worry. So long as the Grim Reaper comes on a Monday morning, perhaps in a nice ski jacket instead of that old cloak.

Nostradamus, the 16th century Provençal prophet, was really rather ambiguous on the subject, and so far the only modern day soothsayer to measure up, June Penn, has remained tight-lipped on the subject. But she did tell Virgos that it might be a good time to spend some savings. That could be a clue.

January 8 Friday

I was out and about this evening for yet more boozing and coarse language. For us shallow, uncultured types, it is the horns of a dilemma to decide between this activity and gawping at the telly all night, with no escape from this quandary for those of us with no idea of how to operate the timer on the video. Indeed, by the time I returned home I could barely operate either my own feet or the floor.

One part of this evening viewing that is unlikely to be entirely lost is *Bang Bang It's Reeves And Mortimer.* I am acquainted with any number of annoying dullards who by tomorrow night will be able to recite the entire script, whether I want to hear it or not.

January 9 Saturday

Liz and I are house hunting at the moment and we had an appointment to view at five o'clock today. I was putting my shoes on prior to getting into the car to go there and had already decided that the place was a dump and not worth half of what they were asking. I had not seen the property at this stage, my opinion being based on the fact that Sunderland were losing at Queen's Park Rangers.

Fortunately, Niall Quinn put in a late equaliser while we were driving there and we gained a point, which meant that by the time the bloke answered the door I had decided to put in a very fair offer. This is a glimpse of just how complex the housing market can be.

January 10 Sunday

Being nothing short of a fashion icon in the south-east High Barnes area, I do not take sartorial decisions lightly. So before I left home tonight, I made pained deliberations over the three way choice of boots, shoes or just socks. Well just a two way choice in effect then.

I would have preferred the boots on a purely aesthetic basis, but there were practicalities to consider. The condition in which I arrive home on a Sunday night out means that the act of taking off my shoes is likely to awaken Liz, whereas removing my boots is likely to dislodge household fixtures and fittings. I always forget to use my hands when I am drunk, so using a key is far from simple too.

January 13 Wednesday

Kevin Bell turned out tonight with a tale of misfortune. A woman where he works had sidled up to him at the photocopier, and with a coy smile had

147

asked him if they were still on for what they had discussed at the Christmas party.

Kevin did not know for sure what she was referring to, but he did what any gentleman in his position would do and readily agreed to whatever she was talking about and hoped for the best. It took him another two hours to establish that his horse riding lessons begin next Sunday. Next time someone sidles up to ME at the photocopier I shall tell them what they can do with their horse riding lessons.

January 17 Sunday

I was at work today where I got to witness our league knacking 2-1 win over Ipswich Town. As we have recently become rather twitchy about litter on the pitch, I was, one minute before kick off, body-swerving round the entire Ipswich defence in pursuit of some blue and white balloons, but more than likely looking like a bit of a tit.

It is the first rule of balloon chasing that getting to within two feet of one of them means that they are likely to be caught in another gust of wind at the point of grabbing. The likelihood of this happening is multiplied by the number of people watching you, so Sky TV were no help either. I am sure I heard Tony Mowbray sniggering at me.

January 20 Wednesday

Every time I have read a newspaper this week I have came across the name of the same dead artist, Monet, who has a big exhibition on London at the moment. I don't know what it is about this man, but I have a theory as to why his repertoire was so small. When I was a child, I became very adept at drawing a boa constrictor devouring a baby elephant and consequently drew little else, meaning that to this day a boa constrictor devouring a baby elephant is the only picture that I can do. It seems reasonable to assume then that Monet had a similar experience with lilies on a pond. Look forward to the Boa Exhibition.

January 21 Thursday

Kerry and I have devised an exhilarating game whereby she reads out the names from the birthday list in the paper, and I have to guess their age and occupation. I tend to struggle on the china watchers and nazi hunters of this world, but this does not detract from this adrenalin-fuelled pastime. Even employees at leading football clubs need their recreation.

One curious inclusion in today's list was that of Telly Savalas who was alleged to be 74. We faxed them to point out that if Telly was going out tonight to celebrate, then the first six feet of his journey would be the most difficult as he has been dead for five years. If they print our fax we might scoop three quid.

January 22 Friday

The day began in disappointment when I bought the paper to excitedly leaf through it and see if they had printed the fax we sent yesterday. Of course they hadn't. We made the clarifications and corrections column, but it is just not the same, shunted down there alongside the spelling mistakes and the split infinitives.

January 23 Saturday

Liz and I had an excursion to watch Sunderland in the fourth round of the FA Cup. There is a certain irony to driving through some of England's most picturesque countryside at full tilt in order to arrive in Blackburn earlier. It struck me as a singularly drab city and I speak as a citizen of Sunderland.

But we were made to pay for snide and hackneyed comments about cloth caps and woollen mills when Keith Gillespie, an ex-Newcastle player, scored the only goal of the game. In fact he played throughout like a man with a bet on.

January 26 Tuesday

We are not having one of our better weeks. Tonight saw our long awaited Worthington Cup semi-final first leg at home to Leicester City. It was a right old damp squib of a game too which we lost 2-1, both of their goals coming from the sprightly octogenarian, Tony Cottee.

There was also a terrific spat between Kevin Ball and Lee Clark. It did not actually come to blows, but if a fist fight is to be arranged after training tomorrow I doubt if any bookmakers would be taking bets on Kevin.

January 27 Wednesday

There was another home game tonight when a ridiculous number of people, 33,000, turned up to see a reserve match with Liverpool. We beat them too, despite the presence of several high profile players in their line up. Alex Rae was hobbling around the tunnel having recently had his knee amputated or something so that he can be fit for next season and uttered the whimsical question, 'If that MacManaman's worth fifteen million then what would you get for me?'

Alex is a decent chap and a good player, but all those who heard could only smile respectfully and assume the question to be rhetorical, rather than give him an honest answer such as, 'About what we paid for you Alex.'

Silence is indeed golden.

January 30 Saturday

This has turned out not to be a good month. We lost 2-1 at Watford this afternoon, which later instigated a furious debate in the Ivy House. This was not because of anything untoward in the Watford victory, but because of wildly differing opinions as to why they have a red moose on their club crest.

February 2 Tuesday

As I sashayed lithely across Market Square, club mobile phone in one inside pocket, pasty in the other, I was accosted yet again by a grubby looking bloke with elbow pads who wanted to know if I would like to buy a lighter for only a pound. Annoyed that he had somehow penetrated my leading club official aura, I said quite curtly that I did not and that nor had I on the previous 15 occasions on which he had harangued me. Furthermore, I would never give him a pound and would see that he was given a minus figure if such a thing were possible.

I then strode away in that superior manner of mine, so it is arguably to his credit that he tried to flog me some nail clippers when I walked past him again. I bet nothing like this happens to Bob Murray. I would ask him if I dared.

February 5 Friday

I saw a dishevelled looking Lesley Callaghan hobbling into reception today. A particularly violent gust of wind had caught her then sent her helplessly into some nearby foliage causing some notable damage to her foot and her hair. No one dared to utter the cliché about being dragged through a hedge backwards as this was precisely what had happened to her.

Shortly afterwards, I was implored by Claire the receptionist to attend to a bollard outside which had become insecure. This just about sums up my esteem at work. Life, limb, property and old people were being put paid to by this passing hurricane, but it was deemed to be perfectly practical for me to be sent into it with an adjustable spanner to mend a keep left sign.

February 6 Saturday

We were at home to Swindon Town today and so confident was I of a good solid victory, that I went to Ladbrokes and slammed a pound on a 2-0 win which was the result, despite Lee Clark hitting the post in the final minute when deliberately trying to score and loosen my vice-like grip on seven entire quid. Swindon were very obliging on the nil side of things.

The possibilities that occur in the wake of a seven pounds windfall are best described as limited, but a bus ride and a turn on the jukebox in the Ivy House is surely quite enough largesse for one year.

February 10 Wednesday

I bumped into Samson The Cat today and he was rather tired, having been to Pride Park in Derby last night for an England under 21 game with France. It turned out to be something of an ad hoc conference for the nation's mascots and he was particularly impressed by Ollie The Owl from Sheffield Wednesday, who thanks to the latest in owl technology, can actually speak.

If Ollie is at the peak of the mascot hierarchy in all his finery then floundering badly, and in danger of dropping into the Mascot Conference League, must be Peter The Pilgrim from Plymouth Argyle who is merely a bloke wearing a big hat with a buckle at the front and he is not even a foam comedy bloke with enormous hands, feet and nose. Disappointing.

February 11 Thursday

I paid a visit to the Charlie Hurley training ground to scrounge some lunch, under the transparent guise of dropping off a bar of soap. Cheered by my success in this and by the enormous jacket potato before me, I had reached a contended equipoise only to see it booted to one side by a steward of my acquaint who was accompanied by a plateful of liver. This makes me queasy to begin with, but to watch him eat it with the alacrity and decorum of a malnourished chimpanzee was quite nauseating.

'Don't you like liver then?' he asked me through a full mouth to make my stomach turn a few degrees more.

'I love it.'

Further to this, much of his lunch was to remain in his moustache and he spent the remainder of the day happily oblivious that part of an animal's internal organ was stuck to his face.

February 13 Saturday

Sunderland won one-nil at Bristol City with a late penalty, which I have not seen yet. Apparently it was rather dubious. I certainly hope so.

February 15 Monday

Dave Nicholson's company car for the last few weeks has been a sort of jeep which used to belong to Lionel Perez. Since Lionel left us, it has been passed round as quickly as people can get rid of it, and I can see why. Today I had to meet a man from the hire place who had come to collect it. In a question clearly loaded with admiration for it, he asked me what I had thought of the vehicle and he looked forlorn when I replied that it was impractical, uneconomical and ugly.

'But it's a fun car,' he said defensively, so I asked what was fun about it.

'The roof comes off,' was a most unsatisfactory answer in our climate, yet he remained unenthusiastic at my lack of appreciation, so we agreed to differ then parted. Fun car my arse! I remember the roof coming off at Strangeways a few years ago and it looked like anything but fun.

February 17 Wednesday

Despite a good show at Leicester City, Sunderland's Cup exploits have petered out for another season. In a 1-1 draw, our goal was scored by the exemplary veteran Niall Quinn who, like a superior claret, improves with age. Meanwhile, their fluke was prodded in again by the decrepit thirty-something Tony Cottee, who should really have been put out to grass by now.

We can now concentrate on the league (of course), while also returning to calling the Worthington Cup a daft little competition for teams with nothing better to do.

February 20 Saturday

Sunderland won 2-1 at home to Wolves, the winner being yet another last minute job against them. My reaction to this was 'Ha!' which was heard by their manager Colin Lee who chose to ignore me.

They did have their fun though. For the second season running, their strike was an own goal by Andy Melville. Their mascot, Wolfy The Wolf had great delight in re-enacting it before the North Stand at half-time, the sort of thing that is hilarious when it happens in your favour, but inflammatory and juvenile when it doesn't.

February 21 Sunday

To make absolutely certain of not having my mind in any way improved this afternoon, I decided to watch any old offal that television might spew out. One documentary showed a woman who in between giggling was keen to tell a waiting world how much she hated Manchester United and that she hoped they would not win anything this season.

This struck me as not being much cop by way of hatred. Wanting another team to finish the season with no trophies is hardly the peak of detestation, considering that Sunderland and Newcastle would prefer each other to finish the season with no oxygen.

I would have turned it off, but the remote control was 18 inches from my hand. This is the laziest I have been since that time I got a lift to the car.

February 24 Wednesday

It is fair to say that I am not as adept as I would like to be at customer relations, but no one is qualified to deal with some of the people I have to speak to. This morning I received a phone call from a supporter who had a concern with the impending North Stand extension as it will not have a roof for some time. I asked him where about in the North Stand his seat was, but he actually sits in the South Stand and was concerned with the stadium not looking good on the television. Eh?! I have found out where he sits anyway and intend to cover his seat with chewing gum.

February 25 Thursday

In the course of my job I am fortunate enough to regularly meet some very interesting and celebrated individuals. Sportsmen, politicians, journalists, entertainers and brutal dictators have all passed my way. Today I met a bloke with no thumb.

He was a rep and I did not notice this defect until I had made an introductory handshake. I noticed then that my right hand had gone further up his right arm than is usual. I was obviously the more embarrassed of the two of us, so I will avoid shaking his hand again. In future I shall adopt an American style greeting by raising my hand high above my head and saying, 'Hey! Gimme four!'

February 27 Saturday

Sunderland played a little part in football history in our early evening kick-off at Oxford United. The reason for this was that it was an experimental 'pay-per-view' game. We did our bit for football by playing our part in an utterly tedious match, so hopefully there won't be any more of them.

March 2 Tuesday

Sunderland were at home to Portsmouth tonight and we won at a trot. Danny Dichio scored a good header, but managed to burst his mouth in the process. It was decided that as no one else in the stadium was in pain, he should play on. But as the game wore on, his mouth expanded, his blood made a dreadful mess in the penalty area and his skin colour went from that of an olive tinged Latin to a far more pallid shade, rather like that of someone who has not been anywhere apart from the Dun Cow for a few weeks. So he was eventually substituted.

As he trudged past me in the tunnel someone asked how he was, to which he replied with the enigmatic, 'Mmfth brrbl nngg!'

March 3 Wednesday

I continue to jockey the discs in the Ivy House, where the quiz, compered by Marcus every Wednesday evening since the Bronze Age, continues to be a triumph of tat over taste. Tonight's Dusty Springfield tribute round (she has passed away) was his worst since 'Which Spice Girl is on which flavour of Walkers crisps?' some time ago.

March 4 Thursday

While in the van heading for the training ground this morning, I was frantically trying to tune the radio to the show where you have to guess who the bloke is impersonating in the style of Scooby Doo, when I inadvertently landed at some crap on BBC Radio Four. Some eggheads were discussing how William Shakespeare had nicked all of the plots for his plays, which they justified with the old chestnut that good artists borrow, but great artists steal. Fair enough I suppose, being too ignorant to argue.

This notion came back to me later in the day when I was in Woolworth's in Fawcett Street, where two snotty little things in track suits were being shoved into the back of a patrol car having been caught pilfering the pick n' mix. What a way to treat two of our great artists.

March 6 Saturday

The club has recently been on the end of some stinging criticism concerning the gaping lack of Zulu acrobatic troupes for pre-match entertainment. Happily this oversight was rectified before today's 1-0 win over Norwich City with the appearance of Black Lightening.

As they stood four high, juggling lighted pool cues on a unicycle, the crowd said 'Oooh!', and feeling full of myself, I nudged no less a personage than Peter Reid and said, 'You and Sacko want to be doing that instead of head tennis.'

He replied with a puzzled expression before sloping off to ask someone who I was. Well I thought it was funny even if he didn't.

March 7 Sunday

Liz, Bethan and I toddled along to Cleadon for Sunday lunch today and most agreeable fodder it was too.

Our eating was accompanied by the strains of the new Cher album, as she continues with her relentless belief in love after love. As each song rolled mercifully by, it became apparent what a fickle old cow she is. Her aforementioned belief in love after love having been firmly established, she then warbled some ditty about doing anything for some lucky cove, even ironing his slacks. However, in the next song she was crooning defiantly about being strong enough to live without him. I assume it was the same bloke. Perhaps there was some sort of altercation between recording tracks three and four.

March 8 Monday

Stanley Kubrik died today. Celebrities are dropping like flies this year.

March 9 Tuesday

There was a beamback tonight for Sunderland's game at Bradford City. There were technical problems and the signal was two minutes late. Even then they had to use microwaves to send the signal, which means that picture quality suffers in heavy rain, which of course we got. On the other hand, the game was done to a crisp.

All of these difficulties were forgotten when we won 1-0. Niall Quinn scored and then had to go in goal for the injured Thomas Sorensen. He was pretty good too and his whole performance put one in mind of the hero in a bad adventure movie. I mean this as a compliment.

March 10 Wednesday
Told you so two days ago. Joe DiMaggio is away now.

March 12 Friday
I had my big health and safety exam today at South Tyneside College and it was Comic Relief Day. My answer to question six may render the two events connected. I was distracted by the low quality of the graffiti on my desk; surely anyone who has reached adolescence should be aware that the F word also has a C in it?

It seemed an eternity to be in there. When I went in Yehudi Menuhin was still alive as far as I knew, which was not the case when I came out. I hope the announcement was not some shabby Red Nose Day joke.

March 13 Saturday
There was another beamback today with more technical problems to annoy the fans who had to miss the first 12 minutes. It might not have been that long but for me. When the receiver van finally picked up the signal, there was a further delay for me to run from the van down to the basement to alert the television people who were putting out Ceefax in a futile attempt at keeping the punters happy. Clearly, my van-to-basement personal best is some way behind me these days. We won 2-0 so all problems were forgotten again.

It is surely worth pondering that live Jack Russell racing from Bondai Beach provides no such difficulties, but our game at Grimsby Town provided a technological mountain to climb.

March 14 Sunday
Today was Mother's Day, so obviously the pubs this evening were crammed with huge gaggles of blokes all celebrating the fact. Among them was Taff who was watching the Spanish football with his usual tenuous grasp of all matters foreign.

We were marvelling at the Nou Camp Stadium and its 120,000 capacity, when Taff sagely declared that this volume of people was only possible because Spaniards are so small and because they are also greasy. It is therefore easier to squeeze more of them into a sports ground. Height and complexion are set to dominate the whole federalist debate.

March 18 Thursday
Another show biz personality has shuffled off to the Great Euphemism in the Sky. This time it was Rod Hull, who had already made a head start there when he fell from a roof when altering his television aerial. I have

155

never known the death of a celebrity to elicit so little sympathy. Already I have heard unfeeling jibes along the lines of, 'Come down Rod, you'll never get it to fly,' followed by heartless merriment from pondering the possibilities of teaming up with the equally redundant Schnorbitz, then the unquestionably funny image that someone conjured up of the bird attending the funeral with his head bowed reverently.

This disrespectful sniggering was not a feature of Stanley Kubrick's passing.

March 20 Saturday

Fate looked favourably upon us today. We took on Bolton Wanderers at home and sent them back to Lancashire with no points, their pride dented, a flea in their ear and a Chinese burn. 3-0.

Furthermore, there was a film crew on the loose around the stadium again, and as a result the chef who normally slaps down our pre-match nosh up was trying to impress the outside world, placing all manner of sophisticated fare under our noses. John Mallan tucked into his coq au vin with great gusto, although after I had polished off my chateaubriand steak I still had to supplement it with a Crunchie.

March 21 Sunday

The great Ernie Wise has gone now, but this did not provide anything like the amusement of Rod Hull the other day.

March 27 Saturday

There is no football this weekend so we have decided to move house instead. I therefore went to Tommy Porter's house to borrow the van. Always a congenial host, he gave me a cup of tea and a biscuit as we discussed cabbages and kings and I asked him how many grandchildren he had, at which point his face contorted to signify that a complex mathematical process was taking place. Eventually he gave up and shouted 'Joan!' as he required the assistance of his wife.

Immediately, she came up with the correct answer, as she is a dab hand at the mental arithmetic. The answer was five, although I don't know why pi had to be calculated to so many places to establish this.

March 28 Sunday

We moved house. I shall not say where to obviate the possibility of inveterate diary fans camping in my garden.

March 29 Monday

Today I was involved in discussions with a high-ranking cabinet minister. The secretary of State for Health, Frank Dobson, was in the stadium for an important conference which concluded that everyone should eat their greens. Afterwards, he went to Executive Box 48 to give television interviews with the pitch as a scenic backdrop. Mr. Dobson is clearly not happy to give answers without my assistance - in fact had I not been on hand to go down and ask Tommy to switch off the noisy lawnmower, the National Health Service could have been in disarray.

Having averted a national crisis, I then nipped to Sea Road to buy some teacakes.

March 30 Tuesday

My feet were absent today, as I had been rushed off them. I just about made time to read the weekend's papers where I noticed that Rod Hull's funeral had taken place. Having fallen to his death from a roof whilst adjusting the aerial to gain better reception of the football on Wednesday, I had reasonably assumed that things would not get any worse for him. But there was the further and final indignity of the only attendee of the funeral to have a tributary quote in print was the nauseating Timmy Mallet.

If you ever read this Timmy, be aware that I do not want you at my funeral, wedding, birthday, bar mitzvah or Nobel literature award ceremony.

April 1 Thursday

At lunchtime today I was walking along Crowtree Road with time to kill, when I remembered that the Everything's A Pound shop is usually a source of amusement, what with their 'Grow Your Own Sprouts' kits, *Black Beauty* cup and saucer sets, combined ornamental rampant horse and pen-holder and the like.

However, the place was closed when I arrived there and I thought for one awful moment that they had simply disappeared, but they have merely relocated to Market Square and changed their name to Superpound. Sheer relief then as there is no finer sight on the High Street than the 'SALE ON' sign at the Everything's A Pound shop, in which circumstances they may just as well change their name to Just Take It.

April 3 Saturday

It was another sell-out today for the game with West Bromwich Albion, except in the visitors' section. Their fans could buy a ticket on the day for the match, provided they could somehow prove their allegiance to that noble club. This made for some amusement when two teenage girls, who were incontestably from Sunderland due to their mandatory sports wear and scrunchies, barged into the ticket office and announced 'Us are from Bromwich!'

So convinced was the woman at the counter of this being a fib, that she only confronted them by asking a deliberately unchallenging question. Who was the manager of West Bromwich Albion? They still got it wrong, in fact

157

their answer of 'Tom' was about as wrong as you can get. Tom's lads lost 3-0.

April 5 Monday

Easter Monday and the end of the tax year. This became a triplicate celebration when Sunderland uncharacteristically got a 1-1 draw at Selhurst Park with Crystal Palace. People will remember days like this, but I am not one of them.

April 8 Thursday

There is a chance that we could be promoted on Saturday if we beat Huddersfield Town, so we had a meeting to organise some appropriate frivolities. However, these will be as nothing compared to what goes on after our final game against Birmingham City.

Dave Nicholson told us that for that game the club has booked a well known band whose name eluded him 'You know them. They've got a singer. Oooh, what do you call them. Begins with a D. Prodigy! That's them. The Prodigy.'

Then he calmed down, satisfied that his much lauded powers of recall had triumphed once again. Satisfied, that is, until Mark the electrician more accurately remembered that it was Republica that we had booked.

'Well you knew who I meant,' responded Dave. Wrongly.

April 9 Friday

There was a fair amount of merriment around the administration building today as the staff amused themselves by contemplating the directors strutting their stuff along to Republica before the Birmingham City game. Given that Dave Nicholson told us yesterday that The Prodigy were coming to town, the thought of this has come as a relief by comparison. Surely it would be of no benefit to anyone concerned to see Bob Murray and his good lady wife jiving gamely to the tuneless strains of *Smack My Bitch Up*.

An obvious compromise would have been for the Prodigies to play something more crowd pleasing, such as the *Hokey-Cokey*, which is something of a favourite of Mr. Murray's as I found out on the 16th of September last year.

April 10 Saturday

The march continued this afternoon with a 2-0 win over Huddersfield Town. The victory was cemented for me by the appearance as mascot by none other than Bethan, who by the time she arrived at the stadium had gone beyond excitement and will probably take a month to come back down. She had sound reason to be excited too as 41,074 people had turned up to see her, although some of them stayed on to watch the football.

As usual I was down in the tunnel trying to look important, but today I had a camcorder in one eye and a tear in the other and I fully expect to bore more people than I regale with this video. Yet this is a small price to pay for being my friend.

April 11 Sunday

I played the video of Bethan as mascot to a busy Ivy House, much to the boredom of everyone else there, apart from a couple of women who said 'Aaah'.

April 12 Monday

I began a four day first aid course in the players' lounge this morning. We will perfect the Heinrich manoeuvre but only on a plastic dummy which is a let down as he isn't very sexy.

April 13 Tuesday

Throw away those calculators and put your fingers and toes back in their rightful place! We are now mathematically promoted to the Premier League after tonight's 5-2 win at Bury! The occasion was marred by some serious disorder when someone pinched Peter Reid's tie in the after match celebrations.

Is there a most glamorous location than Gigg Lane in which to capture a success like this? Well yes, virtually anywhere else come to think of it, but we do not mind.

April 15 Thursday

Having successfully completed my first aid course and been given the badge and 'I'm a first aider me' t-shirt, I rewarded myself with a trip to the town to buy a Devon split.

Coming down the stairs from the car park and past Marks & Spencer, I caught sight of one Gary Smith. I went to school with him and had not seen him since those heady days. So many memories, so many stories to recall, so much to catch up with. I considered whether to embrace him, or whether to just shake his hand and slap him on the back, and I hoped he would have enough time to discuss everything. However, all of these problems were dispersed when he merely said, 'Alright mate,' and walked right past me, never to be seen again.

April 16 Friday

To Barnsley and a sexy 3-1 win which means that we are now champions. Bring on next season! I am arrogant and bored with this one.

April 17 Saturday

We are in Sheffield at the moment, but despite this, I was forbidden by Liz to go to Millmoor to watch Rotherham United play Carlisle. They won 3-1 too. Bah!

April 20 Tuesday

There has been considerable consternation and uproar around Merseyside today after the Home Secretary, Jack Straw, made a comment along the lines of Scousers being a set of thieving shitbags to a man. The disgruntled citizens of Liverpool have had the temerity to complain about this and Mr. Straw has explained by saying that he was only joking, which should do the trick as they have a great sense of humour in Liverpool.

Meanwhile, to be completely chummy again he was going to deliver a fulsomely apologetic speech from Liverpool Town Hall tonight, but had to cancel at the last minute when his briefcase containing the speech mysteriously disappeared along with his mountain bike.

April 24 Saturday

Today's home game with Sheffield United was a goalless draw and an undeniably dull one at that. My attention was thus easily swerved by the Sunderland bench and the incredible Bobby Saxton a few metres from me. His antics have livened up many a boring afternoon.

His wild, receding hair, doughy face, with his amazingly loud and high pitched voice puts one in mind of one of those less fortunate types who can be found in Mowbray Park, hurling abuse at the stone lions. One of these fine days a linesman will smile kindly at him, then chuck him a 50 pence coin and tell him to go away and buy himself a nice cup of tea.

April 27 Tuesday

After work it was off to Sainsbury's to experience first hand their super value and friendly service. Why I was bowled over. I was. Their reward points scheme now extends to other household name outlets. Imagine my excitement when I saw that Scottish Electric was one of these names. But the list was to have some glaring and surprising omissions considering how much they were trying to impress me. They could have given me a few points to splash around Asda! Today, therefore, is the last time I go to Sainsbury's for my box of matches.

May 1 Saturday

I did not travel to Stockport County for our largely academic 1-0 win.

May 2 Sunday
Taff was back in town tonight after attending yesterday's epoch making victory over Stockport County. Perhaps even more notable than this stunning success was the introduction of a new song. To the tune of *By The Rivers Of Babylon*, it goes;

By the Rivers of Pallion,
Where we chopped chips,
Where we ate lard,
And we had balls like stallions.

Clearly, this little ditty is puerile, bad poetry, inaccurate and just plain hopeless, so obviously Taff and a chap called Steve King have become self-appointed standard bearers for this contemptible nonsense. In the interests of fair play, I had to concede that there are not that many words that rhyme with Pallion.

May 4 Tuesday
The reserves had a big game tonight and 20,000 odd people turned up to see them beat Derby County reserves to win their league. I resent this as it meant I had to work tonight.

May 7 Friday
Redge etc. are up for the weekend. To complete an evening of boozing and coarse language, we all went back to our house where we woke Bethan up. She staggered sleepily into the living room and announced, 'I was a mascot,' to all present. Ah, bless.

May 8 Saturday
The continued NATO attacks on Yugoslavia have run into more than a little controversy after they used an outdated map. Perhaps I should not be too precious about this as I recently used a six year old A to Z in the course of my work, although the adverse consequences were pretty small beer by comparison.

NATO managed to accidentally aim missiles at the Chinese Embassy, provoking a major diplomatic incident and international condemnation, whereas I went to a new industrial estate and was unable to locate an outlet that had some drill bits for us, which meant that we were unable to put up a picture of Jimmy McNab in the Sports Bar.

May 9 Sunday
The 1998-99 football season finally came to an end this afternoon when Sunderland beat Birmingham City 2-1, although the game was little more than an interruption for the bands, acrobats, stilt walkers and dancers. My

suggestion of a quiz had been rejected as logistically unsuitable, but at a pound to enter, some lucky winner could have scooped £40,000.

Top of the bill were Republica, led by the lovely Saffron. Their bus had broken down and so her little legs were trotting up the players tunnel where she bumped my arm, luckily not the arm that was holding my Cup-a-Soup. Hopefully this will be enough to inspire a cruel, mendacious tabloid rumour about me being Saffy's new toy-boy.

After the game, the waving around of the Championship trophy was accompanied by the PA announcer, John Foster, playing the expected *We Are The Champions, Cheer Up Peter Reid* and so on. Among the unexpected though was *National Express* and I could think of no possible reason for this, so I asked John what the reason was. 'Oh, I just like it,' was the answer.

Fair enough.

May 10 Monday

'Twas the big civic reception today and when I got home I managed to catch a glimpse of myself on television outside the stadium looking quite imposing and central to the proceedings. This was indeed the case, as a police horse had deposited some manure adjacent to the open top bus that the great and good were about to board and I had to stand guard over it to ensure that no dignitaries would greet the crowd then immediately slip over on a great mound of horse shit.

I thought of allowing Kevin Ball to go ends up with the trophy in his hands for a laugh, but joining the dole queue could not be compensated for, even by giving Dennis Norden something to show for the next 30 years.

May 11 Tuesday

There was more extra work tonight when the stadium held a testimonial game for Jimmy McNab, belatedly by about 30 years. Unlike on Sunday, we struggled to find some appropriate music for him to walk out to. *Jimmy Mac* by Martha Reeves And The Vandellas hardly makes for a dramatic entrance. He still scored a penalty.

May 12 Wednesday

After contending with a flood in the administration building, built two entire years ago, Liz and I got ourselves suited and booted and headed back to the stadium for the Championship Ball.

After a delicious umpteen-course meal with plates full of pandulum that I had never heard of, we listened to a speech by Peter Reid, who was in attendance of this official binge, despite being a confirmed ascetic. He managed to heap praise and gratitude on each and every department except ours. Perhaps he had been in his office since the flood.

162

It was definitely worth going for the free bar and also to see Mr. And Mrs. Murray bopping away to the timeless air of *Sex On The Beach* by top Dutch disco duo, T-Spoon. I would imagine that a quick sift through their record collection would confirm them as committed stalwarts of Euro pop in general.

May 15 Saturday
It was well to be noticed that it was I who had dressed Bethan this morning. I took her into town so that she could strut around in her Sunderland shirt, which was one sure sign. Another indication arose as we strolled into C & A, where a teenage girl tapped me on the shoulder and politely pointed out that the little one's shoes were on the wrong feet. I looked down to see that this was indeed the case, as I frantically thought for a way of camouflaging my embarrassment, which was to say 'Bethan! What have you done?'

I wish I could take her to work with me. Having a six year old around to pass blame onto would be a real asset.

May 17 Monday
Just to prove how unutterably sophisticated I am, I ventured down to London for an exhibition on equipment for stadiums and training grounds at Chelsea F.C. I even had Peter Robertson ringing me on the journey down which enabled me to say that I was on the train.

In a hospitality lounge at Stamford Bridge, we delegates were given a short but rousing speech by Ken Bates along the lines of 'Please spend lots of money in here.' Afterwards, I was able to take advantage of the corporate hospitality, which consisted of the chance to buy some instant tea in a plastic cup for a pound - which is exactly how much it cost Ken to buy the club some years ago. So you can't say the boy hasn't done well for his quid. Even Superpound would struggle to match that particular bargain. It makes you wonder why he didn't get two of them.

May 18 Tuesday
Back at the stadium and my life continues to be punctuated by the regular appearances before me of Malcolm the tour guide. There is surely more than one of him because every time I am approaching a corner he seems to appear from the other side of it.

As ever, he was hovering around the players tunnel after a non-momentous 3-2 win for Liverpool in an exhibition match with a Sunderland side that clearly resented not being in Ibiza. As the victorious but bored looking Liverpool team trudged nonchalantly from the pitch, Malcolm was standing by to congratulate them. And why not? Having played in the World Cup last year, it must mean a lot to Paul Ince to play a pre-season friendly then receive a pat on the back from an utter berk.

May 19 Wednesday

Sara in the marketing department had a birthday today. She was 19 or 37 or something. To top off what must have been an occasion for her, albeit a mediocre one, I bought her a tin of hot dogs while I was out for a paper, stewing steak being out of my price range.

I was feeling quite pleased with this japery, well it amused me anyway, when I noticed a mood of resentment among the others in that department. This was led by Donna who sulkily proclaimed that I had neglected to buy any hot dogs on *her* birthday. True, but I did fork out 18 pence for a card with a picture of a fishing rod on the front for her. Greedy cow.

May 22 Saturday

Today I watched what was easily the funniest F.A. Cup final since the last one. After being merrily routed on the pitch by a semi-interested Manchester United, the best fans in the world then set out on their equivalent of the Notting Hill Carnival, the Annual Bigg Market Riot.

There were the usual festivities, cleverly smashing up the same telephone booths in front of the same security cameras before the same police officers as last year, complete with unattractive females clog dancing at the top.

Every time I had a glance at Ceefax, the number of arrests had risen. This represents a missed opportunity for television. They could have kept a running total as they do on *Children In Need*. It would also account for that bandage on Pudsey Bear's head.

May 23 Sunday

It is fair to say that Bethan displays considerably more enthusiasm for Sunday morning rising than I do. She was up well before me today, but managed to force me out of bed by attrition and her remarkably eclectic taste in music.

After she had played *Tommy Can You Hear Me?*, she then moved on to a bit of Rocky Sharpe And The Replays, Prokofiev (or *Dum De Dum* as she prefers to call it), then Bernard Bresslaw singing *You Need Feet To Keep Your Socks On*. By the time we got to *Rudolph The Red Nosed Reindeer* I was a beaten man and got up. This was all because she wanted some breakfast. Clearly she can operate the stereo with great dexterity, so why not the toaster?

May 25 Tuesday

At work today I was accosted by a Republica fan with a lisp and a real need of deodorant. He asked me whether there were any photographs of the band from their appearance at the Birmingham City game. I told him some piffle about not wanting to deflect any attention away from the players

164

and their achievements of the season, even if it was to a high profile rock band who will now be forever linked to the club blah blah blah . . .

The crowd that day were too far away from the band to know this, but the reason for the absence of any pictures of them maybe that their guitarist was sporting a 'Masturbation is not a crime' t-shirt.

May 30 Sunday

We were dragged gracelessly into work today for a Millennium Christian celebration. The club has decided to treat the event as though it were a match, so there was a full complement of stewards on hand to avert any highly unlikely skirmishes between the Methodists and the Church Of England. Most of the congregation were simply enjoying the singing and the sunshine, but some of them were downright disturbing. We were unable to join in with them, as we do not know any songs concerning the Light or candles or fish.

Needless to say, Jesus did not find us this afternoon. No one did as we were all hiding in Box 26 watching Manchester City play Gillingham in the Second Division play-offs.

June 1 Tuesday

Bethan was all tucked up in bed this evening, but was insisting that she would have to listen to a story before she could drop off to sleep. I could not accurately recall any stories and getting off my big fat arse to look for a book was obviously not an option, so I had a stab at making one up on the spot. How about this?

'Once upon a time, there was a handsome young man called Tony, who went down the pub for a few jars and a conversation about football, before returning home to eat toast. And he lived happily ever after.'

I thought this was a good enough effort, but Bethan was clearly not happy, so I gave her some crisps instead. What a great dad.

June 3 Thursday

It seems that Lee Clark managed to get a ticket for the F.A. Cup final last month. Oh dear.

June 8 Tuesday

Sunderland had a lucky escape today if you ask me. Lazio sold Christian Vieri to A.C. Milan for 28 million pounds. I am glad that this type of player has not come to our club as he has evidently been to a few, a large percentage of his salary in effect coming from signing on fees.

Ironically, I used to make a living from signing on, but decided not to follow this career path in the same ruthless manner as Christian. As I was only receiving 96 quid for each fortnightly signing, we are probably not comparing like with like. I can't imagine that he will be supplementing his income with a fiddle bar job.

June 11 Friday

Kevin Ball's testimonial game is imminent and what better addition to the festivities than the engagement of the Scottish Opera Orchestra? To this end, Dave and I met this pompous, stuck-up gentleman from Edinburgh called Cameron who, apart from his stock response of 'Indeed' was a tiresomely bombastic man. Indeed.

He was keen to call a spade a manually operated horticultural implement, as demonstrated when we asked him if he had received a faxed message, to which he replied, 'I am unaware of this having been conveyed to me.'

This flowery answer struck me as peculiar, because it showed that a man who obviously took pride in his vocabulary should be unable to track down words such as 'No'.

We would have been able to go home much earlier. Indeed.

June 16 Wednesday

I saw a bloke trip over a hosepipe at the side of the pitch today. I shouldn't laugh, but it was brilliant.

June 19 Saturday

I asked Liz if she knew where there were any egg cups, so she put four of them under my nose under the misapprehension that I had a preference on which one to use. This reaffirmed my belief that God is a man because he made the Universe and all of its contents in six days, whereas a woman would still be deciding on the colour.

Liz countered that He couldn't be a man as He wouldn't be able to find anything to get the job done unless there was a Mrs. God to point him in the right direction. But I won the argument by pointing out that God is omniscient and would therefore know where the egg cups were along with anything else required.

Theological discussion is all that we have to do on Saturdays at the moment. I hate the close season.

June 21 Monday

There is a series on BBC1 at the moment called *On Side* in which sporting celebrities are interviewed. Tonight the guests were Martina Navratilova and, for some reason, Stephen Fry. The interviewer, John Inverdale, used the programme to ask them questions on tennis and cricket respectively, which to us lads (rrrr!) means that he has missed a great chance to make a name for himself.

166

Surely it would have been much more of a hoot if he had sat them both down then waded in with, 'Well you two wouldn't be much use to each other then eh?'

It would have brought the house down would that. I'm afraid he made the mistake of putting substance before style. And so to bed.

June 23 Wednesday

I was disc jockeying in the Ivy House again this evening, with Marcus next to me as quiz master as is perennial, displaying his barely credible capacity for depth plumbing, pit scouring and barrel scraping.

For one of his rounds he gave the participants the name of a brand which was either a dog food or a cat food and they had to decide which. Kit-E-Cat and Mr. Dog were one hundred per cent correctly answered. I politely pointed out to him that this was the most contemptibly silly lowbrow and uncultivated round of quiz questions to be devised by any person ever.

Undeterred by my criticism, he turned round and gamely replied, 'Ah yes. But I got them all thinking with Choosy.'

His day job? He is a grocer of course.

June 24 Thursday

The football world is still reverberating from the news that we are to change the dispensing machines in the stadium toilets and that it will be the club's responsibility to replenish them.

This exigent chore has been deemed to be of such importance that I shall be directly in charge of this. I am none too thrilled with this dreary addition to my workload. But it will not be without its compensations, as any chap alive would like to make a name for himself by ordering 20,000 condoms. I have already planned the telephone conversations; 'Just twelve thousand this week please, I don't expect to be that busy'.

June 28 Monday

I met Tonka for a game of five-a-side, during which I was the best and after which he regaled me with the sordid events of his weekend in Liverpool. He had had such a good time that he even bought me some novelty aftershave while he was down there.

I could hardly wait to saunter down to the Ivy House to share this aroma with a waiting world, as there is nothing like the great smell of Fab Four to set the chicks a-swooning. I must say it is very similar to the equally classy J.R. Ewing that was available a few years ago.

July 4 Sunday

There is really nothing to be physically gained from the regular consumption of alcohol. It can lead to physical and psychological difficulties, nutritional and emotional disorders, disease of the heart, liver

167

and peripheral nerves, as well as ravaging the cerebral cortex. One must carefully weigh up these considerations against how crap the telly is on a Sunday night.

Having done this, I then set off to meet Tonka and Taff in the Ivy House, thus confirming our collective opinion of *Heartbeat*.

July 6 Tuesday

The club today finalised the signing of Steve Bould from Arsenal. So far he has cost us £500,039.50. £500,000 to Arsenal and £39.50 to Greenham Trading because his first act upon becoming a Sunderland player was to reverse his four-wheel drive Super-Duper into a signpost in the car park. I have to replace it now because the top of the pole has gone from being three metres from the ground to about ten inches. What a prang!

This most unpropitious of starts has been greeted around the club with a mixture of laughter, dismay and derision, with predictable jokes about him taking the back post, etc., already doing the rounds. He can jolly well help to cement in the new one.

July 8 Thursday

I am sure that Steve Bould would prefer to keep Tuesday's little mishap under wraps, so I sincerely hope that there was only me who read the *Daily Mirror* today. Meanwhile, the club is trying to lure the German international Thomas Helmer, which I am quite excited about, as this would be two signings in a week of players that I have heard of.

July 12 Monday

Kerry is off to Corfu again for three weeks, so in her absence I have been charged with the responsibility of loaning out the Football League Championship trophy to various functions and social gatherings. Alas, I do not have the final say on who gets to have it, as I found out when I applied to take it down to the Ivy House with the expressed intention of 'Waving it around, drinking Double Maxim from it and generally arsing about.'

I have been flatly refused for this admittedly completely unreasonable request, but is goes to prove what a load of old cobblers honesty being the best policy is.

July 13 Tuesday

Bethan has been learning ballet for the past few weeks and the big night arrived as she stole the show with her five minutes as a supporting fairy. She has that Muse. Sadly for Liz and me, the price for this brief flirtation with the finer arts was that we had to sit through about two hours of other stuff that was really quite dull.

Some of the older performers were a modicum on the portly side too. Sitting and watching them clumping around the stage to the strains of *Who*

Wants To Be A Millionaire?, I ruminated that being a millionaire would be pretty handy when keeping that lot in dinners for a few months.

July 14 Wednesday

Sunderland's leading pub quiz master (me) was called for a now rare appearance in the Ivy House. The current affairs round was a gloomy affair and my question about the death of Bill Owen, who played Compo in *Last Of The Summer Wine* was possibly in questionable taste, as I raised the issue of his funeral and whether his coffin would only be placed in the ground having first been rolled about two hundred feet down a Yorkshire Hill.

The sadness of his passing has been heightened by the prospect of no more new series being made; we may have to be content with repeats of the first 34.

July 17 Saturday

Liz's birthday and we also attended a lovely wedding. We have decided to get married ourselves next year. Child, house, wedding. Everything in precisely the wrong order.

July 19 Monday

Dave Nicholson is now on holiday as well as Kerry. This means that I have to go to work and actually do some. I'm a saint me, I really am.

July 21 Wednesday

Today was the 30th anniversary of the first moon landing, when after years of scientific endeavours, Apollo 11 blasted off from Cape Kennedy and four days later docked on the surface of Earth's only natural satellite. Two blokes then jumped out and had a game of golf. I tried explaining all of this to Bethan, but she was clearly not taking any of it in. I don't know why. It's hardly rocket science.

As expected there was a smattering of people on the radio who deny that it ever happened. It must be a terrible social burden for these people to go through life wondering if they have a back to their heads merely because they have never seen it.

July 25 Sunday

I became embroiled in a bizarre conversation in the Ivy House with two blokes who I hardly know about what to do if any of us were to ever win the pools or the National Lottery. One of them expressed the opinion that if he hit the jackpot, he would tell the world on television, in the newspapers and on the sides of buses.

Then the topic was slightly adjusted to what we would be prepared to do for a million pounds. I drew the line at holding a door open, but these two were prepared to commit a homosexual act, although in this instance they would be more keen to tick the 'No publicity box'. Which is good as no one would want to see a big fat arse on the side of a bus.

July 29 Thursday

For some reason, there was an assumption doing the rounds that I was hosting some sort of phone-in for the mentally imbalanced at work today. No sooner had I put the receiver down on a woman who found it quite unacceptable that it had rained the last time she was at the match, than another called to strongly urge us to turn the stadium round a bit because the sun was in her eyes.

Then a man rang up with a gripe about the searchlights. This usually means a moan about the cost of them, but this fellow's indignation was because he is apparently Sunderland's leading astronomer. Our lights seem to have made it virtually impossible for him to see the orange sub-giant Kochab. I would hate that._

July 31 Saturday

Today was the big day for Kevin Ball and also for me as I was put in charge of being blamed for everything that might go wrong. His testimonial game was a 0-0 draw with Sampdoria which Sunderland then uncharacteristically lost on penalties.

But there were a fair number of events going on other than football. In the executive box corridor I passed a little fat chap who was making some daft vocal noises in a burlesque theatrical manner. I was about to cackle loudly and give him an appreciative slap on the back, because at that point I was willing to give my approval to anyone who might like to poke fun at the visiting Scottish Opera. Luckily I realised in time that he was not taking the piss and was in fact their tenor warming up his throat before his recital.

The pubs must have been heaving right up until the kick-off.

August 2 Monday

My week off from work was off to an exhilarating start when Liz, Bethan and I went for a picnic at Finchale Abbey. The tranquillity was soon forcibly removed by the arrival of Mr. And Mrs. Hooligan, their four charming offspring and two dogs, who most have been the loudest and most boorish family at any 14th century ruins today.

Mrs. Hooligan, as I have wildly guessed at for a surname, cut quite a dash as she waded out of the River Wear in her Umbro shorts, XXXL Newcastle United away shirt and record breaking collection of cellulite. Having pitted this vision aesthetically against that of the famous scene with Ursula Andress in *Dr. No*, I have decided upon a decisive victory for Ursula.

170

August 3 Tuesday
My madcap week off work went into overdrive today. In fact, in the words of the current chart topper we were *Living La Vida* Local. Yes, we went to the caravan.

August 5 Thursday
Two days to the start of the 1999-2000 season. Topper!

August 6 Friday
I went up and off to Durham train station where I met Alan Riddell among others who were making the same journey to London on a different carriage. On the platform I asked him for his prediction for tomorrow's first game of the season at Chelsea and he gave me the grim forecast of a 4-0 defeat.

However, when I saw him three hours later at King's Cross Station, he had had time to quaff a few cans and discuss the matter with the other lads and as a result of this had revised his opinion to a hard fought 1-0 win for Sunderland.

It can not be underestimated just how little reassurance this has given me for tomorrow afternoon.

August 7 Saturday
There was a very amicable atmosphere around Stamford Bridge this afternoon before the game. We had a few pleasant drinks in some salubrious Chelsea pubs before strolling to the stadium in the sunshine and taking our seats completely without the threats, stabs, ambushes and bricks of years gone by. This meant that things were going too well and that the only area left for disaster was on the pitch.

We were beaten 4-0, although I have to say that were it not for several incidents of gleeful good fortune we may have been given a real pasting. If we carry that sort of luck for the rest of the season we may win the league. My optimism was not universally shared. Some people were already predicting relegation because the mighty Bradford City won.

August 8 Sunday
I saw Alan Riddell on the train back and congratulated him on being right first time with his scoreline prediction for yesterday.

August 10 Tuesday
The first ever Premiership game at the stadium ended in disappointment. For Watford. Ha! It was 2-0 and we are off the mark.

171

Before the game, I was less than chuffed to be given the less than exacting chore of parking the players' cars, a scheme unlikely to last as they all arrived at once and left me with a traffic jam to clear.

All of the vehicles were pretty nifty, but not all easy to drive. When I put on the ignition of Niall Quinn's car, my ears were assailed by many decibels of cheery Irish music, the Saw Doctors I believe, and I also had some difficulty in reaching the pedals with my fairly average legs. By contrast, I was folded up like a concertina in Kevin Phillips' car.

Steve Bould was concerned with my obvious unfamiliarity with his automatic model and asked if I would be okay. I denied myself the pleasure of saying that it was not me who had flattened a signpost on the 6th of July.

August 11 Tuesday

It was all arranged for the team photograph to be taken on the pitch this morning, but probably not a good idea to have it coincide with the great eclipse. This wonder of nature was not as spectacular in Sunderland as it was in Cornwall, but as the stadium was not immediately plunged into an ebony darkness, patience around the place was in short supply.

People have been waiting since 1927 to look up to the sky and say, 'Is that it? It's crap!', and yet if they had followed by lead, keeping a diligent upwards watch for the next 13 hours, then they would have been rewarded with the sight of a sky with no trace of sun.

August 14 Saturday

I witnessed a little piece of history at about half past two this afternoon, when I witnessed a referee being enthusiastically cheered by the home crowd this afternoon. Now Uriah Rennie knows that sending Alan Shearer off last week will keep him in free drinks in Sunderland for a good few years.

Later, I was mooching around the stadium prior to our delightfully savage nil-nil draw with Arsenal, when I clumped into the irrigation room to misappropriate some paper cups. Before I entered, I faintly heard someone calling my name, only to ignore it and barge in to find Kevin Keegan standing there. If anyone had asked me the name of the last person alive I would have expected to see in there, the answer would have been Idi Amin, but Keegan was a surprise too.

He was waiting to be interviewed for radio, so I just smiled politely and left him to it. Then I wished that I had not been so deferential when I remembered that I don't like him. He should be more like the Prince Of Tomfoolery, Arsene Wenger, whom I observed at close quarters this afternoon.

August 17 Tuesday

I had to concede at work today that it is just about possible to have too much frivolity and arsing about. Dave Nicholson shouted to me, loud and clear over the walkie-talkie, to put down whichever woman I was with and get my fat ugly arse over to the admin. building. I gave the awkward response that I would have come immediately, had I not been in the middle of an ashes scattering at the precise moment he had uttered those badly timed words.

Proceedings had already been off to a bad start when I absent-mindedly turned up for it in a tie that depicts Bart Simpson playing football, instead of the intended and more reverential dark blue one. Only the bloke in the urn remained unoffended.

August 21 Saturday

Sunderland were at Leeds United where we thought we were clever when we scored a goal. But it turned out to be a stupid idea as they scored two.

August 23 Monday

I am not sleeping too well at the moment with an over active stomach. We play Newcastle in two days time and I am terrified of losing.

August 25 Wednesday

I was at work tonight for the mother of all beambacks. We had our first derby match in two and a half years and we beat the Mags at the Temple Of Doom 2-1 in torrential rain. Watching on the big screen from the dugout at the Stadium of Light, I could sense that the soaked ones weren't happy, but when I looked out of a window at the street below ten minutes after full time, the scene put one in mind of the end of *The Wizard Of Oz*.

So far the media have only noticed that Newcastle lost, without also realising that by definition, someone else must have won. Nevertheless, me and my fellow logic scientists have reasoned this one out for ourselves and trouped off to Annabel's nightclub on the strength of it.

Poor Alan Shearer was left on the bench for the beginning of the occasion, as rumours abound that he is causing numerous problems on the training pitch. In his defence, I have to say that he was on the pitch for about 20 minutes tonight and caused no problems whatsoever.

August 26 Thursday

I have to admit that it has been a while since we beat the old Skunks and last night's success followed by the obvious copious drinking meant that I didn't get an awful lot done at work today. We drank anything available. Even Mick Hillam, who usually sticks limpet-like to real ale complete with vegetables, wood and parts of the bloke who brewed it, was seen swilling down random lager in Annabel's.

I saw him this morning, queuing for a ticket for Derby County, and I felt the need to drag him in for a cup of tea and see if we had omitted any

173

aspect of the game during our conversation last night. We hadn't. Once again, ha!

August 28 Saturday

A home defeat to the hated yet clearly superior red and whites has proved too much for Ruud Gullit's tenure at Newcastle United and he announced his resignation this morning. He cited media harassment as the reason for his departure, which is the only possible basis, what with him having created such a thriving team, playing sexy football before an appreciative set of supporters.

These supporters may be heartened to learn that the remaining novelty Gullit dreadlock wigs will not go to waste. They have been snapped up by an appreciative Sunderland fan who will sell them on for a large profit to people who truly appreciate all of Ruud's efforts over the last year.

August 29 Sunday

We had a somewhat anti-climactic 1-1 draw at home to Coventry City today. After the Lord Mayor's show and all that.

Before this, I met Martyn McFadden, who is a local fanzine editor and a good chap, standing in the stadium reception with an horrendous eight feet high painting of the Christ-like Peter Reid beneath a halo, holding a Davy lamp to light the world and a couple of archangels waving a couple of rattles. It is the work of a talented artist and completely tasteless.

For now, I have bunged it out of sight and out of mind. It is difficult to think where we are eventually going to hang it, unless we are about to open a club Blasphemy Lounge.

August 30 Monday

Amazingly, I went to a pub tonight and became involved in an outré argument about football. This bloke contended that Coventry City had been unfortunate to gain only a point yesterday, citing frivolous excuses for them such as their centre forward missing a last minute sitter, their midfielder being unfairly sent off, their being denied an obvious penalty, and the fact that Kevin Phillips' equaliser was clearly offside.

As far as I was concerned, he had argued himself into a corner, as it was obvious from what he was saying that a draw was a fair result. Outlandish bias will always triumph over reason.

September 1 Wednesday

It has been four weeks now since the Ivy House closed for refurbishment, and with another week to go, we now have a shrewd idea of what purgatory will be like. I had largely forgotten that there are other things to do with my spare time, so over the last month or so I have thrown myself whole-heartedly into my latest project. Watching the telly.

Other Ivy stalwarts are less fortunate as they do not have such outside interests and are having difficulty adjusting to their temporary life. Some have been spotted walking up and down Vine Place with wide-eyed, lost expressions on their faces, which is hardly surprising as some of never been that far from the pub before.

September 3 Friday
I had to go back to South Tyneside College today for more health and safety stuff. If you ask me, Section 13 of the Health, Safety and Welfare Regulations 1992 leaves a good deal to be desired, but I shall not dwell on it here as I am unlikely to be able to keep my emotions in check.

Before I set off, the only clean garment that I could find was a Sunderland A.F.C. t-shirt, which I was reluctant to wear as the college is littered with Mags and would run the gauntlet of hackneyed, dim-witted abuse and ridicule. Then I remembered that we had beaten them, were above them in the league, have more fans and a larger and superior stadium, and so swanning around was therefore in order.

September 7 Tuesday
Sing hosanna! The Ivy House is open again.

September 11 Saturday
Leicester City were back in town today and Sunderland beat them for the first time since round about the time of the Roman invasion.

I stood in the tunnel watching Martin O'Neill who was seeing his team trailing 2-0 with a man sent off, his club in considerable political turmoil. Martin was shouting, fulminating, swearing, grinding his teeth and generally looking extremely dischuffed.

At this point I turned to Clare from PR and suggested that she go and tell him that it was only a game and invite him to the Sports Bar for a drink and some Wotsits. She wimped out, so we may never know if he would have come.

September 12 Sunday
I was lying on the settee, seeing how many grapes I could count on a bunch that was four yards away, when for some reason I came over with an inescapable feeling of boredom. Yes, the car racing was on again.

Some bloke called Eric Hakkinen, in the course of his driving round in circles, crashed his machine and immediately burst into tears, as he is evidently a big Finnish ponce. It turned out that he didn't even own the car, will not have to pay for it, can use another one and his no claims bonus will remain intact, so there was no need for this very public face twisting. As I said, big Finnish ponce!

175

September 14 Tuesday
Unlike Sunday, today was all about proper sport. Worthington Cup second round, first leg. Sunderland 3 Walsall 2. Fear no foe.

September 15 Wednesday
This evening saw the return of the rightfully maligned Ivy House disco and quiz. It was yours truly who was responsible for the deeing-and-a-jaying, and as a socially responsible jock I kept the punters up to date with tonight's football scores to give temporary reprieve from their subjection to my records.

One score that I read out with some gusto was from St. James' Park and was Newcastle United 1 Sunderland 2. Of course, this game took place three weeks ago and everyone is fully aware of what the score was, but as this was my first opportunity to gloat about it so publicly, I grasped it with both hands, both of my feet, all of my teeth and a bit of tongue. Rrrr! This was shameless popularity seeking, but it worked.

September 17 Friday
There was high drama at work today when a paper towel dispenser in one of the outside toilets at the admin. building caught fire. Most of the staff responded to the sound of the alarm by immediately ignoring it. We put it out, then I rang the fire brigade to advise us as to whether it was safe for people to clean up, which lead to eight of them turning up dramatically in an engine about an hour later to say yes.

The female staff members who own Fire Fighters calendars were also profoundly disappointed with this octet of confirmed non-hunks. A flabby, balding and generally unsightly crew, they were not the sorts of chaps whose sweating frame a girl would wish to see emerging from a burning building with a puppy under an arm.

September 18 Saturday
Liz and I went to Pride Park to see Sunderland play Derby County, expecting to see a close and hard-fought affair. And much as I enjoy being right, I could not help but feel gratified to watch us administer a Rest Of The World versus Spennymoor type of thrashing.

The problem for the Derby supporters close to us, apart from the obvious anger, humiliation and embarrassment, was trying to taunt and wind up a set of opposition supporters whose team is winning 5-0. Quite a few of them tried to grind us down with inappropriate hand gestures, but they found us to be made of sterner stuff when we managed to somehow ignore the provocation and carry on with our grinning.

September 19 Sunday

Newcastle's first home game under Bobby Robson was also their first win of the season. It was an undeniably spectacular 8-0 win over Sheffield Wednesday. Prepare for months of 'If Bobby had been here for those first few games . . .' and 'You know, next season . . .' and so on.

September 21 Tuesday

In the Worthington Cup second round, second leg, it was Walsall 0 Sunderland 5. I wished that I had gone until I remembered that it was played in Walsall. One of our substitutes tonight was a Brazilian trialist called Bica, but he is pretty sexy so I don't suppose we will pursue our interest in him. Plain looking footballers only if you don't mind.

September 25 Saturday

It was Sunderland's turn to beat the shoddy Sheffield Wednesday, but only by an undeniably unspectacular 1-0. The only point of interest was a negative one and concerned the dreadful 'band' which follows them around the country.

No one in their right mind could call me an old misery guts for wanting to direct this lot in the direction of quicksand - after all it is them and not me who is spreading the misery. They are annoyingly awful with their squeaky trumpets and irritating drums, usually churning out a barely recognisable version of the theme from *The Great Escape*. Each Wednesday corner is taken to the accompaniment of a godawful racket.

The only person in my social circle with any musical pedigree is Tonka, who can manage *We're All Going To The Zoo Tomorrow* on the guitar, which would be enough for him to join this lot.

September 27 Monday

It was my birthday today, so I took some time to go wandering round the admin building with no other purpose than to soak up the good wishes as I am quite fantastically popular.

The Deputy Chairman, Mr. Fickling, who is insistent on not being called a vice-chairman after events at Newcastle last year, walked up to me with a partial smile on his face that led me to assume that he was about to wish me many happy returns, which would have confirmed some sort of standing for me at the club. Of course, my assumption was completely erroneous as his only utterance was, 'When are you going to sort out that toilet that was burned down?'

The moral of this dull story? Know your place.

177

October 1 Friday

Kerry and some of the other girls from the admin building have gone on a girly, womanly, lasses weekend away, to cackle their way around an endless succession of tacky and vulgar theme pubs. As they pulled away in their chartered floozy carrier, complete with streamers and bottles of plonk on their strictly all female sojourn, I gave myself some self-congratulation for being born male. Their trip to Blackpool should provide an interesting prelude to the Conservative Party Conference which will also be there next week.

Doubtless, the ladies will return to work on Monday with hangovers and hats which read, 'Kiss me and that sort of thing repeatedly if you will'.

October 2 Saturday

We were on beamback duty again. Today Sunderland had what seems to be their annual walkover at Bradford City. 4-0. It was one of those games where Kevin Phillips showed why he can be so annoying to opposing teams. He had not touched the ball in the first 87 minutes, but had two kicks in the final three, both of which were goals. I wish I could do that.

October 7 Thursday

There is to be no proper football this weekend, but we still have to go to work as England have decided to play Belgium at the stadium. No *Country File* for me again then.

October 9 Saturday

I was at work today to prepare for tomorrow and there were a fair few people there to see if the Sweden – Poland game could give a result that would assist with England's qualification to Euro 2000.

I was actually in the boardroom for a while where Kevin Keegan was watching the television and egging on the Swedes. I was disappointed to see him calmly sipping coffee and chatting when he should have been gibbering and chewing the carpet in agitation. He simply does not swear enough for a football manager to my thinking.

He was probably more anxious than he looked, but there was no need to be as Sweden gave England's best performance in months.

October 10 Sunday

We finally got the England game out of the way and Belgium were beaten 2-1. We just about managed to applaud a fine Alan Shearer goal, although the applause was almost drowned out by the grinding of teeth. However, that was not the highlight because if it was not worth going to work to see Jamie Redknapp's goal, then it was certainly worth going there to see his wife. The lovely Louise passed me on the stairs, presumably en route to Joan's Cafe.

There was any number of famous faces at the stadium today which set me up nicely for an evening of shameless name-dropping in the pub later.

October 12 Tuesday

Sunderland were eliminated from the Worthington Cup by Wimbledon after losing 3-2 at Selhurst Park. This was every bit as much a shock as all of those numerous other occasions we have been beaten at Selhurst Park.

October 18 Monday

We had a somewhat providential win at home to Aston Villa this evening. As usual, their manager John Gregory was seething with displeasure at the referee, but not without foundation.

Although it was previously unheard of for such a man to chat during the game with riff-raff and scum such as myself, this was precisely what he did, seeking verification that he was not simply being biased. He kept leaning towards me with comments such as 'This referee's terrible,' and 'That was never a penalty you know,' to which I replied with 'Absolutely,' and 'You're quite right,' respectively.

After I had expressed my affinity with his opinions, he turned to his bench and pointing behind at me with his thumb and said, 'See! He's Sunderland and even he says it wasn't.'

I was flattered but very bemused that my opinion should be given such status. A strange manager, but I liked him.

October 23 Saturday

The cream of Sunderland's philosophy circle, Dave Irwing, Kevin Bell and me, were engaged in the usual cut and thrust of intellectual debate tonight, this time comparing the merits offered by going to the pub against those of watching football. An amicable compromise was only reached when *Match of the Day* came on the telly in the Ivy House.

A goal by Liverpool's Titi Camara inspired a spate of high-brow comedy concerning his surname, how he specialised in snap shots, was still developing, was once on the books at Lens, had put himself in the frame, had zoomed into the penalty area, how Southampton had put up the shutters for him and so forth.

We rounded off the evening by moving on to his first name.

October 24 Sunday

There was a double inconvenience at work today when Sunderland's remorseless 1-1 draw at West Ham was beamed back to the stadium while it was also being inspected by a F.I.F.A. delegation for England's 2006 World Cup bid.

For the occasion, we hoisted flags of all nations, well five nations, one of which was the United States Of America. This gave me the opportunity to wear it as a cape and pretend to be Carl Lewis. I think that John Mallan would have liked to join in with this skylarking, but the only flag left at this point was that of the United Arab Emirates and he was stumped on recalling the names of any famous Arab athletes.

October 25 Monday

Marcus the quiz master returned from yesterday's game at West Ham with an injured hand. He claims not to have been drunk when the accident occurred. What happened was that he did not realise what a successful invention the internal combustion engine has been and that there are even cars in London these days. Without this prior knowledge, crossing the capital's roads can be dangerous and so it proved.

The up side to this is that it now appears as though he has a novelty hand as it has swollen to about five times its normal size. This in turn means that he only has to write 'Sunderland R the best' on the back of it to save literally two pounds on one of those foam numbers.

October 28 Thursday

It was Bethan's seventh birthday today. She brought a load of her noisy little friends clumping into our home to mark the occasion which was to give away the lie that children are easy to please. Any party that I have had for adults has had success guaranteed simply by telling them where the fridge is. Entertaining children is far more demanding.

Nevertheless, I think we did well and I have been established as having the second best job of any father of a child in Bethan's class, as I can get Kevin Phillips' autograph. But I still have some way to go to displace the top spot from Bridie Bogie's dad as he apparently has an ice cream van.

October 30 Saturday

Hallowe'en is almost upon us again. Like any occasion with religious connotations, it has been appropriated by teenagers on the make. Two grubby adolescents came to my house and informed me that the sky is blue, the grass is green and could they have some cash in return for imparting this privileged information.

Then some others came along with that crappy Americanism, trick or treat, to which I slammed the door in their faces. I consider this a treat when compared to booting them up the arse instead, although that would have been a good trick.

October 31 Sunday

Sunderland beat Tottenham 2-1 at home today. We had to play them on a Sunday as they have German opposition in the UEFA Cup who have had to alter their fixture list due to an unpropitious backlog in the Bundesliga, and not because it was Hallowe'en, which was what Tonka said.

The great Uriah Rennie was standing next to me in his capacity as fourth official today. After about ten minutes, Peter Reid was enraged and complaining loudly to anyone who could hear about some refereeing decision. Uriah, leaning casually against the wall merely looked over and said, 'Peter. Calm.'

This worked for about ten minutes until another even more dubious decision was made in Tottenham's favour. Peter's fury was plain to see, his shouting and swearing became louder, his neck muscles became more pronounced and his face became scarlet. I was seriously considering hiding when Uriah defused him with the following exchange.

'Peter.'

'WHAT?'

'Can I have a chewy?'

I have never been so impressed by a match official. Even George Graham laughed.

November 1 Monday

It says in this diary that today is All Saints Day, which is quite an honour for them so you can't say that the girls haven't done well in a short space of time. Already canonized too!

November 5 Friday

To Liverpool, not for once because of a football match, but because a bunch of us are flying from here to Madrid in the morning, just to appear suave and debonair although this may be difficult as we are going by Easy Jet and not Concorde as you may expect for 29 quid.

We spent the evening in a dingy little pub behind the Liverpool Empire Theatre, but it was worth going in there to witness a drunken skirmish between two down-at-heel Scousers which, better still, was mediated by a third drunken down-at-heel Scouser, who very amusingly had curly hair and a moustache and was urging the two protagonists to 'Calm down!'

This is completely true, but if they had been wearing shell suits I would not have believed it myself.

November 6 Saturday

The reason our merry group has come to Madrid was to surprise birthday boy Bernie Callaghan who was already here with Lesley who, to her eternal credit, arranged everything. Which was good news because we would have been lucky to get out of the Ivy House if it was left to me.

As soon as we had jumped out at him in a bar on the Grand Via, thereby shocking and possibly disappointing him, we whisked him off to an English bar that we had found on the internet where we guzzled lager all afternoon

181

whilst watching live coverage of Sunderland's foul strewn 1-1 draw at Middlesbrough. Afterwards we had a discussion about this complete change to our usual activities and agreed that it would do us all the world of good.

No wonder the buccaneering Ernest Hemingway was so fond of this great city.

November 7 Sunday

It would seem from our short trip on the metro today that the buskers of Madrid are even better than their Sunderland counterparts. They all play Spanish guitars very competently, complete with twiddly bits and everything. Very good.

Taff and some of the others went to watch Atletico Madrid play. I wouldn't like to qualify how useless he can be at times, but they joined the wrong queue and almost went to a circus instead of the match.

As it was our last evening out here, we decided that we should make the effort to do something different so we all went out and got completely hammered for the first time without jackets in November. One of our party, Julia, was keen to visit a bar that used to be frequented by Frank Sinatra, Ava Gardner and Salvador Dali, but when we arrived it was closed. I suppose that is what happens when all your best customers are dead.

November 8 Monday

Alas and all to soon, we had to come home this afternoon, taking off from the thriving concern that is Madrid's international airport then landing in the bus shelter that is Liverpool's.

When we arrived back in Sunderland we realised that we had forgotten to buy Bethan a present, so we immediately jumped into the car and headed for Asda where we bought a Robbie Williams CD, which we slapped in her hands and said, 'Look what we bought you in Spain.'

This was far from ideal, or indeed convincing, but it was clearly better than our alternative scheme of giving her a couple of pairs of socks from the bottom of my suitcase, which was undisguisably feeble.

November 13 Saturday

There was no proper football today because Scotland were playing England at Hampden Park to establish just who is the best team in the world. And on this afternoon's evidence I would have to say France.

After all the hype that has been used over the last month, it was obvious that the game was going to be a wash out although England won 2-0. People must have felt proud to be foreign. Any nation capable of droning on about a 700 year old battle must hold a longevity world record for either gloating, grudge bearing or both.

November 17 Wednesday
England managed an inauspicious scrape into the European Championships. I was rooting for England, but would have found it difficult to suppress a guffaw if the Jocks had actually pulled it off. Nevertheless, it was still amusing to see Don Hutchison bag the only goal of the game for Scotland.

When you see some violent simpleton in a designer jacket singing *No Surrender To The IRA*, without the faintest idea of what this means, you can only wish misery and misfortune for them. Whereas someone who knows the limitations of his team and therefore has to drink copiously while wearing a kilt and an orange wig to enjoy the game somehow provides an endearing spectacle.

November 20 Saturday
Sunderland had the first home defeat of the season, 2-0 to Liverpool, but what will stay longest in my memory is their coach, Phil Thompson, who is the most biased person I have ever seen watching a football match (bear in mind that I have been to games with Taff).

Backing your team is one thing, but this was pathological. He was delivering yet another loud jaundiced rant at virtually any old innocuous decision that was given in our favour. I stood near him in quiet admiration, but not so Peter Reid who had clearly had enough and gave him a volley of what I can only presume were expletives, as I did not recognise all of the words. I love swearing, it's the dog's c***!

November 26 Friday
I bumped into a rather relieved looking Samson The Cat today. Before the Liverpool game on Saturday, he was over exuberant in the course of his customary shenanigans and incurred the wrath of a spectator who saw his Robbie Fowler style touchline coke snorting celebrations. The spectator took exception to this and wrote a humourless letter to the club to say as much.

The outcome was that a contrite Samson stood before a disciplinary hearing, whiskers lowered, claws behind his back, to receive a written warning. Disciplinary action was deemed necessary, but fears that he may have to pay the ultimate price were assuaged by the sight of panel members pissing themselves laughing. This is good news as there are a distinct lack of vacancies for seven foot cats.

November 27 Saturday
Sunderland claimed another worthy victory today when we won 3-2 at Watford with Kevin Phillips claiming two goals. I use the word 'claiming' advisedly as the first could not have been more of an own goal if the fellow

had put in a diving header then ecstatically punched the air before the visiting supporters, but Kevin is still claiming.

Undeterred by his tenuous connection with the goal, he expects full credit. But from what I saw on *Match Of The Day* tonight, I may as well throw my hat in the ring too because it was as much my goal as his and I was 250 miles away.

November 28 Sunday

I drove about 200 yards around the corner, only for the car to die on me. It transpired that some chirpy neighbourhood prankster had cut the fuel pipe and pinched all my petrol. My obvious annoyance at this was exacerbated by the fact that the thief had merely made off with the unleaded without showing any interest in the actual car.

December 3 Friday

We play Chelsea again tomorrow and one of their followers that I know, a bloke called Tim, came with some friends for a look round the stadium. He had a sit down in the visitors' dugout on the seat which he says will be filled by Gianfranco Zola when he is given a rest after completing his hat-trick with about 20 minutes to go. He may be right, so I hockled on it.

December 4 Saturday

We exacted spectacular revenge for the August fiasco by barbecuing Chelsea 4-1. It was 4-0 at half-time. It was Graham Rix's first game back on the Chelsea bench after he completed his prison sentence. He seemed to be undecided over which was worse, the game or the songs which have been written about him while he was away.

One minor personal regret came about when I was hanging around after the game, smirking. Ray Wilkins came up to me and asked, 'Do you know where Peter's office is?' to which I replied that Mr. Reid could be found in the office on the left.

I should have said, 'Peter who?', or 'Who's asking?', or better still, 'How come they call you Butch then?'

Of course, the truth and a good story tend not to be so matey, so in the Ivy House this evening I wisely chose to employ the version that would further cement my immense popularity.

December 5 Sunday

There is no point in pretending otherwise. I am having pleasurable difficulty in wiping the smile from my face. Multi-million pounds, Champions League, cosmopolitan, household name, King's Road, city slickers Chelsea were completely humiliated yesterday. So today my hobbies consisted of gloating as well as the usual gluttony and sloth.

Gloat! Gloat! Gloat! Gloat! Gloat! Why, I almost gloated my head off. Gloating is an ungracious and very annoying trait in others, but you can't beat having a go yourself.

December 11 Saturday

Every team in this season's FA Cup third round has been forced to play a month earlier because Chelsea prefer it. Ours is not to reason why, with the visit of the not-even-a-bit-mighty Portsmouth, who are managed this week by Kevin Bond.

Our lot were not quite stopping at random to nip out for a fish supper or back a few horses, but it is fair to say that they did not exert themselves either in a perfunctory 1-0 win. About the biggest obstruction to our process was the famous and never dull Pompey Chimes. An insipid afternoon ensued, before the well below capacity crowd ambled away home in the drizzle.

Hey, doctor, get me a cure for Cup fever!

December 12 Saturday

Undeterred by the onset of Ramadan, I met Tonka in order to guzzle in simply disgusting quantities of alcohol. To drink any more we could probably have only managed it intravenously. We also discussed current affairs, if saying that Christmas is coming up counts as current affairs.

This led to a conversation about Gary Glitter and whether he was still on the Christmas compilation these days, so someone went over to the jukebox to investigate. The answer was affirmative; he was indeed still having a *Rock n' Roll Christmas* and was after *The Little Drummer Boy*. Well, quite.

December 14 Tuesday

Dave Nicholson was today complaining about the temperature control on his company BMW. My discernible lack of sympathy stemmed from the fact that temperature control in my own mobile bucket consists of stamping your feet and blowing a bit. He was griping over the fact that his car interior is not comfortably warm on the journey home until he reaches Peterlee, although at the speed he drives this is no surprise. I suggested that he take a different route.

December 18 Saturday

We dispensed with tradition today by beating Southampton 2-0 at home. Not far from me on the substitutes bench sat the great Matthew Le Tissier who has regularly scored winning goals against Newcastle down the years. One of the lads down the Museum Vaults, Simon, is so impressed with this that on each of these occasions he has sent him a fiver and told him to get himself a drink.

I though briefly about popping over to the bench and telling him that there are certain parties who are willing to up the ante as far as £7.50 if he can repeat the feat this season. However, I do not want any personal involvement with corruption and inducements and besides, it was probably a bad time to mention it.

December 21 Tuesday

I wandered into the canteen at lunchtime where the lads from Football In The Community were having their daily chimps tea party. It is fair to say that their conversational parameters tend to be limited so I was surprised to find them discussing language.

They were disgruntled that in the French language each noun is either masculine or feminine. It was ludicrous, they concluded, that a window was feminine and a door was masculine and so forth, the ultimate conclusion being that the French as a nation were therefore stupid and crap. However, with a scrupulous regard for fair play, they did concede that a door has a knob.

December 26 Sunday

Redge and I went to Everton where we lost 1-0, or was it five? It's so difficult to tell these days. Anyway, at least we didn't pay as we were the guests of Kate Johnson, who is the daughter of the recently resigned Everton chairman, Peter Johnson.

Kate was accompanied by her husband Ray and sister Charlotte, the latter I found to be uproariously funny if only because she is the first person I have met to actually have attended a finishing school where she learned how to eat an apple with a knife and fork, handkerchief folding, and other life saving skills. Her education in refinement and finesse did not prevent her from mooning at us outside the pub tonight, although she carried off her performance with such etiquette.

December 27 Monday

We popped in to Mr. Johnson's house this morning although he wasn't in. It was fortunate that we had come in Redge's car, which is presentable enough, rather than mine, which I would have been embarrassed to park outside a house like that. Kate gave us tea in cups with handles. They also have an inside toilet.

December 28 Tuesday

At work today there was all manner of things happening, including Sunderland being conned out of two points by a diving little git called Solksjaer in a 2-2 draw with Manchester United. Not that I am bitter.

The highlight of the day came after the game when I saw Sir Alex Ferguson in the basement complaining about how long the lift was taking to come. I suppose he is entitled to feel like the most important person in the country as he is generally treated as such, so it was most gratifying to inform him that the lift had been deliberately retained on the third floor so that Tony Blair could walk straight into it. Yes, the P.M. himself was at the match tonight, which meant that even Malcolm the tour guide was shoved down the pecking order.

Mr. Blair seems to be fanatical about shaking hands with people whether they want to or not. He shook mine when I was merely trying to walk past him and his posse in the basement. I was actually in a bit of a hurry, but did not feel confident enough to tell him I was a bit busy and could he greet someone else.

However, I must refrain from all of this name dropping as it is a practice which I deplore as I pointed out to Sir Tim Rice in the tunnel just before he drew the half-time raffle. I overlooked the fact that he was responsible for us having to sing all of those songs from *Joseph* when we were at school, and allowed him one sentence of conversation for which he chose, 'Shit! That was close!' when Michael Gray cleared off the line.

I was dazzling the company with this anecdote later in the Ivy House, but then spoiled everything with a completely fictitious account of Dame Judi Dench being chucked out of the Sports Bar after going mental on pints of snakebite.

December 30 Thursday

I have decided to devote the rest of the century to sitting about. What is more pleasing about this is that I have read in a newspaper that there is not long to go until the new millennium, just over a year in fact. Everyone is pretending that it is this year so that we can have longer off work, or perhaps they just can't count.

Whatever the reason, we are all pretty sick of the mere mention of the word and what is actually a bog-standard New Year's Eve is being elevated from its mere piss up status. However, I have decided what I will be doing in the new millennium, as I am sure to be dead for most of it.

December 31 Friday

We managed to reach the end of 1999 without the world coming to an end which is nice. On television we had Peter Snow keeping tabs on any disasters that may have befallen us due to the much-vaunted Millennium Bug. There was a brief moment of unease when it was discovered that the Russians had accidentally launched some missiles, but relief when it was confirmed that they were not nuclear, but good old scuds being delivered the quick way to Grosny.

This will have brought particularly good cheer to the people whose houses they landed on who must have thought that they were in for a really rotten New Year's Day.

2000

January 1 Saturday
It becomes ever more difficult with each passing year to think of expressions that accurately depict just how utterly boring New Year's Day is. However, when I put on the television and saw the words *World's Strongest Man* on the screen, I could only think that these words would suffice. Watching a load of blokes juggling with buses or whatever is not as exhilarating as feeding the ducks, so it was off to the park for Bethan and me.

Even the ducks were a rather jaded looking set of lads and they had obviously not been watching *World's Strongest Man*. Lucky then that the country's media has camped down at the Millennium Dome and not Barnes Park.

January 2 Sunday
I must say that Armageddon has been a complete flop so far, the main reason being the most incompetent Millennium Bug in living memory. It was rubbish!

We were promised all sorts of spectacular mishaps, such as life support machines switching themselves off, production lines halting, cruise missiles going off, and, of course, planes falling from the sky. In actual fact, all we got was the odd garage door becoming stuck and a couple of burglar alarms going off. I wouldn't have thought that many film directors would bother to make a disaster movie out of it.

So the Apocalypse was a right old washout, but it's not the end of the world.

January 3 Monday
Sunderland lost the first game of the year 1-0 at Wimbledon in a match that was somewhat brutal. Fancy that! One foul was particularly eye-catching, an elbow in the mush of Nicky Summerbee was very audible, as was the wind he expelled at the point of contact and the agonised sounds he made as he writhed around on the turf. And I was only listening on the radio. What a foul!

I would imagine that the offender, Ben Thatcher, was sorry to see a concussed Summerbee being substituted as a result, as presumably he would have liked to have gone back and finished him off with half a brick. Next time we go to Selhurst Park we should play Clint Eastwood on the wing.

January 4 Tuesday

We at Sunderland A.F.C. have only had one day at work since Christmas Eve, but it was wrong to assume that we would all be revivified and brimming with vitality. I could no more be arsed to get out of bed than attempt a triathlon.

Nevertheless, when I did get to work I got immediately knuckled down to it, firstly sticking my head out of the office window to ensure that the stadium was still there. That done, I then strode purposefully along to the kitchen to put the kettle on before entering a debate with Kerry about whether rich tea biscuits are more fattening than digestives. I tell you, the morning's just not your own.

January 8 Saturday

Sunderland lost the second game of the year at Tranmere, yet again. A truly bizarre day for Liz and me began when someone had unsuccessfully tried to steal the car last night, which is weird. As I have said before, a cursory glance is enough to realise that it is more likely to pass an A level than an MOT.

Yet the same old heap took us to Prenton Park where the day became even dafter. Tranmere had a man sent off, but then simply replaced him with a substitute to play on with a complete team, which apparently is against the rules. We cleverly allowed them to do this so there is a chance that the game may have to be replayed. Hurrah then for the superior footballing prowess of the Premiership.

January 10 Monday

From the outset of the working day, everyone was holding their breath as we waited to hear if the F.A. was to reinstate us into the F.A. Cup and order a replay with Tranmere. As the announcement was not made until five o'clock, this was also highly dangerous.

The outcome was that Saturday's result stands and we are still out. This came as a disappointment because the only appropriate course of action would have been to put Tranmere Rovers out, reinstate Sunderland to the fourth round with a home tie against Cambridge United and boot out the Mags while they were at it.

Of course, none of these obvious options were taken up because they are all biased at Lancaster Gate these days.

January 11 Tuesday

Having finally lost a 48 hour Cup tie yesterday, today was taken up with putting the champagne back in the fridge and welding the top back on to the bus. But everyone at the club has perked up since someone brought in a big box of scones.

One can only be positive and being still in the Cup would have deprived us of the opportunity of commenting that there is always next year. I cheered myself up further still when I returned to my car and found one of those 'Want to earn extra cash?' cards jammed into the driver's window. Very covertly, I sneaked over to Bob Murray's Mercedes and popped it under a windscreen wiper while his chauffeur was asleep.

January 12 Wednesday

To the Ivy House as ever this evening, where I ear wigged some dismal blarney from a student who was trying to impress a girl with an apocryphal tale of how close he had come to inventing the steam driven helicopter. I was not about to make critical judgements upon the lad, as he put me in mind of myself a few years ago. My own lamentable patter in those days ranged from how I had once written a novel called *The Hobbit*, how I was actually Eric Idle's love child, and how the Tan And Tone solarium shop on Chester Road was jointly owned by myself and my friend Tan.

January 15 Saturday

Sunderland lost the third game of the year at Arsenal this afternoon. I was working in the stadium as the game was being beamed back and we were awash with complaints concerning the screens, the lighting, the beer, the room temperature and anything else that could have a grievance attached to it.

This was strange, as the only difference between this and any of the other beambacks was that we were shafted 4-1. Clearly, the direct correlation between the match score and the screens, the beer, etc., always baffles us non-scientists. It is at times like this that I wish I had stuck in at school.

January 17 Monday

There was another ashes scattering for me to attend to at pitch side this morning. I am aware that most of the mourning has been done by the time these ceremonies take place, but sometimes there is a level of cheeriness which does not seem somehow decent.

Today's group, for example, brought along a camera, which is actually not unusual. In fact camcorders are not unheard of. But what was odd was that the mourners lined up for a team photograph, some standing, others on one knee, with the ashes as a sort of trophy. This was in questionable taste, as was their raising of the F.A. Urn.

Eventually and thankfully, they scattered the ashes and went home to discuss tactics for whoever they may have to cremate in Europe next season.

190

January 23 Saturday

Sunderland lost the fourth game of the year at home to Leeds United. This is getting out of hand. The score was 2-1, but it was easier for them than that would suggest and their lovely supporters were left with nothing to complain about. At half-time they still went ahead with their not completely unexpected riot anyway.

The police waded in accompanied by the stirring chorus of 'You don't know what you're doing!', but this was an erroneous chant. The officers prodded them in the direction of the backs of uncomfortable looking vans, where I could not say what happened afterward as they closed the doors. The next step presumably is prosecution, so in other words, they really DID know what they were doing.

January 25 Tuesday

We had a staff meeting this morning which we all went into steeled by good intention, setting out to discuss how this new era would be hallmarked by Sunderland having the most envy inducing and efficiently run stadium in the country. But this grand conclave soon descended into a noisy squabble about who should fetch the milk from the admin building.

The edict from Adrian the groundsman to Mark the electrician that he should shut his clanker was a fitting conclusion to a vulgar slanging match which threatened to get out of hand when the subject of biscuits were thrown to the symposium. This is not a typical department meeting as sometimes they are banal and unproductive.

January 29 Saturday

There was no football today so it barely qualifies as a Saturday really. The only event I can properly remember from today came this evening in The Pilgrim when a bloke on a bar stool in the middle of the pub began to vomit copiously in a striking shade of crimson, a spectacular reintroduction of the many 'Pink Kangaroos' he had gorged down earlier.

As it sprayed outwards through his fingers, people oohed and aahed because it was a display that put one in mind of the Trevi Fountain. A couple of punters even threw some coins in and made a wish. If their wish was for the bouncers to come and throw him out, then it came true.

February 1 Tuesday

I had to buy a wheelchair today for the impending visit to the stadium of Bob Murray's auntie. Auntie Hilda, for 'tis she, mustn't be as sprightly as she once was and requires the chair to be shown around. We have no proper use for it beyond that, apart from the occasional race along the concourse against the mobile stretchers that the St. John's Ambulance mob uses.

I received a free gift upon buying the wheelchair, an implement to help frail people to sit up in bed. I am hardly frail myself, but I am interested in simultaneously eating, drinking and watching television in bed, so it is just the ticket.

February 3 Thursday

· Germaine Greer gave her dominoes evening a miss tonight in order to appear on *The Late Review* as a critic and Rottweiler. She pounced on a new film with a paedophile for a baddie for being homophobic, and for being manipulative and only representing the loss of material items while representing a completely ossified genre.

Having missed the first five minutes, it was quite an achievement on my part to work out that she was discussing *Toy Story II*. Still, even listening to this highly arcane patter was preferable to the alternative of watching *Ally McBeal* or *Whinging Bitch* as the less enlightened among us tend to call it.

February 4 Friday

Everyone was extremely jumpy today. We play Newcastle again tomorrow.

February 5 Saturday

Sunderland finally managed to play a game this year without losing. This was a good thing too as we were playing the Mags and would have had to hang ourselves otherwise.

They could only manage a draw with us, even though we very sportingly gave them a two goal lead. Kevin Phillips scored even more goals, the second of which was declared to be offside by Bobby Robson, who had an ideal view of it from the dugout. Of course he was wrong, but many of us wish that this were not so as it is an appealing thought to have an equaliser that was half a pitch or so offside.

There was personal embarrassment for me. Until today I had never asked any player for an autograph, but I was asked by a Mag uncle of mine to acquire some. The first footballer I ever asked for an autograph? Alan Shearer. Ugh!

I had hoped that he would react to my request with an ignorant and obnoxious refusal, so that I could get down the pub and give him some first hand slagging off instead of the usual stuff that we make up. Instead he was courteous, polite and actually seemed grateful to be in the privileged position of being asked. In short, a perfect gentleman. The bastard! He spoiled my day.

February 6 Sunday

Liz and I spent the morning in supine laziness, the only reprieve from this being when we summoned the energy to check last night's lottery numbers on Ceefax. We actually had four numbers worth a hundred and thirty quid. This galvanised us into immediate bickering over who should take credit for this, which I claimed on the grounds that I had ordered Bethan to go and retrieve the ticket from the mantelpiece.

Having completed these tasks, we went out and invested a good portion of our winnings on a massive Sunday lunch. Quantity not quality I say, the only testimony to a good meal is if you can barely walk at the end of it.

February 7 Monday

I made a quick inspection of the graffiti left by the Newcastle supporters in the male toilets on Saturday and a pretty sorry affair it was too. Among their daubings was a highly prophetic piece concerning the undoubted superiority of Alan Shearer over Kevin Phillips, as well as other highly articulate epigrams such as 'Kill Sunderland' and 'Ashington Magpies – hard as fuck.'

Yes, evidently some people called the Ashington Magpies are so incredibly hard, so superlatively tough, such an inestimably hardy set of stalwarts, that they locked themselves in a cubicle so that they would not be seen carrying out a minor act of vandalism. Cross them at your peril.

February 10 Thursday

There was more bad news for the mass murderer, Dr. Harold Shipman. On top of his 15 life sentences, he has now been struck off the medical register. The General Medical Council had what I presume was a fairly short meeting to decide this. That'll teach him.

February 12 Saturday

I was on beamback duty again today, so that Sunderland could unveil their latest debacle at Coventry City. Unlike most people who watched the game, I was actually paid for doing so, yet somehow it did not seem enough today.

The 3-2 defeat seemed like tough luck on our resolute defence, which had stoically negated the onslaught with great aplomb until that fateful 94th second. After that we were never really in it.

I comforted myself by harking back to the days when we had one of the most revered team in the land. In fact I did not have to hark too strenuously as it was only two months ago.

February 13 Sunday

I encountered some of the poor unfortunates who had returned from the wounding defeat at Coventry City yesterday; tales of crying children were heard. A seven year old was wailing outside Highfield Road after the game, until a kindly Sunderland supporter went over to establish that the little one was alright and to ensure that the lad was only a Coventry supporter.

There was no need to blub. He may have lost his parents, but he had got the three points.

He was passed over to the tender and loving care of the West Midlands Constabulary who should by now have beaten out his whereabouts on the 21st of November, 1974.

February 14 Monday

My appeal for St. Valentine's Day calm among the ladies of Sunderland was a resounding success. There was an absent horde of shrieking maidens hindering my path to the car, no pound of choccies in a heart shaped box, and definitely no need to wade ankle deep through perfumed cards in order to reach the front door. A lower than expected gas bill was the most romantic item in the post this morning.

However, there was to be no dampening of Liz's ardour as she proved when she presented me with a boiled egg, a fond compliment that I later returned when I gave her three quid so she could nip out to the garage and buy some tights.

Romance not dead then, but clearly unwell.

February 19 Saturday

No football yet again this weekend, so Liz and I had a jaunt up to Edinburgh where we had a richt braw nicht oot ye ken, despite not doing the usual touristy things such as visiting the 12th century castle, strolling down the Royal Mile and shooting up heroin. Nevertheless, we can now chalk off another major city in which we have got ourselves absolutely blotto. We now only have Burnley and Rio de Janeiro to go.

February 20 Sunday

We returned to England this afternoon after our successful binge in Edinburgh. There was no duty free as such, but we still came home with exotic gifts such as red cola, a pound of aromatics and one of those delightfully stylish Wee Jock MacTavish dolls, which the shop keeper assured us was *haute couture* in the more urbane Scottish country residences.

We drew the line at buying any 'Beware of Nessie' t-shirts, as I am sure that she bears us no ill will and also resides in Loch Ness, about 150 miles from Edinburgh. No real need to beware in this instance then, surely only the undiscerning and gullible tourist would purchase such an item.

February 23 Wednesday

England played Argentina tonight, but curiously did not select Kevin Phillips, presumably for scoring too many goals. This ploy worked very well as there was not a single goal in the game, thus saving a great deal of paperwork, which is what football is all about.

Meanwhile, there was sad news with the death of Stanley Matthews who has died at the age of 85. He will be forever synonymous with the 1953 F.A. Cup final, known as the Matthews Final because Stan didn't score while a bloke called Mortensen got a hat-trick and a chap called Bill Perry hit the winner. There is therefore still hope for a Gillan Final.

February 24 Thursday
I was sitting wistfully in the living room tonight when a hugely innovative idea struck me like a thunderbolt. Why not go down to the Ivy House for a drink?

Emboldened by revolutionary vigour, I marched down there and met a sturdy fellow called Jax. A few metres down the bar stood a bearded gentleman with a ruddy complexion and swept back hair who will never know of the amusement he caused us with his striking similarity to George V, albeit dressed in the unlikely monarchic apparel of a Def Leppard t-shirt.

I could have spent the remainder of the evening standing there sniggering at him, but the band came on and forced us to leave, 12 seconds into an appalling version of *Pretty Vacant.*

February 26 Saturday
Our pithily uninspiring 1-1 draw with Derby County today will probably be best remembered for what the more mannerly among us will refer to as an indiscretion in the tunnel after the game.

Derby's midfielder Darryl Powell had been the victim of a rather nasty looking elbow from Alex Rae. The method of retribution that he employed was not terribly scientific. Using the law of averages, he had a go at anyone close enough, including Peter Reid (I hid), in the hope that his next victim would be Alex. Not a good memory for faces then.

Eventually, the team were dispatched to their respective dressing rooms and everyone calmed down, when the relative quiet was halted by a booming, 'Come on then!' We turned round, startled, but were relieved and slightly annoyed to see Bobby Saxton and Jim Smith engaged in a rather elderly fun fight.

February 28 Monday
I was involved with another meeting at work, which was so top-level that only the maintenance department was invited.

A while ago we had discussed suitable accommodation for the security guard at the Charlie Hurley training ground, before I took the bull by the horns and bought him a 95 quid hut from a DIY shop, which he assembled himself. Job done.

Or so we thought until it was pointed out to me that this inexpensive shanty had been blown over several times. Suggested solutions were invited, at which Mark the electrician chimed in with 'Well, it wouldn't blow over if he stayed in it.'

This uncharitable rejoinder was swiftly agreed upon, so that the agenda could move on to the weightier matter of who had pinched Ronnie the plumber's banana yoghurt.

February 29 Tuesday

February the 29th and the local media seized their once every four years chance to wheel out some old biddy on this the occasion of her 21st birthday, when in actual fact she is 84, the issue of her being born on this date in 1916 having some hilarious consequences.

The only noteworthy event to take place on this quadrennial day was at work when I saw Leanne flouncing around the office with a 1999 Canford Audio catalogue balanced on her head to improve her slovenly deportment, pronouncing, 'Eee! Look at me! I go to lady classes.'

THAT should have been on the local news.

March 2 Thursday

I strode cheerily into accounts where the currently with-child Sue Kay was waiting for me with an expense form. In the course of small talk, I asked her 'How's everything downstairs?'

For one truly horrible, blood draining split second I thought that I might have made an awful mistake. What if she was not pregnant at all and I had just asked her the most impertinent question possible.

Thankfully, this was a fleeting moment of horror as she was successfully up the duff after all; it was just the slight pause before she answered that panicked me.

March 3 Friday

Dave Nicholson, Graeme McDonnell and I nipped over to Houghton to see the splendour of the McEwan's Centre. Our visit began with a jolt when the door was answered by a woman who appeared to be labouring under the misapprehension that it was Hallowe'en, but it seems that she was merely a fanatical follower of Max Factor.

The purpose of our meeting with Mr. Roseberry was to check the feasibility of the venue for an additional beamback for our game at Liverpool next week. Dave thinks it is a goer because of the easy compliance with regulations and the straightforward logistics of the event. I think it is a goer because you get such lovely tea and biscuits, Hallowe'en or not.

March 4 Saturday

Liz and I were invited by my celestial colleague, Leanne, to a club this evening for her engagement party. It was probably naïve of me to expect it to be busy with peers of the realm sitting in high-backed leather armchairs, sipping brandy and smoking cigars, but the Castletown Working Men's Club has alternative allures, such as Davie's Mobile 2000 Disco and a quite splendid line in ham sandwiches. A very good do.

March 5 Sunday

This is becoming plain silly. Sunderland lost what seems like the umpteenth game this year. This time it was Leicester City who cuffed us 5-2. Stan Collymore was in inspired form as we were on the receiving end of the biggest thrashing since his last girlfriend.

At least I only watched it on television and could alleviate the gloom by making an immediate return to the pub. This was not the case for Jim Fox who had made the mournful journey back from Filbert Street just in time for last orders when he burst through the double doors and filled the room with spite. Thank Buddha for obscenities, otherwise his speech would not have made a single dram of English sense.

March 7 Tuesday

Shrove Tuesday, so it was left to me to traipse around the shops scouring for shroves, but to no avail and we had to settle for pancakes.

As happens every year, the occasion was marked in several Yorkshire backwaters by a glorified punch up thinly disguised as a football match. Hordes of unemployed louts and yahoos gather to mete out all types of violence while a ball is chucked about. Not for them the silky first touch or the deft in-swinger from the outside of the boot. The winner is whoever is not dead.

It is a shame that Kevin Ball opted to go to Fulham.

March 8 Wednesday

Ash Wednesday and therefore the beginning of Lent, so I went down to the Ivy House with the others for a skin full of drink to pave the way for abstinence. It is impossible to abstain without first indulging.

We are fond of the high life and so asked Bob the manager to put the subtitles on the telly so we could watch *Coronation Street* without missing any of Darren's Disco. This was good news, as we would have otherwise missed Ken Barlow tearing a much needed strip off Blanch Hunt. As Ken rose to his theme, so did the patrons of the pub, encouraging him vocally as though he were a tricky midfielder on a promising counter-attack.

How about that for a night out!

March 11 Saturday

There was more beamback duty for us at work today. After the game, we were left to ponder the disconcerting trait of Sunderland teams down the years to be annihilated by mediocre sides, then take points from clubs that

197

should really have taken victories as well as our dinner money. So it came that we irritated Liverpool 1-1 today and deserved to.

Later in the Ivy House, we had some fun at the expense of one Tom Pescod who perseveres with his claim to support Liverpool despite being seen at Anfield less often that Halley's Comet. Undaunted, he still plods on with his use of the pronoun 'we' when referring to that great club, owns a couple of Beatles records and has been known to watch *Brookside*. Unrivalled commitment there then, in fact if you were to cut his arm it would undoubtedly bleed red.

March 14 Tuesday

Dave Nicholson was not in today, so I was called upon to deputise in a meeting connected to a forthcoming B.B.C. Music event in the stadium.

The music professor from the Beeb asked persons assembled if there were any musical connections at the club, such as an Italian international who could treat us to an aria or two. The implausibility of this was met with wry smiles. I suggested alternatives such as Danny Dichio's disco or Chris Makin on the spoons, but my efforts did not earn me any sort of plaudit apart from a hefty kick on the shin.

I was slightly peeved at this as it was no worse than the cheesy gimmick suggested by Phil Clarkson from the ticket office of 'Three Tenors for a Fiver'. Anyway, one of them is a baritone, so there.

March 15 Wednesday

Liz, Sue from reception and I were all persuaded by Kerry to drive down to Old Trafford to watch Manchester United play Fiorentina in the Champions League. Upon arriving, we met Kerry's Italian friend, Dimitri, whom we plied with traditional English fare in the nearby Pizza Hut before whisking him off to a hovel called The Dog & Partridge, which I wrongly supposed could not be any worse on the inside than the outside.

Academy award winning scenery makers could not have contrived a grottier setting. It is perhaps forgivable that the place may not have been decorated in the last 30 years, but it also appeared that in the same time scale they had not got round to giving the bar a bit of a wipe.

This pub and a 3-1 defeat for Fiorentina will have done little to hasten Dimitri's return.

March 18 Saturday

As far as today's visitors were concerned, the 1-1 draw represented a pride saving point salvaged from the evil grasp of a mortal enemy, whereas to the Sunderland contingent it represented an irredeemably drab draw with Middlesbrough. Common courtesy should be enough to ensure that hatred is reciprocated, but this is not the case. How terribly ill mannered of us.

The seething cauldron of hatred that the stadium became in its one and only derby game thus far was not in evidence today as Sunderland supporters tend to invest most of their hatred in one team (guess who?), with a little left over for Leeds. The absence of enthusiasm for today's game was amply demonstrated by a bloke sitting near me who at one stage counted 37 seagulls perched along the East Stand.

March 20 Monday

Your actual Peter Reid came bounding into the office today for one of his infrequent chats. His jaunty disposition was unbleached by the double downer of not having won a game this year, coupled with his recent acquisition of endorsements on his driving license.

Coincidentally, he had also been to that game at Old Trafford last Wednesday, but unlike me he had been nicked for speeding in Leeds on the way home. The traffic policeman in attendance said that he admired Peter's abrasive and down to Earth approach to football management, but was nevertheless duty bound to give him three points. Some very obvious jokes are now doing the rounds.

March 21 Tuesday

A drunken chain smoker and motorist drove past me as I went for a paper with a definite angry expression on his face. This was probably because it was budget day and he had been clobbered on the usual three fronts. There was good news for me when a five per cent reduction on capital gains tax was announced. This is a levy on a person's assets, so the government must owe me a few quid looking at the state of my car.

March 23 Thursday

The big news in North East football today was the resignation of someone called Freddie Fletcher as the Chief Executive of Newcastle United and his imminent replacement, David Stonehouse, who is Sunderland's Financial Director at present.

The reverberations of this top-level desk shuffling have not been as seismic as had been supposed. The only response that I have so far heard to this news, official or otherwise, was from the lads in our department who said, 'Good. We might get a decent van now.'

As my financial qualifications are confined to an 'O' level in maths, I am unlikely to be offered Mr. Stonehouse's job, but I wouldn't mind having his office as it has a fridge and could easily accommodate a dart board.

March 24 Friday

The club is currently making laudable attempts to counter racism at football matches. For tomorrow's home game with Everton, a poster campaign has been launched with the legend 'Kick Racism Out Of Football', complemented by a photograph of a Sunderland player in action.

At the time when these posters went to print, Sunderland did not have a black player on the books, yet the choice of the Indo-European, Nordic, blond haired and blue-eyed Stefan Schwarz may have been something of an injudicious selection, although his surname in English does mean 'black'.

March 25 Saturday

Our good form continued still further with a pulsating 2-1 win over Everton, which bolsters our total number of victories this year to one. The city centre was in boisterous mood this evening, surfing on this tidal wave of success.

Amid the merriment, I heard a catchy new ditty lilting its melodious way through the doors of The Borough. The theme of the song was Alan Shearer's resemblance to a horse's arse, but it fell down lyrically because the best the librettists could manage as a word rhyming with 'arse' was 'shite', which means that it is unlikely to attain classic status. This was a pity, as I thought for a moment that we had another *Keegan Is A Wanker* on our hands there.

March 27 Monday

It was an extended working day for us today, due to a reserve fixture with Manchester United in the stadium tonight. The game was notable for the first appearance in a Sunderland shirt of the Honduran, Milton Nunez. He goes by the sobriquet of Tyson after the thoroughly unpleasant heavyweight boxer. This was also the name of a Labrador that used to come in the visitors centre and Milton is only slightly taller.

Honduras expects, so let us all hope that he is a success at the Stadium of Light. If this is not to be, then at least he would have the consolation of being able to get in for half price.

April 1 Saturday

Sunderland managed to win 2-1 at Southampton today, which one could be forgiven for presuming was an elaborate April Fool's joke, as the last time we won at The Dell neither side had a fully formed homo sapien in their line-up.

A slight exaggeration perhaps, but our last victory there coincided with Frank Ifield's *I Remember You* dropping out of the charts and the Cuban Missile Crisis. Not only has this now been put right, but Frank was soon back at number one with *Lovesick Blues* and a nuclear war was averted, so good news all round. If we win there again, it will be an achievement for me just to be alive to see it.

April 8 Saturday

We were at home to a godawful Wimbledon side today in a dour and largely uneventful game. Who would have thought it? It was the type of afternoon that brings out the legendary native wit of the North East crowd. I shall never forget the *bel esprit*, who upon seeing their crappy deflected equaliser hitting the net came out with, 'That's shite!'

This was complemented by another fellow's, 'He wants his arse kicking!', the memorable 'Bollocks!' and other *bon mots*.

All of these sentiments had been dispelled by full time after we had contrived to actually win the game. Kevin Kilbane's gleeful response to scoring the winning goal was tinged with regret for me as it served to remind me that I was supposed to have arranged for his fridge freezer to be repaired last week.

April 9 Sunday

I did not bother to watch today's Cup tie between Chelsea and Newcastle, as foregone conclusions are of little interest to us neutrals. Sure enough, a 2-1 victory to Chelsea ensued and local television decided, rather negatively, to gauge reaction from fans in pubs around Newcastle, which were absolutely funereal, choosing not to concentrate on the Wearside equivalents, which were in vibrant and celebratory mood.

One lucky punter in The Londonderry had the further good fortune to have correctly placed a bet on the outcome. With some relish, he was showing anyone who would look his betting slip, which was worded 'Scum to lose two-one'. Even in Sunderland he may have difficulty claiming his winnings.

April 10 Monday

Liz and I attempted to pit our knowledge against the intellectual heavyweights gathered for The Lansdowne's pub quiz tonight.

It is one of those establishments where they attempt to enhance the cosiness of the room by having shelves full of books, all of which are glued together to prevent people from stealing them, although the chances of anyone wanting to swipe *The Scarlet Scimitar* by Osbert Fondling are slight, unless Osbert himself has lost his own copy.

Luck was against us in that 'Who wrote *The Scarlet Scimitar*?' did not crop up. Yet despite this handicap, we managed a creditable third place, winning two pint tokens that we were unable to spend and an entire 75p in cash, a prize that only barely qualifies for the description of being better than nothing. I allowed Liz to keep it.

April 11 Tuesday

In Dave's absence, I was called upon to chair a Stadium Debrief meeting, in which any issues to arise after the previous home game are discussed. All persons present were pleased with the change in the chair, as my cheerful amateurism ensured that the gathering had dispersed in about half an hour, and ten minutes of that was taken up with the subject of the mooted return of *Crossroads* to ITV. Some argued that this programme was extremely lowbrow drama. While it was no *Albion Market* or *Eldorado*, it was certainly better than that *Madame Bovary* rubbish that was on again tonight.

All of this has been put in the minutes, but I hope it is never leaked to the press, as we wouldn't want supporters to imagine that these meetings are taken lightly.

April 13 Thursday

There will be another beamback on Saturday, as no Sunderland supporter would want to miss seeing us lose to Manchester United, so a large screen is being erected on the pitch.

The contractors for this task are led as usual by a big chap from Somerset called Denzil, who arrived this afternoon bearing gifts of jars of real scrumpy. They were transparent jars, unfortunately, which put me off rather as all of the impurities therein were clearly visible. Animal, vegetable, mineral.

I declined this kind offer for health reasons, unlike some of my colleagues who are probably dancing round a maypole as I write.

April 15 Saturday

Oh dear. Much as we did at Coventry, Sunderland were making favourable progress for the first 150 seconds at Old Trafford this afternoon, before our play was notable for a marked vitiation. I also reckon that Manchester United are even better than Coventry. The final score was 4-0, which to the layperson would seem a plaintive outcome. How right they would be.

I watched the game at the beamback in the Stadium of Light, where at around 4:35pm there was talk of an equaliser, but this talk was employed solely for the purposes of black comedy. As viewing spectacles go, it compared favourably to *Ground Force*, but that is the only positive comment I can come up with, other than the fact that it is finished now.

April 18 Tuesday

Consternation and dismay were in evidence at work today after the news that Dave Nicholson has handed in his notice. This is indeed a blow. There are other persons at work who, in order to be replaced, would first have to explain what they actually do. I refer, of course, to people like me, but with Dave this is not the case.

It has already been suggested by ill-informed friends of mine that I should step into his shoes. This will be a distinct possibility if I can qualify as a civil engineer, structural expert, quantity surveyor and draughtsman by Friday week. I would have a stab at cramming all of this in were I not in the middle of a really good book right now.

April 22 Saturday

When I bought the tickets for today's game with Sheffield Wednesday at Hillsborough, my only reaction upon seeing the word 'UNCOVERED' printed upon them was to utter the word 'Pah!' and make a dismissive backwards motion with my left hand.

This clear invitation to a torrential downpour to come and do its stuff was taken up enthusiastically, the clouds opened at the stroke of three o'clock and continued spitefully until half-time. This discomfort, combined with a listless performance on the pitch, caused some disquiet amongst my fellow uncovereds, but this agitation was dispersed and a heavy letter writing campaign averted by two late goals. Final score 2-0. Evidently it is impossible to get wet if we win away from home.

April 24 Monday

I arrived at work this morning and was quietly relieved to see Ronnie the plumber still intact after the condition I found him in on Saturday in Sheffield. He tottered up to me beneath the stand at Hillsborough and loudly slurred something about having been for a drink in Wrexham. This was obviously all a fib, his drinks quota was no way in the singular and Wrexham is in North Wales. With a far more sedate countenance today (sober), he admitted that his drinks had been indisputably plural and that he had actually been to Worksop.

All of this is of far more interest than Sunderland's dire 1-0 home defeat to Bradford City today. I mean, who wants to hear about that?

April 28 Friday

It was Dave's last day today. This is the end of an era, so we gave him a pen. I am sorry to report that I have failed in my efforts to become a qualified civil engineer, structural expert, quantity surveyor and draughtsman in the last ten days, so someone else will have to replace him. Perhaps I could have been successful if the telly hadn't been so damn good recently.

His last act as Stadium Manager was to attend a meeting on the North Stand extension, which he insisted I sit in on. This was scheduled to last for around three hours, but as he had been copiously plied with champagne by Peter Reid earlier it was considered prudent to wrap things up after 40 minutes.

I left him as I shall remember him, standing outside the stadium waiting for his lift home, drunk and holding four pink balloons on strings.

April 29 Saturday

I listened attentively to the radio to hear all about Sunderland's swashbuckling, heart stopping encounter with Aston Villa, a 1-1 draw. After Niall Quinn's equaliser, Paul Butler made what was described as a 'no nonsense clearance' from the six yard box, which seems a shame when he could have carried out a completely nonsensical clearance with three feet long football boots in a green curly wig, before hilariously falling face down in a muddy puddle. The game is crying out for some honest to goodness buffoonery.

April 30 Sunday

Liz, Bethan and I had a jaunt along to South Shields this afternoon, as not only is Monte Carlo lacking in a certain chic at this time of year, but is also about a thousand miles too far to simply pop over for a Ninety Nine.

All over South Tyneside there are prominent road signs proudly proclaiming it to be 'Catherine Cookson Country'. There may therefore be a chance of immortality for me yet when a waiting world finally gets hold of these diaries. If I can whip up a yarn about an orphan who is brought up on a diet of dead bats and coal, but goes on to become the owner of a successful chain of handkerchief shops, then who knows? I could even have an honorary plaque to me put up outside the Ivy House.

May 2 Tuesday

Today was my first day without Dave Nicholson, and my ignorance in all matters technical had been shown before I had even dunked the first digestive into my Adam Rickett mug when somebody asked me which type of fixings we would be using on the roof trusses on the North Stand extension. My answer of 'Good sturdy ones' only revealed me for what I am.

My hopes of seeing a lorry pull up with the legend 'Good Sturdy Roof Truss Fixings Ltd' emblazoned on the side were not well founded. The club seems to have decided that I should adopt a heuristic approach to my new duties.

Incidentally, the Adam Rickett mug was a novelty gift from the girls who went to Blackpool and in no way denotes puffiness. Oh no no.

May 5 Friday

As our leader has now left us, it has fallen upon me to attend the progress meetings for the North Stand extension. It appears that these meetings have been crying out for the presence of someone who is completely unqualified, out of his depth and with virtually nothing to offer the discussion, so thank God I was there!

All too quickly, the agenda moved on from topics in which I have considerable expertise, such as tea and biscuits, and on to subjects such as extraction and ventilation to the new kiosks, where I had rather less to contribute. It is as well that I am practised in the art of nodding sagely and saying 'Good point,' every now and again, a most invaluable debating tool.

May 6 Saturday

Kevin Phillips put away his 30th goal of the season in a 1-0 win over West Ham. This was the last home game of the season, so we put on a few festivities such as bands, fireworks, stilt walkers, unicyclists and others who were imbued with similar life saving skills.

I intend to send a stern letter to one particularly incompetent juggler who would in future be better advised to use tennis balls instead of lighted clubs. This would have obviated the embarrassing trail of scorch marks that he left along the synthetic track. He was truly talentless.

At least we were spared the odious pastime of plate spinning. Had I spotted an exponent of this particular animus I could not have been responsible for my actions.

May 7 Sunday

Newcastle can't catch us now. Ha!

May 8 Monday

Someone shoved the Sunday papers under my nose at work today, to show me photographic evidence of the behaviour of one of the men who was supposed to be working on the extension during the game on Saturday. He had been watching the match, but wearing a hard hat and holding an architect's drawing for verisimilitude. He was most convincing too until Sunderland scored.

At this point he leapt into the air, which resulted in his hat coming off and he also began to wave the drawing ecstatically above his head. The game was up as far as his pretence of inspecting pop rivets was concerned. I expect he will be discussed under Any Other Business at Thursday's meeting.

May 14 Sunday

I did not buy a ticket for today's last game of the season as I had expected it to be beamed back. Mysteriously and annoyingly, it wasn't.

We lost 3-1 to the preposterously entitled Tottenham Hotspur who were named after a character from *Henry V,* and symbolic of their inability to remove their head from their arses ever since. Worse than that, Henry Hotspur was the son of the Earl of Northumberland, which effectively means that they were named after a Mag.

May 15 Monday

The 1999-2000 football season has ended with Sunderland limping out of it rather at Tottenham. Nevertheless, we finished in a highly respectable seventh position and can consider this to be a success. We actually finished a trifling 33 points behind Manchester United, although they also have a superior goal difference. The acquisition of another eleven wins and a draw would see us in our rightful place at the top.

As ever, there is always next season and with a couple of new signings, a snort of good fortune and mindless optimism in our hearts, we may do even better.

May 17 Wednesday

We are barely into the close season so there have not been any new signings so far, nor indeed has a new Stadium Manager been appointed. However, we are not wholly without new arrivals as our new club hawk was ushered in today, a tough looking lad who has been employed as a kind of bouncer to keep the pigeons from our newly laid pitch.

He has the eminently cool name of Red, which is befitting of the meanness, moodiness and magnificence of this resplendent bird of prey, and so much more befitting of such a creature than Sandy, which is what I mischievously informed Yvonne from P.R. was the name of the beaked one.

May 19 Friday

It was the birthday of Sara in Commercial today. I did not buy her a present, as it would have been impossible to top the tin of hot dogs that I presented her with last year, although I almost gave her a quite stunning cactus that was available for £1.25 from Wilson's of Whitburn. But no one else would chip in.

May 20 Saturday

The *Stars in Their Eyes* final was a disappointment. The winner was supposed to be Freddie Mercury, but he bore a closer resemblance to Captain Darling from *Blackadder Goes Forth.*

May 23 Tuesday

I arrived at work to be greeted by the sight of Cathy Kerr from Commercial at the top of the stairs, gazing down at me with an expression that I had not seen since arriving home at an unearthly hour from a nightclub at the age of 15.

My mind flashed over the possible reasons for this mien. Had there been a mishap with the stadium extension, the pitch renovations or the impending renewal of the safety certificate? But thinking of these possibilities only served to show how misplaced my priorities were. The imbroglio of issue was the two bonsai plants that remained in the players lounge when they should have been in the admin building and I was directly responsible. Club shares so far remain at four pounds and ten pence.

May 24 Wednesday

The passing away on Sunday of Dame Barbara Cartland, the mad old purveyor of slop, brought shameful unalloyed joy for one woman in a Nottingham factory who had drawn the slushstress in a stiff stakes, which meant that she stood to win about a grand.

But her elation lasted for just 24 hours until news came through of the death of Sir John Gielgud, who also had his dentures removed for the last time on Sunday. His agent had deliberately withheld the announcement, presumably to piss off people in factories who organise stiff stakes. Until the exact times of death are made public it can be considered a dead heat, if I may use that expression.

May 26 Friday

I was startled to come across the news today that Alan Shearer had actually put someone in a coma just by talking to him. While it is well documented that his skills as a bon viveur and raconteur are not quite honed to perfection, this seemed rather a dramatic outcome even for one who has attained his soaring heights of monotony.

But the truth of the matter was that I had read the *Newsround* page on 510 of Ceefax in too cursory a manner. The bloke had actually been raised from unconsciousness by the sound of Alan's voice, which sounds even less plausible to me.

As the patient in question was a Mag, the likelihood is that the hospital staff parked his bed closer to the kebab shop and inspired him to wake by the medium of smell.

May 29 Monday

Another bank holiday might imply having little to do, yet no sooner had I drank four cups of tea and done the lounging about than it was time to go to the Little Sisters Garden Fete where society gathers to dazzle, with the paparazzi insidiously concealing themselves around the tombola stall. I went home with the bounty of an Elkie Brooks album, on offer at the jumble stall for 30p, although I managed to violently haggle the woman down to 20p as it was for charity. When I got home though, I found an audible crack in the middle of *Lilac Wine* and the devious bitch hadn't given me a receipt.

June 8 Thursday

There was a monthly meeting for the North Stand extension which is far more important than the Friday weekly meeting. Oh yes. Not only was John Fickling in attendance today, but there was a meticulously prepared pile of sandwiches of various flavours. I even said something today, even if it was to express obsequious agreement with anything that Mr. Fickling said.

June 10 Saturday
Liz had her hen night in Durham tonight. What a state to come home in.

June 12 Monday
There was football on the television tonight, only international mind, Euro 2000 in fact. At half-time I read the paper, which was all about today's Burns Report that was supposed to establish whether fox hunting was a dastardly and barbaric activity or just a rather flash way of staging a picnic. Lord Burns was eager not to appear partial when describing the animal being pursued by a pack of frenzied bloodhounds that have not eaten for two days and had got out of the wrong side of the kennel. Instead of just saying that this was curtains, the peer suggested that this could 'seriously compromise the welfare of the fox'.

England seriously compromised their own welfare tonight when they lost to Portugal. Well, I wouldn't want to be partial and call them crap.

June 17 Saturday
England beat Germany 1-0 tonight. An enquiry is underway.

June 20 Tuesday
England were put out of Euro 2000 by Romania. There is no shame to this as we were beaten by the probable champions, and besides, England are just not Sunderland, so what does it matter?

June 23 Friday
A pile of us are in Edinburgh for my stag weekend where there is a greater concentration of theatres, art galleries and museums for us to ignore. This city is awash with culture and our contribution to it was for Peter Cain to sing the incidental music from the *Carry On* films when an attractive female walked past. He will probably be asked back to perform it at the Fringe.

I was berated by Taff for not consuming 17 cans of Harp on the train journey up and for being able to stand up at midnight. But I still had trouble finding my way back to the hotel as the landmark third heroin addict on the left had been moved on, possibly to a slab.

June 24 Saturday
Marcus finally lurched in this morning as I was finishing my breakfast. He had taken full advantage of Scotland's more liberated licensing laws. He promptly lay on his bed and became immovable, even when we poured

cold tea in his ear. This was a problem as he was supposed to be changing rooms.

As the spiritual leader of this expedition, it was down to me to ponder this predicament. 'What would Napoleon have done?' I wondered. There was only one available course of action and we took it when we hid his shoes and pissed off down the pub.

The stag weekend later hit fever pitch when we plumped up the cushions to watch Romania play Italy. Us lads, eh?

June 25 Sunday

Back in Sunderland I put the hair of the dog theory into practice. What a load of cobblers it is.

June 26 Monday

Well it was certainly all happening today. Scientists have unravelled the genetic code to our human existence and the seats have started to be installed in the North Stand extension. This is all very clever stuff. There was further drama when I went home from work with tonsillitis.

June 29 Thursday

Liz and I are getting married tomorrow. We may as well as it is the close season and there is not much else to do. I am staying at Redge's mother's house tonight. We all went out at seven o'clock for my final evening of bingeing as a bachelor, with Eileen's stern motherly advice of 'No daftness mind,' ringing in our ears.

June 30 Friday

Proceedings of the day got off to a bad start, when my best man Redge, Rachel and I got in a Thorney Close Taxi to the registry office. Spotting our buttonholes, he rather morosely asked, 'Funeral is it?'

We ignored his sarcasm and politely replied that it was a wedding.

'That's what I said; it's the same thing! I've been dead for 14 years now.'

I thanked him for his encouraging words, but did not tip him. This would have been the low point had they not played *It's A Kind Of Magic* immediately after the ceremony.

Liz and I later had to treat the evening guests to the risible sight of us leading off a dance that no one else joined in. We were left to wish that we had selected *Agado* or the *Hokey-Cokey*, or certainly something where they give you some instructions.

July 13 Thursday

Middlesbrough are giving a trial to a player called Joseph Desire-Job. This has to be the best name ever for a triallist at any club.

July 15 Saturday

Liz and I are on honeymoon in Paris for a couple of days. This morning, in a quiet side street off the Champs Elysees, we spotted a bloke wearing a Sunderland shirt. As he approached, I decided that he would appreciate a hearty greeting from one devotee to another, but I was wrong. He merely gave us a quick shufti askance then clumped straight on past.

Later we called in on Carl Redman, who lives out here with his family. He took us to the palace of Versailles, which, while no Crowtree Leisure Centre, is not a bad job. A bit more effort with the gardens, a couple of waltzers and a few hot dog vans would make it seem more complete.

July 16 Sunday

There was more tourist type stuff on the agenda, starting with an exhaustive walk to the top of the dome at Sacre Coeur. Later we went for a drink at Notre Dame, where the prices were not so much steep as vertical. It was there that we had arranged to meet Redge, who was out here for work purposes.

He came with information of Don Hutchison signing for Sunderland. Meeting your mate and talking about footy is enough to top off any honeymoon and cement the romance of Paris.

July 18 Tuesday

We are home again. The only transport that we have been on in the last few days to be horribly overcrowded and unpleasant was the last section of our journey. It would be expected on the Calcutta to Dacca route, but we had naively expected better of the Newcastle to Sunderland train.

July 21 Friday

There was a mound of invoices for me to approve back at work today. One that really caught my eye was from an orthopaedic consultant and was for Steve Bould's bilateral forefoot realignment. I could not say why this bill ended up with our department, but I have refused to pay for it unless Mr. Bould fancies coughing up for the hire of the pallet barrow that we used last week, which I doubt.

Incidentally, the price of having a forefoot bilaterally realigned is £65, which seems rather expensive for just the one. Although to have both feet done would be nothing more than vanity.

July 25 Tuesday

It would seem that my car is finally coming to the end of its long life. The cost of putting it through another M.O.T. has made it non-viable as we executives say. I thought briefly about trying to sell it (after all it only says two thousand miles on the clock), but any mug can see that this is not the first time it has said this and possibly not the second or third time either.

For my colleagues, this does not so much represent the end of an era so much as the removal of an eyesore from the club car park. I have to concede their point. The coat hanger aerial just adds that final cliché, while it has always been a source of mirth that I bother to put an anti-theft device on the steering wheel.

July 28 Friday
Worse than having to scrap the car, it now transpires that I will be lucky to get ten quid for it. I sent an email round the club today, making the superficially attractive offer of a free car for anyone who wanted it. So far nobody does, not even the Chairman.

August 1 Tuesday
I wandered over to the Sports Bar this afternoon to discuss the possibility of starting a quiz there. How well the discussions went is a matter of opinion. I intend to be the finest quiz master in the Premier League.

The manager there is the former Newcastle player, John Cornwell. My finely honed negotiating skills led me to ask him for sixty quid, the idea being to haggle £50 out of him, but all the fun of the haggle was dispersed when he said, 'Sixty quid. Fair enough.'

So I actually came away from discussions with more money than I was trying to get, but felt quite forlorn when wondering just how high he would have gone. I actually don't need the money, it's just that I am very very greedy indeed.

August 3 Thursday
With one hand passing over the V5 form and the other wiping away a tear, I finally took the car to the scrap yard today. I got fifteen pounds for it, which means that the petrol I left in it is probably worth more than the vehicle.

August 11 Friday
Myself and the rest of the civilised world are just killing time until the football season begins. The close season is a pointless exercise and ought to be stopped.

August 16 Wednesday
I was in the chair for the Stadium and Events meeting, but my main contribution to it was to gaze aimlessly out of the window, which needs doing. In the course of this toil, I spotted a contractor gambolling along the roof of the stadium, no harness, carrying a pot of paint and a ladder, chatting happily with his friend who was equally unshackled but carrying

nothing, save for the Space Rocket ice lolly that was protruding from his mouth.

With not an inch of safety rope in sight, I used my extensive health and safety knowledge to divine that this behaviour was probably contrary to regulations. I referred the matter to John Davidson, the Safety Officer, who after sifting through reams of legislation confirmed that this was the case. We have decided to have a word.

August 19 Saturday

Sunderland opened the new season as expected, with a stylish win over an outclassed Arsenal. Our one effort on goal went in whereas their constant bombardment of the Sunderland penalty area was utterly fruitless. I for one thought it a convincing victory.

Patrick Viera was sent off, but Arsene Wenger was indignant at this injustice on the grounds that Darren Williams was not actually dead. I had noticed during the match that Arsene spends much of his time in dour resentment. 'Zut alor!' he was heard to shout, his diction also peppered with many a 'Mon dieu!' and 'Oo la la!', and on one occasion an 'Avec fromage!', but that was when someone offered him a cream cracker in the players lounge.

He gave me what can only be described as a dirty look when he stomped down the tunnel on the final whistle. My French may be rubbish, but he could clearly understand a smirk. Immediately after this glower, he apparently landed himself in trouble in an incident with the fourth official, but like all of the fun, I missed it.

August 21 Monday

Patrick Viera was sent off *again* tonight. This is twice in 48 hours, so credit where it is due.

August 23 Wednesday

My new car is still off the road despite the five hundred quid that I parted with to buy it, so Bernie Callaghan offered us a lift to Manchester City this evening. With the benefit of hindsight, this can only be described as spite. We lost 4-2 and Paulo Wanchope scored a hat-trick, so God only knows what he was trying to do.

Sunderland were fairly awful tonight, but the main thing is that everyone did their best, surely?

August 24 Thursday

My debut as the Sunderland AFC Sports Bar quiz master had been backed up with an advert in Saturday's match programme, many e-mails and a poster campaign, and such is the power of advertising that we managed to pull in six entire teams. This means that in a room with a legal occupancy of 400, we only need another 360 or so people to fill it.

August 26 Saturday

We played at another promoted club this afternoon when we lost 1-0 at Ipswich Town. The consensus amongst those of us who did not actually attend the game was that these tractor people must have been extremely lucky and will probably be relegated.

One such fellow-me-lad in the Ivy House tonight was in the midst of a bitter (though rather eloquent) rant about how much they stink of fish when his gusto for his subject receded by someone asking if he wasn't getting mixed up with Grimsby Town. It is very easy to confuse the primary industries at that time of night.

August 28 Monday

Bethan has been hounding me to take her to Euro Disney. I compromised by whisking her off to Bamburgh to see Grace Darling's tomb.

August 31 Thursday

The Sunderland AFC Sports bar quiz has already said farewell to the angst-ridden days of only having six teams. Another one turned up tonight making seven.

September 3 Sunday

The school holidays are mercifully all but ended, yet there was still a bit to be done to entertain Bethan for another afternoon, so I was shanghaied into going to the cinema to see *Stuart Little*. Having already shelled out for the tickets, I was not then ambitious to remove the price of a box of popcorn from the funds. As such, I informed Bethan that a damaging strike had taken place in the popcorn industry. The notably militant Popcorn And Truffle Makers Union had decreed that no corn would be popped until their extravagant demands were met.

All hopes of saving £1.20 were cruelly dashed when she noticed the large illuminated sign behind me that said 'Get your lovely popcorn here'. To decent minded people like me, this represents the unacceptable face of capitalism.

September 5 Tuesday

It was generally a disappointing evening. There were hundreds of West Ham supporters in town tonight and not a pearly king among them. What kind of way is that to support your team? Then there was Davor Suker.

I was pretty excited about seeing him having been impressed with his achievements in international tournaments. He scored the equaliser in tonight's 1-1 draw, but it was such an extraordinarily shoddy affair that I consider it unprofessional of him to have celebrated it. The ball bobbled off his studs then bounced three times on the ground before trickling into the net. If Ronnie the plumber's work was as sub-standard as that then the stadium would barely have a lavatory in operation.

There was an interesting moment at half-time in the tunnel where Frank Lampard Jnr. was taking great exception with the new Argentinean, Julio Arca, over something that had occurred on the pitch. Julio merely stood and smiled politely at this diatribe, which was not due to any restraint as much as, being unable to speak a word of English.

September 7 Thursday

There was another game at the stadium this evening when Sunderland reserves took on those of Manchester United, two days before the first teams compete at Old Trafford. United were generous enough to field a team of teenagers which allowed us to biff them 4-0.

Upon bumping into some of the chaps as I wandered round the West Stand, I pointed out that this was likely to be an omen for Saturday. Bernie and Taff agreed with me, but only in a negative, cynical way, decrying the augury and saying that we would again witness a large yet casual victory for the home team against a side consisting of players that no one in the ground has heard of.

Dreadful attitude. I'm afraid that where there's hope there's also the likes of Bernie and Taff.

September 9 Saturday

Bernie and Taff were of course right. For some reason there are no beambacks these days, so I listened to the radio to hear the lads do even better at Manchester United than last season, only losing 3-0 this time.

September 13 Wednesday

The country is currently in the midst of a fuel crisis, brought about by a blockade which is being staged by people who like being seen on the telly. I am alright as I wisely panic-bought on Sunday. I urge everyone to do the same as this will ultimately bring the country to a standstill and we can all have a week off.

September 15 Friday

Tonight saw the end of a television series called *Big Brother* in which some people were locked in a house for a few weeks during which time it was hoped that something interesting would happen.

As they were being let out, it was curious to think of all the events that they could not know about, such as the fuel crisis, Mo Mowlam resigning and Sunderland drawing Luton in the Worthington Cup. Above all, it is worth pondering how agreeable it must be to have completely missed this very dull and completely pointless television series during which time nothing happened apart from some minor altercation when someone apparently smuggled in a pencil. A must see.

September 16 Saturday

We beat Derby County 2-1 at home, but it wasn't as good as last season's game with them here. This afternoon there was not even the suggestion of a punch up.

September 19 Tuesday

There was another home game tonight, but with the greatest of respect (as people always point out insincerely on these occasions), it was difficult to become too excited by a Worthington Cup tie against Luton Town. This general lack of interest, compounded by torrential rain, spread among staff, supporters and players alike. The positive aspect to all of this was that the apathy had extended to the media, with the welcome side affect that there was a veritable embankment of sandwiches left over in the press lounge.

It was a long old day, but ultimately a successful one as we secured a 3-0 win and I didn't have to call in at the chip shop on the way home.

September 23 Saturday

Sunderland secured a 1-1 draw at Liverpool, the third time in a row that we have drawn there. This is something that the Scousers find terribly irritating and as usual they rang up radio stations to say as much. I was not at the game, but listening to these phone-ins it seems that Sunderland have resorted to deliberately defending our goal while also trying to kick the ball in the direction of theirs. Is this what football has come to?

September 26 Tuesday

Sunderland won 2-1 in the second leg at Luton. I am consumed with indifference at this.

September 28 Thursday

The Sunderland AFC Sports Bar quiz has already undergone a spectacular surge from a position of a low profile to the dizzy heights of mediocrity. The picture round was fairly easy as even the team of dimwits by the pool table did well, although they took no chances with number eleven. Having correctly guessed and written down the answer of Hitler, they then made absolutely sure of the point by putting in brackets afterwards Adolph.

The picture round was popular, but my questions on anteaters were sadly less well received.

October 1 Sunday

Sunderland's goalless draw with Leicester City will only linger in my memory because of the amusing fracas in the tunnel at half-time. There had already been some argy bargy on the pitch between Niall Quinn and Gerry Taggart which carried on as they made their way to the dressing rooms with the good grace of being heated rather than violent. Then Don Hutchison, who had had nothing to do with the altercation, entered the fray by winding Taggart up further by snarling, 'You started it!' before completing the process by adding, '. . . you fat bastard!'

That was it. All hell then broke loose with a solitary policeman in the middle of the hostilities, rather lamely telling everyone that it was 'Only a game'.

The incident was disgraceful, so almost by definition it was also a right laugh.

October 4 Wednesday

I threw off the shackles of tradition before wisely putting them back on to stroll to the Ivy House. I was halfway there when I felt an object strike me on the hip, as the car with my assailant in sped off. Closer inspection showed that I had been hit by an egg.

I returned home to change and finally made it to the pub where I gave a dramatic account of this sinister drive-by egging. However, it seems that only death attains any kind of sympathy as I discovered when I was given only a barrage of sarcasm about grassy knolls and calling out police helicopters. I don't know why I bother.

October 8 Saturday

England's qualification for the 2002 World Cup is now looking decidedly ropey as Germany won the last ever game at Wembley. Kevin Keegan has resigned on the back of it. It seems he wanted to spend about two hundred million quid on foreign players but was not allowed.

October 11 Wednesday

Just when it seemed that England could not become any more amusing, they pulled off a quite hilarious 0-0 draw with the invincible Finland, although it was the away fixture.

To be scrupulously fair, Finland is about twice the size of England, and even though only eleven people live there, when they get together they have a pretty nifty football team. Obviously, it was not a good evening and there was further ignominy when so-called England supporters couldn't even be bothered to smash up Helsinki. Fortunately, not many people watched it as it was pay-per-view and was only England after all.

October 12 Thursday

There was more unfettered euphoria in the Sunderland AFC Sports Bar that only quiz night can bring. Tonight's pictures round included a photograph of George Orwell, just next to Bobby Davro. However, Orwell fans were not in attendance en masse as demonstrated by the hopelessly inaccurate guesses for him such as Peter Mandelson, although I have to concede that he is not entirely unlike the bloke who used to be in Sparks. The place was simply bristling with intellectualism.

October 14 Saturday

It was a trying day to say the least for the maintenance team.

Just before one o'clock we put the kettle on, only to find it ceasing to boil after a minute, much to the chagrin of Mark the electrician who had not had a cup of tea at that stage. We soon realised that the situation was even more serious than that and that the game with Chelsea might have to be postponed, there being no electricity or tea. Some oaf on a nearby building site had sliced through a cable, but after some frantic splicing and welding, we managed a four o'clock kick-off. The match ended just in time for a floodlight to catch fire.

Sunderland won 1-0, which was about the only thing to go right today.

October 15 Sunday

As is usual on a Sunday night, I bumped into Keith and we discussed our respective theatrical experiences of the weekend, his being *The Marriage Of Figaro* at the Theatre Royal, while mine was *Tarzan On Ice* at the Arena. It seems to me that he had chosen unwisely, as despite the title, it was not the show where the fellow sings 'Figaro! Figaro! Figaro! Figaro! Fiiiiigaro!!!' which seems a bit of a swizz to me.

The production that Bethan and I watched came complete with the requisite Tarzan, Jane and some classic Phil Collins tracks. Tarzan 1 Mozart 0. And so to bed.

October 16 Monday

Discussions took place this morning to decide upon preventative measures in the aftermath of Saturday's floodlight fire. One suggestion was to place a fire extinguisher adjacent to each floodlight. My response to this was that we should make very sure that they were securely fastened because if one of them should fall from the roof and clonk a Premier League footballer on the bonce it could conceivably leave us in a bit of a pickle.

The financial consequences of such an accident do not bear thinking about. We would however be guaranteed a 'What happened next?' spot on *A Question of Sport*, but this should not be our first consideration.

October 17 Tuesday

I got home late tonight, as there was a Roker Liaison Group meeting, which is an assembly between some supporters' representatives, influential people from the club and me. The provision of egg mayonnaise sandwiches was enough to secure my presence.

The Chairman opened the meeting with the highest placed items on the agenda, such as the annual pre-tax profits, transfer activity and the forthcoming academy project. Meanwhile, I was not exactly pivotal to the proceedings, even if I did emerge as top sandwich eater.

Yet I did fleetingly come into my own when we arrived at item ten, long after the Chairman had gone for his bus. This was the issue of some graffiti on a bog wall. My answer was full yet very concise as all of the good sandwiches had gone by then.

October 18 Wednesday

We all arrived at work early in order to check the generators after Saturday's near miss. But it was not all bad news, as the club was obliged to pay for sausage sandwiches from Sizzlers. The City does not know about this.

October 19 Thursday

The Sunderland AFC Sports Bar quiz has now reached the giddy heights of 12 whole teams. The snowball question was for 60 quid and even the daftest teams had a stab at 'In which country is the town of Banana?' One particularly dim group was first to race up to me with their three guesses, eager to know if any of Africa, the USSR or Scandinavia was to be their passage to riches.

It was not easy for me to break it to them that none of their offerings were actually countries and that their chances of actually winning were exactly the same as if they had not entered, but they did have five minutes of excitement. Incidentally, the answer was Zaire.

October 20 Friday

This is not just any job that I do. Today I was walking out of the tunnel with another ashes scattering party, and in doing so had to walk past a bloke that I recognised from the Ivy House posing with his new wife for wedding photographs. I just thought I would mention it.

October 22 Sunday

We watched Sunderland's game at Aston Villa in the upstairs living room at the Ivy House. The game was all but devoid of any notable incident until Liz removed a table lamp from the top of the television set, upon which, Kevin Phillips battered a shot against the Villa crossbar. There seemed to be an obvious and direct correlation between the two events, so we set about rearranging the whole of the furniture in the hope of securing all three points.

In the end all we could manage was a goalless draw, so in my personal experience the merits of feng shui are highly dubious.

October 25 Wednesday

I have a few days off, money, a car and an extravagant imagination, so we have all gone to Kilmarnock.

October 26 Thursday

This afternoon, we made the short pilgrimage to Rugby Park, where we invested in a bottle of Killie Beer and watched the lads in training prior to their undoubted victory over Rangers this coming weekend. The former Sunderland player, Ally McCoist, did not bother to turn up, the rumour among the locals being that he had gone for a manicure as he is on television more often than he is on a football pitch these days. Actually he is on television more often than the news these days.

October 29 Sunday

Sunderland beat Coventry City 1-0 this afternoon thanks in no small part to some interesting decisions by the referee. Gordon Strachan was keen to discuss these issues with him as he scampered down the tunnel at full-time. I must say Mr. Strachan's much-vaunted sense of humour seemed to have let him down at this point. I, on the other hand, was giggling uncontrollably.

October 31 Tuesday

It's official. Tonight's 2-1 win in the Worthington Cup means that Sunderland are even better than Bristol Rovers.

November 2 Thursday

After a frankly dismal Sunderland AFC Sports Bar quiz, I shuffled off up the stairs to the Director's Suite to attend the staff Hallowe'en party. In the absence of cocaine, I took with me this evening's picture quiz, something that seemed to intrigue Bobby Saxton.

He agonised long over number 12, which happened to be Keith Chegwin, before deciding upon the answer of, 'Oh yeah. It's er . . . the lad off the telly . . . yeah.'

I told him that what he was saying was correct as far as it went, but before I could press him for a name he had walked off towards the bar with a fist clenched to signify success. Strictly speaking, he had not done enough to ensure a point but I let it pass.

November 4 Saturday

Under the current climatic conditions, it is obvious that only the hardiest of stalwarts would have made the journey to Tottenham today, which would seem to exclude the likes of me.

The flooding continues across the country so rail travellers could possibly alight at Stevenage, then complete the journey to King's Cross by hovercraft. One wonders what type of biblical scourge will be the next for us to endure. It was not too long ago that we had a drought, although locusts are unlikely to be next up as they would drown at present. Losing 2-1 to Spurs is enough affliction to be going on with.

November 7 Tuesday

Rivers around the country are continuing to rise and burst their banks causing devastation and chaos, but we in Sunderland are unaffected by this, so sod 'em.

A perpetual source of intrigue in all of this is that no news item on the subject is complete without footage of a cyclist making a tortuous journey up a High Street in four feet of water. Call me an old quitter if you will, but when it starts sloshing around the handlebars then surely the best available option is to dismount and go to the pub in a kayak.

There is no chance of small children being swept away, but there's fun to be had by telling Bethan the exact opposite.

November 8 Wednesday

As the weather becomes dafter by the day, it was time for Radio Five Live to hold a debate on the consequences of global warming upon the climate, and who better to contribute than a procession of old people who think that the greenhouse effect will simply mean better tomatoes.

One old boy, who was adamant that no one needs to change their ways, came up with the robust but perplexing line of defence of 'What about the volcanoes? Eh?' as he seemed to want them to be banned because of all the stuff that they expel into the atmosphere. Which I suppose is a reasonable standpoint if you are a old loony.

November 9 Thursday

It was back to the crazy thrills and spills of the Sunderland AFC Sports Bar quiz. Writing this week's current affairs round was no easy feat as there has been little aside of elections and floods in the news this week. I was sitting at home desperately scouring for questions when I discovered that the bloke who organises Miss World had died and that the Queen Mother had fallen down a flight of stairs. What a stroke of luck.

My best question, apart from those two, concerned Hartlepool United's mascot, H'Angus The Monkey (good grief). He has been suspended from duty for making lewd and suggestive gestures at a recent game. This really was scraping the barrel and proves that *The Times* is not the organ of gravitas it once was.

November 10 Fridday

This morning I was called upon to conduct an ashes scattering in the stadium. This is a regular occurrence, but no one told me that today I would have to meet and greet the Beverley Hillbillies.

This vast tribe of the shabbiest most boorish mourners I have yet to meet, when not swearing down mobile phones, were arguing with each other as to who would be the first to sprinkle some ashes. This went on for some time and at some volume until a small and previously anonymous little woman chimed in softly with, 'Well he *was* my husband.'

I mused silently to myself that the bloke in the urn was probably glad to be there.

November 11 Saturday

Glen Hoddle's Southampton came up today and gained a 2-2 draw. They should really have won the game, but missed a sitter that had to be seen to be believed, then laughed at. The bloke who missed, someone called Tessem, must have done something greatly reprehensible in a past life.

November 17 Friday

The stadium was a hive of activity all day as the big screens went up again. We play Newcastle at the Temple Of Doom again tomorrow. I have not eaten since Thursday morning.

November 18 Saturday

Although I watched this afternoon's beamback on my own in a darkened room, this, along with my abstention from food for 48 hours, was not due in any way to worry. Oh no. Worry is a wasted emotion, especially in the light of Sunderland beating Newcastle at St. James' for only the second time in the last two seasons there. I apologise if this sounds a little triumphal, as it was intended to sound completely, utterly and wholeheartedly triumphal.

Between the hours of about 5.00pm and 3.00am, the ambience of the City of Sunderland bore a resemblance to nothing less than VE Day, but with better songs. The unfamiliar chanting of 'Shearer! Shearer!' after the lad's tragic penalty miss was simply childish, but what the hell, I had a very happy childhood. There is another long day of gloating ahead of us tomorrow too.

221

November 19 Sunday

Got up. Had a gloat. Breakfast. More gloating. Read the match report in every single available newspaper, which cost me a fortune, and then I settled down for a relaxing gloat.

Liz, Bethan and I then went through to Eldon Square for the first time in an immeasurable period of time to facilitate my relentless swanning around in a Sunderland shirt before large portions of the populace of Newcastle. The only item we bought was the Baha Men's anthemic masterpiece, *Who Let The Dogs Out?*. I could have bought it round the corner from our house without travelling 13 miles, but you don't get into the Gloating Premier League without putting a bit of effort into it.

I gave myself a break from all of this gloating upon my return home by watching a video of yesterday's game.

November 20 Monday

In common with all civilised people, I was pretty keen to stride into work this morning. There was an e-mail waiting for me that showed Niall Quinn's winning goal on Saturday, but what I did not realise was that this seven seconds of footage was the equivalent of about a thousand regular e-mails. Hence, when I sent it on to another 30 people around the administration building, who then each sent it on to another five people each externally, there were apparently some problems with the system.

At least, this is the explanation that Graham from I.T. gave us when he blocked it from being sent out any more. It is, however, worth noting that Graham is a henchman of the hopeless, an aficionado of the laughable, a foot soldier of the pitiful, a Mag.

November 23 Thursday

This evening's Sunderland AFC Sports Bar quiz was mindful of what people like and of the spirit of the times. Well, the spirit of this week anyway. As quiz master, I surpassed my own already impressive personal best for the number of times that I mentioned the score of Saturday's match. Such was the appeal of this disorderly gloatathon, we could conceivably have had the proceedings sponsored to raise a few quid for charity.

Team nine won, but only because of the extra points they attained for the most imaginative abuse of a third rate football team.

November 24 Friday

It is Friday now, and yes, if anyone is interested, we are still crowing about that game.

November 25 Saturday

Sunderland won another away game, 1-0. But it is fair to say that it was not the auspicious and ecstatic occasion of seven days ago, especially coming against a club as inoffensive as Charlton Athletic.

Some dreary old sod in The Borough tonight tried to persuade me otherwise. 'You only got three points last week as well you know. It doesn't matter who you beat really as long as you do. A place for everything and everything in its place. Ow! Stop hitting me.'

He finally paid the price for not realising that football is a mere fraction of itself without petty hatred and inveterate gloating.

November 28 Tuesday

Our Worthington Cup game with Manchester United this evening ended in a 2-1 win for us, a most welcome piece of news as absolutely nothing else went right. There was another fire in one of the floodlights, followed by a deluge of water from a toilet into the executive box below and general disquiet in the Directors' Suite over the lack of central heating.

All of these afflictions were quite biblical, except for that last one about the Directors' Suite, which was not the sort of thing that Moses would have landed the Egyptians with. They got off lightly if you ask me, a few locusts are nothing compared to the state of Box Eleven tonight.

In the game itself, Dwight Yorke was sent off after almost removing the kneecap of Emerson Thome. After he had been changed, he came back up the tunnel and asked me how bad it had looked on the action replay. I thought it best to give a succinct reply by making an 'O' shape with my mouth. I did not want to upset him because I wanted to hear all about Jordan. Besides, Alex Ferguson said that the referee was to blame.

December 1 Friday

At this afternoon's Stadium And Events meeting, I actually had something to contribute. Oh yes. At the urging of our electrician Mark, I raised the issue with our PR department of him not being given due credit for tackling Tuesday evening's floodlight fire, although I probably overdid it with my description of him risking life and hairstyle to save some recently orphaned kittens from the blaze, and likening his role to that of Paul Newman in *The Towering Inferno.*

Other prominently noted minutes from this meeting concerned fans of Monday's opponents Everton, who are known around the country for stealing drinks from stadium bars and attempting to gain entry with unwarranted concession tickets. This is not a joke about thieving Scousers, which is a pity because as I have already noted in this diary, they have a great sense of humour.

December 4 Monday

Tonight we managed to cope with Everton and their supporters, described in the minutes of our Friday meeting as 'noted for petty theft'. I would be the first to dispel this offensive stereotyping of Scousers if they would only stop nicking things. In the event, all concerned were a credit to Everton Football Club, as not only were all of the toilet roll dispensers left intact, but they also presented us with three points without putting up as much as an argument or a 'by the way'.

December 5 Tuesday

Bethan and I have travelled down to Oxford to see my new nephew and a splendid chap he is too. The journey down was a smidgen dull though, but was enlivened for Bethan by three hours worth of S Club Seven tapes and for me by the occasional amusing road sign. The sign for the Royal Armouries Museum in Leeds is forever good for a giggle as the symbol thereon never fails to put one in mind of a lady's internal reproductive organs. And who could fail to titter at the sign in Northamptonshire, which reads 'Welcome to Silverstone – please drive carefully'.

Come to think of it, the whole journey was excruciating from start to finish.

December 6 Wednesday

Bethan and I had the afternoon to ourselves in Oxford and were burdened with a wide choice of activities. As everyone knows, it is an internationally famed seat of learning, the alma mater of many literary and scientific luminaries, containing many sites of historical importance. In the end, we decided to see Pizza Hut again.

December 9 Saturday

The complete absence of panache that accompanied Sunderland's undeserved 1-0 win over Middlesbrough this afternoon was somehow in-keeping with the opposition's home town.

It is true that Captain James Cook originally hailed from there. While this is a source of justifiable local pride, I should caveat this by pointing out that Captain Cook is famous for his epic voyages and discoveries of foreign lands. In other words, his celebrity stems from the fact that he spent most of his life trying to get as far away from Middlesbrough as possible.

December 11 Monday

Usually I am too much of a towering intellectual to take any notice of tawdry downmarket tabloid newspapers, but as there was a picture of me in one of them today I made an exception. Your number one, first with the facts, soaraway *Sun*, printed a photograph taken on Saturday afternoon, which showed me at the tunnel in between Terry Venables and Brian

Robson, in what appeared to be a top level football symposium. This centre spread hunk pageant should make me a celebrity around the Middlesbrough area, which should last until they read what I wrote on Saturday.

Tel and Bri have yet to contact me on the matter.

December 12 Tuesday

I dashed home from work, leapt athletically into the shower then wolfed down my tea. This was all done with the intention of getting down to the pub to watch Sunderland at Crystal Palace. However, the game was postponed at the last minute, so we had to be content with a pub quiz. Pah!

This was all very frustrating and we all felt rather dejected and disappointed. But then I was reminded of people like Taff and Jim Fox who had actually travelled to London to see the match, thereby making a completely pointless 600 mile round trip. Thoughts of these poor unfortunates made me feel less unhappy and from there it was only a small step to hearty derisory laughter.

December 14 Thursday

Tonight saw our staff Christmas party and for the second year running I had my camera with me, but everyone is wise to me by now. What I do is stick the photographs into our own version of *Hello! Magazine* in which I pretend, for instance, that Kerry is Esther Rantzen and that Ronnie the plumber is Robbie Williams, so that everyone gets a cheap laugh.

Peter Reid was in attendance and for some reason was eager to have his picture taken with me. Yes me. This snap is yet to be developed, but the caption for it has already been worked out. 'A LEADING FIGURE IN FOOTBALL has a drink with Peter Reid', should just about satiate my massive ego, if not get me the sack.

December 16 Saturday

Sunderland lost away from home today, but as it was at Leeds United, noted for fair play, friendliness and always wanting the better team to win, we do not mind too much.

This splendid occasion and festival of decency and loveliness was further enhanced by the fact that their first goal was put away by the delightful and charismatic Lee Bowyer. Everyone in the pub tonight was echoing these sentiments. Surely this fine upstanding young man is not about to be given a custodial sentence. It is not as though anyone is a hundred per cent dead because of him.

December 18 Monday

I was at work today for the first time since the Christmas party on Thursday night and found Ronnie the plumber still smarting from his

225

encounter with Peter Reid. It all stems back to the Hallowe'en party when Ronnie, bloated with lager, exhorted Peter on team selections, transfer activities and tactics.

Reidy had obviously resented having his considerable ear bent, so on Thursday, before he had even had a drink, he marched straight up to Ronnie and announced, 'Before we go any further. I'M picking the fucking team on Saturday!'

Ronnie was forlorn, but there may just have been a trace of Schadenfreude about Ronnie in the wake of our 2-0 defeat.

December 19 Tuesday

For the second time in a week, we moseyed on down to the Lansdowne in the hope of seeing Sunderland play Crystal Palace in the Worthington Cup. This week it went ahead. Unfortunately. We went into the game as favourites for once, but still managed to lose 2-1. This seemed like a swizz to me and we had intended to ring Mr. Worthington to get to the bottom of it, but the barmaid assured us that everything was in order. In pique, we went to the Ivy House in a taxi, but the result was no better in there.

Gerard Callaghan was in, wetting the head of his new son. This was all very nice, but in all honesty not as good as a place in the semi-finals would have been.

December 22 Friday

Someone at the club with a fanatical interest in inconvenience decided to have the Annual General Meeting at the stadium today, the day before a home game.

Peter Reid came over to chat with the chaps, possibly because he is not all that comfortable in the company of City financier types, but more likely because we were standing next to the bacon rolls. In the course of our platitudes, I pointed out that the AGM was usually quite a tedious affair involving unintelligible financial jargon, with people only understanding the sections in which football is discussed, to which Mr. Reid made the faintly disturbing quip of 'And that's when I'm done for', except that being Peter Reid, he did not actually use the expression 'done for'.

December 23 Saturday

Sunderland 1 Manchester City 0. Merry Christmas and good will to all men, except for the one who was copiously sick near to Access Eleven this afternoon.

December 26 Tuesday

With there being nothing better to do on Boxing Day, we popped down to Bradford for the match. When we arrived there we asked some old boy the way to the New Beehive and were given the worst directions I have ever heard, which were; 'What a great player that Len Shackleton was, I remember when he left Park Avenue . . . ' and so on, which was vague to say the least.

Eventually we watched a thumpingly fine 4-1 win, complete with a hat-trick for Kevin Phillips and Elvis Presley running on to the pitch in his traditional rhinestone jumpsuit to congratulate him. This was Bethan's first away game and it will be a hard lesson for her to learn that they are not all like this.

December 30 Saturday

If Sunderland's mission for this season was to irritate Arsenal, then we have completed this task with some aplomb. Niall Quinn scored the only goal of the game with virtually our only touch of the ball in the first game of the season. Today they only managed to put away two of the 98 chances they created in the first half, and this meant that the game was to end somehow in a 2-2 draw. So we came away from Highbury with a point and, frankly, a fit of the giggles.

2001

January 1 Monday

A New Year's Day home fixture with Ipswich Town deprived me of the opportunity to become obnoxiously drunk last night and then stay in bed until about tea time. *Superman II* was also rendered out of the question along with *Animals Do The Funniest Things* and *World's Strongest Man*. Bah!

Denial of this cultural extravaganza notwithstanding, it was a productive afternoon with Sunderland winning 4-1 to go jointly second in the league, on purpose too. But the main advantage to having to work on New Year's Day is that something has actually happened on this date this year. Previous diaries reveal that my talent for protracted descriptions of sitting on my fat arse and eating biscuits has been stretched well beyond what is usually thought possible.

January 2 Tuesday

After an entire day at work yesterday, I thought it was prudent to take the next couple of days off. I had several pressing engagements to attend to, but they all had to be postponed on account of the amount of Quality Street still in my possession. Why, I barely had time to watch *Countdown*.

January 4 Thursday

After the thrill seeking escapades of the previous two days, it was something of a respite to go back to work. The pinnacle of today was the Stadium And Events meeting, in which we discuss whatever Saturday's game might throw at us. As we shall be playing Crystal Palace in the FA Cup, the short answer was 'Very little.'

Nevertheless, there was a murmur of excitement in the room when it was announced that Sweet Female Attitude were to perform a couple of numbers before the game, and a murmur it remained as most persons present had never heard of them. Sadly, I was among this number, but at least I am ahead of John Davidson who has not heard of any artists to perform in the stadium since the inaugural performance by Status Quo.

SFA (as we fans call them) consist of just two teenage girls, but there was fun to be had by telling Adrian the groundsman that they are a marching band.

January 5 Friday

The biggest news at work today concerned Helen Smith who announced that she is soon to leave. She is taking up a position in Glasgow as an ice cream salesman or a hod carrier or something. The daft bitch. I shall miss her, probably quite narrowly with a glass ashtray.

News of a far lesser eminence is that Bobby Robson is to attend the match tomorrow. For some reason, we have decided to give him a rather plush seat in the Directors box. Pah! I say, get him in the South-West Corner with the lads! He would find it far easier to savour the atmosphere and he could buy a round of pies with his money.

January 6 Saturday

I was asked by Geordie Barker to collect autographs in the tunnel at the match today. I hate doing this as I am so arrogant that I think that people should be asking me, but as they were for his cute nine year old daughter, Stella, I could not very well refuse.

The game itself was a 0-0 draw with Crystal Palace, the mesmerizing sort of affair that only the white heat of the FA Cup can produce. There were two sendings off, the second of which was for Sunderland when Stanislav Varga was dismissed for a professional foul. As he trudged miserably past me, it occurred to me that he would be at a loose end for the remainder of the afternoon. Yet all things considered, it was probably wise of me not to ask him for his autograph at that particular moment in time, less still to see if he would give the lads a hand with a shutter jam at kiosk 18.

Ah well. We are still unbeaten this century.

January 7 Sunday

As usual, there were few reasons to get out of bed on a Sunday; in fact I only did so because of Liz's unreasonable refusal to bring me Sunday lunch in bed since I spilled cabbage on the duvet that time.

After watching Newcastle's turgid draw with Aston Villa, it was time for the FA Cup fourth round draw. I was hoping that Sunderland would land an away tie with someone hopeless, so that we could progress to the fifth round easily without me having to do any work, which made a possible game at Kingstonian a most appealing proposition.

Ipswich at home. Tch! Perhaps Crystal Palace will spare us the chore by doing the decent thing on Wednesday week.

I cheered myself up by annihilating Bethan at Buckaroo then going to the Ivy House to boast about it. And so to bed.

January 8 Monday

The never ceasing roller coaster of events embarked upon by those of us who work for this leading Premiership club just kept on moving today. The sandwich shop over the road to us has introduced a whole new range of fillings, the pick of which is Mexican chicken. I knew it was Mexican because I saw it wearing a sombrero on the way in (boom! boom!).

229

Sizzlers are to be congratulated for this bold gastronomic step forward. As far as I am concerned, this century is going from strength to strength.

January 11 Thursday

The Sunderland AFC Sports Bar quiz was this evening infiltrated by a Newcastle United supporter. He had employed some elaborate subterfuge to disguise this fact, namely, not wearing a black and white striped shirt and speaking English, but his companion offered me a hint of this by strolling up to me and saying, 'See him! He's a Mag you know!'

I then gave the rest of the room a clue by announcing his Magness over the microphone.

This resulted in the other quizzers giving a loud, vein-necked rendition of 'We beat the Scum 2-1!' to the tune of *Blue Moon*.

When it died down, he replied in the same melody that 'You've only got one song!' This was meat and drink to me, because although his chanted comment was not without foundation, I pointed out to him, with the same tune being given yet another airing, that 'We only NEED one song!'

He had a stream of ripostes to follow up with, which may have been the finest witticisms ever tailored by the human mind, but they were never going to be of any avail as I had a whacking great PA system on my side and was therefore guaranteed victory in any slanging match, probably by two slangs to one. Ha!

January 12 Friday

The first task of the day at the stadium was rather a jolly affair as far as ashes scatterings go. The bereaved were quite taken with our new method of bunging the remains in a hole in the ground then burying them instead of the previous method of making a grubby mess on the pitch.

There was a good deal of death on the agenda today. Soon after the scattering I went to the Sports Bar kitchen where there was lobster on the menu. Young Kelly-Ann who works there was most upset at the prospect of these two live crustaceans meeting their end by being plunged alive into boiling water. In fact she was in tears and refused to speak to the chef who was only doing his job.

There was widespread amusement at this display of feminine sensitivity. Even the lobsters seemed to be having a laugh. They were certainly making some sort of noise back in the pot anyway.

Later this afternoon, Helen Smith had her leaving presentation. She was well thought of at the club, but we gave her some Ikea vouchers despite this.

Then there was another ashes scattering and a pretty awful one at that, although as a rule they not usually noted for high jinks and tomfoolery. There are another two lined up for Monday. I tell you, we're ashes scattering MAD round here.

230

January 13 Saturday

Sunderland's game was in theory quite prominent in today's news. We won 2-0 at West Ham United to establish second position in the league, but let us not flatter ourselves that we are newsworthy for any other reason than the new England manager attending the game.

It is difficult to ignore a team that is doing as well as we are at present, but clearly not impossible. The analysis on *Match Of The Day* was entirely concerned with West Ham's Joe Cole, whose contribution to his side losing at home was apparently only surpassed by his boyish charm, impeccable table manners and kindness to animals, so pick him Sven!

In terms of comment of what actually happened in the world of football today, the programme did not have very much to offer. I shall ask one of the lads to fax them with some information on Monday morning.

January 14 Sunday

As there only seemed to be my friends and me who realised yesterday that Sunderland are second in the league, I must confess that I woke up this morning in something of a panic. Was it really true? And if not, exactly how much did I have to drink last night?

The Sunday papers had good news and bad news for us. The good news is that we really are second in the league, the bad news is that we are scum and riff-raff, completely devoid of talent and only there by default.

Undeterred by the bad news, the Ivy House was still in a buoyant mood this evening. The general conversation was memorable, if severely limited. In fact, all that anyone bothered to say to each other was, 'Ha! We're second!'

Pithy, articulate, and above all, correct.

January 16 Tuesday

These must be tough times to work in Sunderland AFC's PR department. At around half past seven this evening, Lesley Callaghan rang me at home. She was still at work and making assiduous efforts to coax people into being filmed for Sky Television, to say on camera how wonderful, groovy, super-duper and tops it is to watch our football team at the Stadium of Light. Come to think of it, her appeal must have been tinged with desperation, as she was keen to use Liz, Bethan and me. We have agreed and are to be filmed tomorrow afternoon, although so far only Bethan has displayed any enthusiasm for the project.

January 17 Wednesday

The working day began with me sending out the usual juvenile e-mail to publicise tomorrow night's Sports Bar quiz. This week it said that anyone not attending ran the risk of all of their teeth dropping out over the course of the next 60 years. I thought this was rather amusing, but the Football In

The Community office replied by saying that my teeth would come out much sooner that that if I didn't find someone to attend to their squeaking door.

It has been pointed out to them that the correct procedure to have used would have been to complete a work request form, for us to properly register and prioritise, and not to simply issue a gangland threat. Mind you, it has been sorted now.

Sunderland's replay with Crystal Palace took place tonight and we have finally beaten them. The game was not on Sky as they had opted for Newcastle's latest defeat at Aston Villa, so in the Ivy House tonight I had to simultaneously watch that, whilst listening to our game on headphones and competing in a pop quiz. This is actually more difficult than it sounds and is why we only came fifth. We are not ignorant. Oh no.

January 18 Thursday

I was struggling to think of ten current affairs questions for tonight's Sunderland AFC Sports bar quiz, but at the last minute I heard about a sex shop owner in York who had been prosecuted under the Trade Descriptions Act 1968 and 1972 because the films he was selling did not contain the requisite amount of smut. What a great question this made. I would still like to know who first raised the complaint and how he worded it. The bloke in the dock claimed that he had never checked the contents of the videos. Presumably he is not the type of person who watches this sort of thing.

The quiz itself went quite well. One question asked whom an organisation called the Sons Of The Desert was set up in honour of. The correct answer was Laurel and Hardy, but the best answer that I came across, Sadam Hussein, was worth the Gavin McCann key ring that I gave them for the sheer joy of ignorance that it brought.

January 20 Saturday

Tonka and I did the decent thing today and popped down to the Victoria Ground to watch Hartlepool United sloshing about in mud in the hope of beating Carlisle United while they were at it. They didn't, it was a 2-2 draw. But this disappointment was tempered by the fact that we managed to buy a pie each this time, having previously missed out due to popular demand. Hartlepool's pies have received much favourable publicity in recent months and I must say that I can only concur.

On a less interesting note, today saw the inauguration of President Bush; something that I am personally glad has finally happened, as it means that we are now in the final 1,460 days of his term in office.

January 21 Sunday

Sven-Goran Eriksson was at the Stadium of Light for the first time today, but will probably never know how close he came to being clonked around the left ear by some stepladders that John Mallan was carrying. Mind you, neither will John, although plenty of bystanders observed the near miss and made a noise similar to the crowd reaction when somebody hits the post.

Not that anything approaching this level of interest occurred during the game itself. The amount of entertainment to be derived from Sunderland 0 Bradford City 0 was every bit as much as would be expected. The lack of glamour that the media are keen to associate with Sunderland was sadly underlined further after the game when our Danish international goalkeeper gave an interview to a journalist while clutching a 'I Love Copenhagen Airport' carrier bag. Fortunately it was for radio.

January 25 Thursday

It is fair to say that the Sunderland AFC Sports Bar quiz has not gone into popularity orbit in the way that had been hoped. Tonight we had five entire teams, which meant about 26 people in there to swell the coffers. The pitiful nature of the number of entrants was complemented by some of the answers. While I do not expect every man, woman and child to know who succeeded Oliver Cromwell as Lord Protector in 1658, I at least expect a better stab at the answer than team four's Sir Lancelot.

A good tip when making a wild and hopeful swipe at a historical question is to plump for someone who actually existed. That said, team three's offering of Abraham Lincoln was hardly any better.

January 27 Saturday

It was FA Cup fourth round day and our opponents, Ipswich Town, confirmed their status as the nicest club in football. Their supporters were officially described as 'nice' in the minutes of last Thursday's Stadium and Events meeting, and the number of arrests and ejections of their fans from their previous visit here on New Year's Day totalled exactly zero. One of them did tut and raise his eyebrows at kiosk staff when he was told that there was no mayonnaise left, but we have since received a letter of apology.

This genial benevolence extends to their coaching and playing staff. Our cleaners went into the visitors dressing room after Ipswich had left and found that their job had already been done for them. Most teams do not manage to pull the plugs out of the baths or even flush the lavs. They lost 1-0 too!

In his post-match interview, their manager, George Burley, said that even though he was disappointed to see his side eliminated from the competition, he did not really mind. How nice.

January 28 Sunday

West Ham pulled off a surprise in the Cup this afternoon when they went to Old Trafford and beat Manchester United. In the fifth round draw that immediately followed, they drew Sunderland away, which is frustrating for us, as we would have undoubtedly stuffed Man. Utd, but are now left with a tricky tie. Bah!

January 31 Wednesday

There was an inordinate number of hangers-on and lickspittles attaching themselves to the stadium today. The reason was that Manchester United were in town again, so we all had to wash behind our ears and stand to attention.

The ensuing 1-0 defeat was not without controversy, the goal being highly dubious. Perhaps in the years to come we shall see the humorous side of this, but this is most definitely not the case at the time of writing. Three sendings off and a streaker were the games other talking points, all of which were dubious for different reasons. The referee appeared to be the pivotal member in a sub-standard vaudeville skit.

I was musing on all of this in the lift after the game when in stepped none other than Sir Bobby Charlton. It is always difficult to know what to say in a lift to anyone, so Bob, as I now call him, broke the ice by asking what I had thought of the referee. Not wishing to say 'crap' before a Knight of the Realm, I confined my response to a polite euphemism about having seen better.

'Seen better?' replied the great one, 'he was absolute shite!'

So we can add forthrightness and eloquence to his already long list of qualities.

The good news is that Roy Keane is shorter than me.

February 1 Thursday

There was much uncomplimentary discussion at work today about last night's streaker. It is agreed that we would have won easily but for her flabby intervention.

The background to her performance was unfolded in this evening's *Echo* by their crime reporter, who could really do with a spate of juicy murders to sink his teeth into if this is all he has to keep him occupied. Anyway, this woman was sadly misled into believing that she was undertaking a highly original form of publicity seeking, but she is not the first and is probably not even among the first couple of thousand. There have also been streakers at rugby, cricket, snooker, darts and even bowls. Round the world yachting seems to be the only sport that is immune.

Suffice to say that she is unlikely to land a record deal in the aftermath of her antics, so why did she do it? According to the *Echo* she is not just a common or garden show off. Oh no. Apparently she raised a staggering £50 for charity, which might be put into perspective when she goes to court next week and is fined £60.

234

February 2 Friday

As I sat at my desk this afternoon, the boss ghosted in behind me and politely mentioned that we should have a chat. I knew immediately that this meant bad news because he had an avuncular hand on my shoulder as he said it.

The chat was a one-sided affair, in effect a carefully worded speech to inform me of the 'risk of redundancy' before I was handed a letter saying much the same thing. The words 'creek' and 'shit' were not immediately apparent on the page, but were somehow still discernible. I have, however, been invited to apply for three new positions at the club, but I may as well apply to be Dalai Lama while I am at it as I stand a roughly equal chance of becoming spiritual leader of Tibet. I may have to flog this diary.

February 3 Saturday

Ah yes. A jaunty excursion to Derby County to watch a moribund 1-0 defeat. There is nothing quite like it if one discounts past visits to Leicester, Coventry, Tottenham, Wimbledon . . .

Bethan was with us today and she thoroughly enjoyed the first 15 minutes as that is how long it took her to eat her chips, but her interest clearly waned from that moment on and rightly so.

As the weekend was plodded through with the extra ingredient of impending unemployment, it was quite impossible for Liz and me to find a bar that would be open late enough, although common gluttony also played a part in this.

February 5 Monday

I was despatched to Darras Hall this morning to see how Stefan Schwarz's kitchen repairs are progressing. It seems that Mrs. Schwarz set fire to it through the medium of a chip pan.

While in Darras Hall, I found that it has such nice residents that the whole estate would not be out of place in Ipswich. In one sandwich shop where I ordered a cup of tea to take away, the woman returned from the back of the premises with the demeanour of surgeon leaving the theatre after losing a patient who had everything to live for. This was reflected in the gravity of her tone as she grimly informed me, 'I'm afraid there aren't any lids for the cups.'

This was when my natural survival instincts came to the fore as I managed to negotiate the awkward journey back to the van by walking slightly slower than I would have done normally.

Sadly, I am more used to customer service being, 'What do you want? There you are! Piss off!'

February 6 Tuesday

During the morning, I made the effort to be civil to one of my colleagues, which is worth noting in itself. I passed Gail from the ticket office and delivered a cheery and breezy 'Yo bitch!', which for some reason she took exception to. I explained that this was a perfectly convivial and acceptable greeting in the 'hood, but she was having none of it. I don't know why I bother.

I was instead going to give her a hearty slap between the shoulder blades, but then thought better of it. Actually, bearing in mind that she was walking down a flight of stairs and carrying a tray that was heavily laden with cups of hot tea, I think my restraint was nothing short of gentlemanly altruism.

February 7 Wednesday

I had another interview regarding my future or otherwise with Sunderland AFC. So far the smart money has gone mainly on the otherwise. I have applied for the new position of Facilities Manager and my application is rich in comic potential.

Intended as a forum to establish something positive for me, it was more of an exercise in straw clutching for all concerned. I was asked if there was anything I am particularly good at. After an uncomfortably long pause to think, I said that I was a capable writer, despite the overwhelming evidence to the contrary in these diaries. They humoured me by saying that this was 'interesting' but it probably isn't, unless I have failed to notice a vacancy for a club novelist.

February 8 Thursday

The astounding standard of ignorance displayed by certain teams in the Sunderland AFC Sports Bar quiz (Thursdays 8.30pm, top prizes galore, arrive early to avoid disappointment) continues all at once to stun, amuse and elicit pity. This evening's star dumb-arse wrong answer was a real standout. The question was 'Which famous Australian landmark was built in 1973?' The answer is Sydney Opera House, but look away now for a minute and see if you can guess what team eight put.

That's right. They put down Ayer's Rock, which to be fair was only built a couple of million years before 1973.

February 9 Friday

Davie Smith is up from London for the Liverpool game. For the occasion, he had come up with a song about Alan Shearer, Bobby Robson and Mags in general to the tune of the verses of *Bread Of Heaven* (not the chorus, that would be twee), but there was quite an involved aesthetic debate in the Ivy House over what the last line should be.

As Davie had thought of all of the song apart from this elusive final line, it was he who was leading the creative process and I could easily imagine him, à la Stephen Sondheim, tie loosened and sweating over a piano with the song sheets before him, a pencil behind his ear. Yet it was Taff who came up with the definitive dénouement amid much cheering, hand shaking and clinking of glasses. It was a privilege to be present at such a markedly salient cultural moment.

As a matter of interest, the last line that was agreed upon was 'And their dogs as well', so it is probably best left unrecorded as to how the rest of the song went.

February 10 Saturday

I still have a job for now, so today I was back down the players tunnel, earwigging the proceeding of the respective dugouts while we were playing Liverpool. This meant that we had to put up with Phil Thompson on the visitors bench, clinging jealously to his mantle of Most Biased Man In Football.

The game finished at 1-1, due in no small part to a refereeing display that can be most kindly described as imaginative. The Liverpool equaliser came from an incident about two metres outside of the Sunderland box, which culminated in the referee awarding a penalty by way of a reward for Gary McAllister gamely attempting to swallow dive into the South Stand from a distance of fully 60 paces.

A point salvaged for the reds then, but Mr. Thompson did not see things in this positive light as he bellowed, 'Your best man was wearing black out there!' to anyone with a Sunderland connection within earshot. Bemusing.

Other headline news emerged tonight when Taff was admonished by the barmaid in the Dun Cow for falling asleep again. It's all been happening today.

February 13 Tuesday

There was quite some controversy raging around the club today. A while ago, Ronnie the plumber installed a WC in the maintenance office, but after a couple of unpleasant incidents it was decided at a top level meeting that it would be used strictly on a number ones only basis.

However, it transpired today that this rule has been flagrantly and shamelessly disregarded. The first that I heard of this gross malefaction was over the walky-talky from Mark the electrician who did not think of this episode as in any way amusing. In fact, were it not for his Birmingham accent, his speech would have struck a chord with anyone who had also heard Chamberlain broadcasting his declaration of war with Germany.

'This is to anyone who can hear,' began the solemn disclosure. 'There are skid marks in the pan. Repeat. Skid marks in the pan. Over!'

Given the subject matter, I think he did very well to inject such gravitas.

February 17 Saturday

Today's FA Cup fifth round tie with West Ham United was a 12 noon kick-off for two reasons. The first was to accommodate Sky Television; the second was because there was not a more inconvenient time available to annoy travelling supporters.

A Sunderland game live on television is a virtually guaranteed non-event and so it proved with a 1-0 defeat to a slightly better side. There were not even any histrionics down the tunnel to liven up the early afternoon. I even contemplated spitting in Harry Redknapp's ear then blaming it on Peter Reid, simply to instigate a newsworthy altercation. I decided against it in the end, which was probably wise, although as with any missed opportunity there is always an element of regret attached. I shall always muse on the fact that had I delivered one of those good stringy efforts, I may have copped for Frank Lampard Snr. too with a decent following wind.

Plain disgusting, I know, but all part of a generally disappointing day.

February 18 Sunday

Gerard Callaghan was out and about this evening and is yet to get over the novelty of fatherhood. Nevertheless, he is still not enamoured of being made to push a pram around the streets of Sunderland, something that I find worthy of sneering. But he hit back by claiming that in the days when Bethan was of an age, he would wager that I had never been near a pram. This was, of course, a dirty lie. I did push a pram and can vividly remember the occasion. Admittedly it was filled with coal, but facts are facts.

February 19 Monday

There was a reserve game at the stadium tonight, which would not have instilled much enthusiasm had the opposition been provided by anyone other than Newcastle United. Happily, Sunderland won 3-1, a most welcome result, as we could not stand to lose to them in a reserve game EVER. The same applies to youth matches, women's matches, cricket, tug-of-war, billiards, chess, Monopoly, Twister and anything else except kebab eating.

Afterwards, I stepped into a lift already occupied by Bobby Robson, whose expression was as perturbed as mine was smug, but as it was a lift I made the usual polite but strained conversation with him.

'Who are you playing on Saturday?'

'Er . . . Manchester City at home. How about you lot?'

'Er . . . Leicester away. Tough one.'

My word. It seemed like an awful long time to go down two floors.

February 20 Tuesday

This afternoon we had a visit from Princess Anne who had evidently been given the royal short straw and dispatched to a boys club in

Southwick. The mayor seems to have diverted her visit to the stadium in a late bid to impress her.

There were only two types of reaction among club staff to this visit. One was, 'Ooh. Princess Anne.'

The other was to place a completely unnecessary expletive between the words 'Princess' and 'Anne'.

My big job for the day was to raise the flags and I was only allowed to do this as I wear a suit to work. The blue-collar members of staff were hidden away somewhere in a sluice cupboard and rightly so. We do not want her Royal Highness to leave Sunderland under the impression that there are people here who carry out manual labour.

February 24 Saturday

The lure of Sunderland's almost certain defeat at Leicester City this afternoon was matched only by that of sitting bare-arsed on a mound of rusty nails. The expected 2-0 reversal duly arrived, but at least those of us who opted to stay at home have so far been spared the nails.

February 25 Sunday

The only thing to happen today was that the great Australian batsman, Sir Donald Bradman, passed away. Of course this is bad news, but as he was 92 years old at least he has given us the opportunity to say that he had a good innings. No doubt I am the only person to think of this joke.

February 26 Monday

Foot and mouth disease is all la mode at the moment, with huge numbers of cattle being torched like a gigantic spit of kebab meat awaiting a 200 feet long piece of pitta bread.

As I nibbled at my roast buffalo luncheon, I set my mind to scientifically deal with this knotty agricultural problem and came up with an ideal solution, which is to let's just ignore it because it is probably a load of old tosh. I mean, when eating a carcass of any description, I for one always scrupulously avoid any feet or mouths that might be left, especially when there is still a scrumptious helping of offal to tuck into.

The only foods with no chance of making it onto the Gillan menu at present are whale, tiger, anaconda, Time Out bars and celery.

February 28 Wednesday

Interest was fixed firmly upon events at Villa Park this evening for England's first game with Mr. Eriksson. Spain were beaten 3-0 which, according to the excessively biased masses coalesced in the Ivy House, was due entirely to the contribution of Sunderland's own Gavin McCann who came on as substitute in the second half. Collective opinion was that Gavin's performance merited at least another 20 caps, a player of the month award, some Pyrex crockery and a Nobel Prize for something or other. I can only agree.

March 1 Thursday

The enormously popular Sunderland AFC Sports Bar quiz is no more. I was in the very act of printing off what would have been tonight's questions, when our Commercial Director, Mr. McDonnell, came into the office and announced that the bar was closing with immediate effect. Crumbs!

The midas touch I have had with pub quizzes down the years has spectacularly deserted me. Most of the other establishments in which I have plied this dubious trade still have a quiz today and all of them are at least open for business. I wonder if I can have anywhere else closed.

March 3 Saturday

There was no football today, which is always problematic when it comes to holding a conversation in the pub on an evening. Thus it was that our rather aimless discourse turned to the subject of popular music. The latest girly warblers to hit the big time are called Atomic Kitten and they currently top the charts with a ditty entitled *Whole Again*. This led to a tasteless comment from one of the more vernacular members of our company, and as it was a vulgar pun on the word 'whole' I have no intention of recording it here.

March 5 Monday

Sunderland versus Aston Villa was tonight's Sky game, and just the same as last season, John Gregory proved to have the strangest touchline behaviour of any football manager I have so far observed from close quarters. He talks to absolutely anyone during the game, the opposition bench, officials, stewards, ball boys and me all included.

At one stage, the Sunderland coach Adrian Heath took issue with the Villa bench when the ball landed at their feet. They were winning at the time and therefore in no mood to return it.

'Come on Inchy!' shouted back Mr. Gregory with a smirk. 'You'd do the same!' - a comment that caused further annoyance to Mr. Heath with its accuracy.

Shortly after our eventual equaliser, a nearby spectator urged Sunderland to press home their advantage as Villa were 'shitting themselves'. Unusually for a manager, Mr. Gregory turned to this punter to sagely agree. 'You're right mate,' he replied to the surprised fan. 'In fact we're worse than shitting ourselves.'

My contention that there was nothing worse than shitting yourselves, especially collectively, was glossed over.

Immediately after the final whistle, he rounded off the evening in fine style with some very amusing close range abuse of the officials. It is impossible not to like him.

March 7 Wednesday

I had to attend to another scattering of ashes today, so I later felt justified in having a jaunt to the Ivy House. This was due to neither grief nor crocodile tears, it is merely the way I am. I generally fancy going to the Ivy House after a scattering of ashes, a royal visit, a home game, a concert, my tea . . .

March 9 Friday

I conjured up yet another excuse to go to the training ground at the time they were serving lunches there, although checking for puddles was not one of my better ones. It was there that I chatted to my oldest and closest personal friend, Kevin Phillips. Kev began our conversation, having been inspired to do so by the amount of pasta I had managed to put on just the one plate.

'Are you hungry then?' asked Mr. Golden Boot of Europe.

'Pardon?'

'Are you hungry?'

'Er . . . yes.'

'I thought so.'

'Well, I didn't have much for breakfast.'

'Oh. I see.'

We were getting along famously and could have nattered like that for hours, but he had to go and clean his ears. Still, I have another dazzling celebrity anecdote to throw on the pile. I must remember to tell him that the weather is not too chilly for the time of year.

March 16 Friday

Liz, Bethan and I have come to London where tomorrow I shall watch Sunderland take potluck with Chelsea. About a mile north of Watford, Bethan was becoming unbearably bored, so we made a lame effort at entertaining her with a game of the never gripping 'I spy'. It was at this point that the car conked out. I rang the AA and gave them an extensive description of the mechanical problems involved. 'The car's conked out,' I told them.

The AA towed us to Redge's house in Kingston, but are unable to take us back to Sunderland on Monday, so we shall join the RAC in the morning. In the meantime, there is to be a complete ban on 'I spy' in the car.

March 17 Saturday

At Stamford Bridge this afternoon, Sunderland upset as many lazy journalists as Chelsea supporters by bopping them 4-2 and with quite some brio.

Redge excelled himself at the match. At first sight he is just another abusive and foul-mouthed football supporter, but closer inspection shows that he is a gifted linguist and therefore able to shower foul-mouthed abuse on the entire Chelsea squad. They would need to sign an Eskimo to escape him; even then he probably has a smattering.

After the game, a few of us skipped back to the pub for a drink and a gloat. It was in there that a Chelsea supporter whom I recognised from last season informed us that we 'Oughta git aht of 'ere, sam o' your boys 'ave bin a bih naw-ee 'dis arfernoon an' aar firm ain' 'appy.'

Obviously, even Redge had very little chance of understanding him, so we just nodded solemnly for a while then ordered some sandwiches.

Newcastle lost at home to Middlesbrough today, thus ensuring that tonight's *Match Of The Day* should clean up at the next BAFTAs, being particular favourites in the category of Biggest Hoot.

March 18 Sunday

We had to travel from London to Oxford for a christening by bus because of our continuing car trouble, a difficult journey made excruciating by having to carry bottles of champagne and a huge cake, as well as Bethan's singing. It was as well that the driver accepted Liz's cheque, as we had no money about our persons after yesterday's celebratory binge. The nearest bank to the bus station was the Bank Of England, which apparently does not have a cash point.

March 22 Thursday

The Mir space station is due to enter the Earth's atmosphere. It is supposedly going to land safely in the Pacific Ocean, yet this is not a complete certainty and there may yet be danger involved. We at the Sunderland AFC are not particularly concerned, as the chances of part of it hitting someone on the bonce as they nip out to Southwick Road for a paper are minimal.

However, the blokes who regularly walk past the ticket office pushing barrows with old bikes on board will have the prayer mat out. If they could manage to wheel a space station round to the Wearside Metal Company then they could rake in at least four hundred quid.

March 24 Saturday

There was no proper football yet again this Saturday, so we had to be content with watching England beating Finland 2-1 in a rather unexciting game. Winning was all that mattered and if we can cobble together another couple of results like this then we may even have some decent racism back on the front pages.

We now have four days for the players to recuperate and for the fans to think of a derogatory expression for the Albanians. After all, only three million people live in Albania, so we ought to be able to beat them in a fist fight.

March 28 Wednesday

Having established themselves as the world's greatest team by scourging the legendary Finnish side on Saturday, England went one better tonight by casting aside the all-conquering Albanians 3-1. I was pleased with this. By no twist of the imagination could I be described as a racist, but I find it difficult to empathise with a nation of Norman Wisdom fans.

The big news at club level today was Sunderland's announcement of an annual turnover of £25.5 million. However, shareholders should be aware that turnover and profit are not the same thing and that the maintenance department has yet to pay Sizzlers for a stupendous quantity of sausage sandwiches.

March 29 Thursday

I attended another Stadium and Events meeting to discuss Saturday's game. Malcolm the tour guide continues to attend for some reason. This must be part of his mission to irritate as he does not actually have anything to contribute. Alas, this does not prevent him from speaking - today a ten minute dissection on the shortage of paper cups.

At the last home game with Aston Villa, he was loitering around the players tunnel, sucking up to footballers and trying to appear important, when I asked a nearby policeman if he would carry out his duty or turn a blind eye if he saw me beating up Malcolm to within an inch of his life. His answer, that he would join in, has been well received at the club.

Everyone else at the table was brief with the exception of John Davidson, the Safety Officer. When it came to his turn we all made ourselves comfortable and poured a cup of tea. It was well to be seen that we are playing Leeds United on Saturday.

March 31 Saturday

Our home game with Leeds United was a quite dismal 2-0 defeat. Frankly we deserved to lose, but the game could have swung our way when Rio Ferdinand was not sent off for bringing down Kevin Phillips. Peter Reid ventilated his displeasure at this in the usual manner to the referee at half-time, although he had not actually seen the incident in question at this point in time. He had been in the lift and his first account of the skirmish came from me as we passed each other in the tunnel and he asked me what all the noise was about.

Before that, Olivier Dacourt had to be carried off and the stretcher bearers asked me if I would walk ahead of them and hold open the double doors that are on the way to the treatment room. I did this, but not with anything like good grace. I was trying to watch the match and it was not as though he had sustained any lasting damage to his legs, it was only his neck.

April 2 Monday

April Fool's Day fell on a Sunday this year, so it was not the same to think of people opening our letters a day late, even if they were dated the first.

We sent three pretty darned good efforts to the club. One was to Adrian the groundsman, asking to take ashes scatterings one step further by asking if we could bury a relative beneath the penalty spot. The second was to Lesley in PR, requesting a commission to make a club totem pole featuring the faces of Peter Reid and Bobby Saxton to ward off evil spirits and consequently assist with the club's push for a place in Europe. The last letter was to Graeme McDonnell, the Commercial Director, requesting that George Baker who stewards the tunnel on match days should wear a sandwich board, advertising a pan shop, Pete's Perfect Pot And Pan Emporium, on Hylton Road.

Actually they might go for that last one.

April 4 Wednesday

I was involved in a meeting this morning concerned with the Football Association's customers charter. We discussed at length the most efficient methods of fobbing off punters who ring up for a whinge. Also on the agenda was the issue of feedback from fans on whichever project the club is undertaking.

I was relieved to note that no reference was made to recent written suggestions from supporters for the burial of a deceased relative beneath the penalty spot, the commissioning of a club totem pole and stewards being made to wear sandwich boards.

April 5 Thursday

The impending demise of my job does not appear to have much longer to impend. I received an e-mail today which asked me to attend a meeting tomorrow with the boss and Mandy from personnel. The room has been booked for an hour and that is an oversized lump of time to simply ask me to turn up for an interview a week Tuesday.

April 6 Friday

After performing my final official duty for Sunderland AFC, appropriately enough a scattering of ashes, I traipsed back over to the admin building to be given my cards.

The meeting did not last for anything like the allotted hour. After some mandatory waffle with compulsory phrases such as 'restructuring', 'obsolete' and 'package' (alongside the studious avoidance of 'we're sacking you'), we cut to the chase and establish how much I am getting. The amount is enough to keep me in socks for the next six weeks and I get to keep a biro of my choice.

I then slunk out of the building in a blaze of anonymity.

April 9 Monday

I made my first underwhelming journey to the Job Centre this afternoon, where I rubbed shoulders with the rest of the Great Unwashed. They play pop music in there these days to give the place a more upbeat feel. It hasn't really worked.

Tonight we all stampeded to the Lansdowne to watch Sunderland's 0-0 draw at Middlesbrough. It was actually an entertaining game, but the most amusing aspect of it was the sight of the dozen or so visiting supporters dressed again in full white chemical protection suits and dust masks in a clear reference to the Teesside atmosphere, taking sarcasm that step further.

*   *   *

This morning an e-mail was circulated at 'work' informing everyone of my departure. At about 11.30 this morning the phone rang and I answered it to find none other than Peter Reid on the line. He had called to say how sorry he was to hear that I had been shoved off ship. I was genuinely touched and quite flattered that he had taken time for this gesture and it also gave me the chance to eke out one final bit of name-dropping for this diary.

Index
By date

246

Bridges, Michael; 3-10-98
Bristol City FC; 8-9-98, 13-2-99
Bristol Rovers FC; 31-10-00
The Broons; 27-9-97
Brown, Robin; 9-5-97
Bullimore, Tony; 14-1-97
Bullock, Sandra; 8-6-97
Burge, Mr. (referee); 7-12-96
Burley, George; 27-1-01
Burnley FC; 26-8-97, 26-3-98
Burns Report, the; 12-6-00
Bury FC; 16-9-97, 22-11-97, 28-3-98, 24-10-98, 13-4-99
Bush, President George W.; 20-1-01
Bush, Kate; 24-3-97
Butcher, Terry; 1-7-97
Buxton, Mick; 20-7-97
Byrne, Mike; 1-2-97
By The Rivers Of Pallion; 2-5-99

Cain, Peter; 25-12-96, 4-1-97, 23-6-00
Callaghan, Bernie; 25-1-97, 19-3-97, 23-8-97, 28-8-97, 29-8-97, 11-1-97, 1-11-97, 26-12-98,
6-11-99, 23-8-00, 7-9-00
Callaghan, Gerard; 29-9-96, 30-11-96, 25-12-96, 25-1-97, 23-9-97, 23-9-97, 22-11-97,
16-1-98, 5-2-99, 19-12-00, 18-2-01
Callaghan, Lesley (nee Coates); 24-7-96, 2-8-96, 15-10-96, 4-2-97, 28-8-97, 29-8-97,
11-10-97, 26-12-98,6-11-99, 16-1-01, 2-4-01
Callaghan, Paul; 6-8-96
Camara, Titi; 23-10-99
Campbell, Sir Donald; 16-10-97
Carlisle United FC; 2-8-99, 17-4-99
Carrier, Mark; 26-5-98, 8-4-99, 25-1-00, 28-2-00, 1-12-00, 13-2-01
Cartland, Dame Barbara; 24-5-00
Cats; 27-9-96
Chamberlain, Neville; 13-2-01
Charles, Prince; 15-11-98
Charlesworth, Alan; 30-11-96
Charlesworth, Julia; 7-11-99
Charlton Athletic FC; 4-11-97, 15-3-98, 25-5-98, 1-6-98, 25-11-00
Charlton, Sir Bobby; 31-1-01
Chaucer, Sir Geoffrey; 18-7-96
Chelsea FC; 15-12-96, 14-3-97, 16-3-97, 22-8-97, 6-8-99, 7-8-99, 3-12-99, 4-12-99, 5-12-99,
9-4-00, 14-10-00, 16-3-01, 17-3-01
Cher; 7-3-99
Chester City FC; 15-9-98, 22-9-98
Churchill, Sir Winston; 17-5-98
Clancy, Paddy; 18-11-98
Clark, Frank; 18-2-98
Clark, Lee; 2-6-97, 15-7-97, 1-11-97, 8-8-98, 26-1-99, 6-2-99, 3-6-99
Clark, Paul (Tonka); 24-8-96, 30-8-96, 18-9-96, 29-9-96, 28-10-96, 31-1-97, 21-2-97, 20-4-97,
22-11-97, 12-12-97, 17-12-97, 8-4-98, 30-4-98, 1-1-99, 28-6-99, 4-7-99, 31-10-99, 12-12-99,
20-1-01
Clarkson, Phil; 14-3-00
Clay, Cassius; 28-2-98
Clinton, Leanne; 4-9-98, 10-12-98, 29-2-00, 4-3-00
Coates, Lesley, see Callaghan, Lesley

247

Cole, Joe; 13-1-01
Collingwood, Chris; 9-9-96
Collins, Nick; 11-9-96, 14-3-97, 16-3-97
Collymore, Stan; 5-3-00
Cogdon, Claire; 26-2-98
Cook, Captain James; 9-12-00
Cooke, John; 27-1-98
Cookson, Dame Catherine; 30-4-00
Cooper, Gary; 5-4-97
Cornwell, John; 1-8-00
Coronation Street; 27-5-98, 8-3-00
Coton, Tony; 19-10-96
Cottee, Tony; 26-1-99, 17-2-99
Coulthard, Sarah; 25-2-97
Coventry City FC; 21-9-96, 1-1-97, 29-8-99, 30-8-99, 12-2-00, 13-2-00, 29-10-00
Craddock, Jody; 6-8-97
Cram, Karen; 14-7-97
Cram, Steve; 14-7-97, 25-5-98
Craven, John; 21-1-98, 22-1-98, 25-1-98
Crewe Alexander FC; 20-12-97, 18-4-98, 3-11-98, 27-12-98, 28-12-98
Crown Jewels, The (dance troupe); 8-8-98
Crystal Palace FC; 15-12-98, 5-4-99, 12-12-00, 19-12-00, 6-1-01, 7-1-01, 17-1-01

Dacourt, Olivier; 31-3-01
Dalglish, Kenny; 27-8-98
Dali, Salvador; 7-11-99
Darling, Grace; 28-8-00
Davidson, John; 16-8-00, 4-1-01, 29-3-01
Davison, Tony; 14-8-97, 26-9-97, 24-11-97
Dawson, Les; 10-5-97
Day, Sir Robin; 24-7-96
Deng Xiaoping; 18-2-97, 20-2-97, 26-2-97
Denver, John; 13-10-97
Derby County FC; 14-9-97, 26-12-96, 4-5-99, 26-8-99, 18-9-99, 26-2-00, 16-9-00, 3-2-01
Desire-Job, Joseph; 13-7-00
Diana, Princess; 31-8-97, 1-9-97, 2-9-97, 6-9-97, 22-11-97
Dichio, Daniel; 26-1-98, 11-8-98, 24-10-98, 2-3-99, 14-3-00
DiMaggio, Joe; 10-3-99
Dobson, Frank; 29-3-99
Dr. Hook; 16-4-98
Dowell, Davie; 11-10-96, 5-4-97, 25-8-97, 30-12-97
Duncan, Bernie; 1-11-96
Dunn, Katherine; 1-3-97
Dunn, Keith; 1-3-97
Dunning, Rachel; 30-11-96

Egglestone, Ronnie; 26-5-98, 18-6-98, 28-2-00, 24-4-00, 5-9-00, 14-12-00, 18-12-00, 13-2-01
Eriksson, Sven Goran; 13-1-01, 21-1-01, 28-2-01
Everett, Johnny; 20-10-96
Everton FC; 30-11-96, 3-5-97, 11-11-98, 26-12-99, 24-3-00, 25-3-00, 1-12-00, 4-12-00

Fairlie, Bob; 15-7-96, 9-2-97, 22-1-98, 16-12-98, 8-3-00
Ferdinand, Rio; 31-3-01
Ferguson, Sir Alex; 28-12-99, 28-11-00
Ferranti, Demitri; 15-3-00

Fever Pitch; 20-4-97
Fickling, John; 29-7-97, 29-8-97, 26-1-98, 23-7-98, 1-9-98, 21-12-98, 27-9-99, 8-6-00
Finnegan, Judy; 26-4-97
Fiorentina FC; 15-3-00
Firth, Colin; 20-4-97
Flynn, Errol; 25-7-96
Football Focus; 21-4-97
Forrest, Jackie; 3-1-97, 15-1-97, 9-3-97, 15-3-97, 2-4-97
Foster, John; 9-5-99
Fowler, Robbie; 25-3-97, 9-4-97, 26-11-99
Fox, Jim; 5-1-97, 19-1-97, 22-1-97, 25-2-97, 15-5-97, 5-3-00, 12-12-00
Freeth, Rob; 24-7-96, 22-9-96
Fry, Stephen; 21-6-99

Gail from the ticket office; 5-4-01
Gascoigne, Paul; 12-10-98
Gates, Eric; 1-10-96, 31-1-97
Gielgud, Sir John; 24-5-00
Gillespie, Keith; 23-1-99
Gillingham FC; 30-5-99
Ginola, David; 21-1-98
Given, Shay; 31-8-98
Glitter, Gary; 12-12-99
Goldberg, Whoopi; 11-7-96, 16-7-96
Gordon, Andy; 11-9-96, 31-1-97
Goulden, Mandy; 5-4-01
Gower, David; 1-7-97
Graham, George; 31-10-99
Gray, Michael; 15-7-97, 28-12-99
Greer, Germaine; 3-2-00
Gregory, John; 18-10-99, 5-3-01
Grimsby Town FC; 27-10-98, 7-11-98, 13-3-99, 26-8-00
Guivarc'h, Stephane; 12-7-98
Gullit, Ruud; 22-8-97, 27-8-98, 30-8-98, 28-8-99
Gurney, Bobby; 9-4-97
Gurney, Molly; 9-4-97

Hall, Sir John; 27-10-97
Hale-Bopp, Comet; 21-3-97
Halliwell, Geri; 15-11-98
Hamed, Prince Nasem; 2-5-97, 4-5-97
H'Angus the Monkey; 9-11-00
Hannah, Lord Justice; 10-6-97
Hardy, Billy; 2-5-97, 4-5-97
Harris, Police Sergeant Selby; 12-12-98
Harrison, Eddie; 10-10-96
Hartlepool United FC; 2-12-97, 9-11-00, 20-1-01
Heath, Adrian, 5-3-01
Hello Magazine; 26-4-97
Helmer, Thomas; 12-7-99
Hemingway, Earnest; 6-11-99
Henry V; 14-5-00
Henry, Simon; 18-12-99
Herbie Goes Bananas; 21-10-96
Hillam, Mick; 26-8-99

Hitler, Adolph; 28-9-00
Hoddle, Glen; 9-11-00
Howey, Lee; 19-4-97
Huddersfield Town FC; 18-10-97, 24-2-98, 21-10-98, 8-4-99, 10-4-99
Hughes, Ted; 29-10-98
Hull City FC; 2-12-97
Hull, Rod; 18-3-99, 21-3-99, 30-3-99
Hutchison, Don; 17-11-99, 16-7-00, 1-10-00

Idle, Eric; 12-1-00
Ifield, Frank; 1-4-00
Ince, Paul; 18-5-99
Inverdale, John; 21-6-99
Ipswich Town FC; 28-2-98, 28-4-98, 29-8-98, 17-1-99, 26-8-00, 1-1-01, 7-1-01, 27-1-01
Irwing, Dave; 9-1-97, 23-10-99

Jackson, Tony; 24-2-00
Johnson, Charlotte; 26-12-99
Johnson, Kate; 26-12-99, 27-12-99
Johnson, Mickey; 19-9-98
Johnson, Peter; 26-12-99, 27-12-99
Johnston, Allan; 21-4-97
Jones, Vinnie; 7-12-96
Jordan; 28-11-00
Junhinho; 2-10-96

Kay, John; 18-4-97, 27-6-97
Kay, Sue; 2-3-00
Keane, Roy; 31-1-01
Keegan, Kevin; 8-1-97, 14-8-99, 9-10-99, 8-10-00
Kerr, Cathy; 23-5-00
Kershaw's Sea Foods; 14-7-97
Kilbane, Kevin; 8-4-00
Kilmarnock FC; 23-5-97, 24-5-97, 26-10-00
King, Steve; 2-5-99
Kingstonian FC; 7-1-01
Kingston Windows; 25-9-96
Klinsman, Jurgen; 18-2-97
Knight, Gerard; 5-12-00
Kubrick, Stanley; 8-3-99, 18-3-99

Lampard, Frank jnr.; 5-9-00
Lampard, Frank snr.; 17-2-01
Last of the Summer Wine; 14-7-99
Lawrence of Arabia; 11-10-96
Lector, Hannibal; 25-7-96
Lee, Colin; 20-2-99
Lee, Steve; 17-4-97, 21-4-97
Leeds United FC; 2-11-96, 22-2-97, 21-8-99, 23-1-00, 18-3-00, 16-12-00, 31-3-01
Leicester City FC; 17-8-96, 26-2-97, 22-9-96, 29-1-97, 26-1-99, 17-2-99, 11-9-99, 5-3-00, 1-10-00, 24-2-01
Lennon, Dave; 10-8-96, 13-3-97
Lennon, Neil; 30-4-97
LeTissier, Matthew; 18-12-99
Lincoln City FC; 2-1-99

Lindon, Christine; 30-10-97
Liverpool FC; 24-8-96, 2-4-97, 27-1-99, 13-4-97, 18-5-99, 20-11-99, 26-11-99, 11-3-00,
23-9-00, 10-2-01
Lloyd, Rob; 16-9-98
Lowerson, Christine; 8-11-97
Luton Town FC; 1-12-98, 19-9-00, 26-9-00

MacAllister, Gary; 10-2-01
MacDonald, Malcolm; 12-10-98
MacMahon, Steve; 21-10-97
MacManaman, Steve; 27-1-99
Mack The Knife; 25-12-96
Madely, Richard; 26-4-97
Madgwick, Martin; 1-10-96
Makin, Chris; 14-3-00, 14-5-00
Mallan, John; 15-8-97, 2-9-97, 23-9-97, 18-11-97, 12-12-97, 11-3-98, 7-5-98, 20-3-99,
24-10-99, 21-1-01
Mallet, Timmy; 30-3-99
Manchester City FC; 15-8-97, 17-1-98, 17-4-98, 30-5-99, 23-8-00, 23-12-00
Manchester United FC; 21-12-96, 8-3-97, 17-12-98, 19-12-98, 22-2-99, 22-5-99, 28-12-99,
15-3-00, 13-4-00, 15-5-00, 7-9-00, 9-9-00, 28-11-00, 9-12-00, 28-1-01, 31-1-01, 27-3-01
Marriage of Figaro, The; 15-10-00
Martin, Steve; 30-1-98
Matthews, Sir Stanley; 23-2-00
Maynard, Bill; 26-12-97
McCann, Gavin; 2-1-99, 18-1-01, 28-2-01
McCoist, Ally; 26-10-00
McDee, Paddy; 6-8-96
McDonnell, Graeme; 12-11-96, 23-7-98, 3-3-00, 1-3-01, 2-4-01
McFadden, Martyn; 29-8-99
McNab, Jimmy; 8-5-99, 11-5-99
Melville, Andy; 23-11-96, 24-3-97, 20-9-97, 20-2-99
Melvin, Catherine; 10-9-97
Menuhin, Yehudi; 12-3-99
Middlesbrough FC; 14-10-96, 16-4-97, 19-4-97, 26-9-97, 28-9-97, 15-10-97, 21-2-98, 17-4-98,
18-4-98, 19-12-98, 2-10-96, 6-11-99, 18-3-00, 17-3-01, 9-4-01
Minogue, Kylie; 18-2-97, 24-3-97
Mir Space Station; 22-3-01
Monet; 20-1-99
Mortensen, Stan; 23-2-00
Mowbray, Tony; 17-1-99
Muggeridge, Malcolm; 24-7-96
Mullaney, Jill; 13-2-97
Mullard, Arthur; 9-2-98
Mullin, John; 26-3-98
Murray, Bob; 9-8-96, 15-8-96, 15-11-96, 15-12-96, 11-6-97, 29-7-97, 29-8-97, 7-1-98, 31-1-98,
10-3-98, 16-9-98, 2-2-99, 9-4-99, 12-5-99, 11-1-00, 1-2-00, 17-10-00

NATO; 8-5-99
Navratilova, Martina; 21-6-99
Newcastle United FC; 12-7-96, 17-8-96, 5-4-97, 8-1-97, 16-5-98, 12-7-98, 27-8-98, 30-8-98,
31-8-98, 21-2-99, 22-5-99, 23-8-99, 25-8-99, 26-8-99, 28-9-99, 15-9-99, 19-9-99, 4-2-00,
5-2-00, 7-2-00, 23-3-00, 9-4-00, 7-5-00, 1-8-00, 17-11-00, 18-11-00, 19-11-00, 25-11-00,
7-1-01, 11-1-01, 17-1-01, 19-2-01, 17-3-01

Nicholson, Dave; 4-4-97, 9-4-97, 23-4-97, 28-4-97, 11-6-97, 23-6-97, 31-1-98, 10-3-98, 8-4-98, 23-4-98, 21-5-98, 16-7-98, 9-10-98, 19-10-98, 9-12-98, 27-12-98, 15-2-99, 8-4-99, 9-5-99, 11-6-99, 19-7-99, 17-8-99, 14-12-99, 3-3-00, 14-3-00, 11-4-00, 18-4-00, 28-4-00
Nixon, Keith; 22-9-97, 15-10-00
Nookie Bear; 9-2-98
Norwich City FC; 30-8-97, 28-1-98, 29-9-98, 6-3-99
Nottingham Forest FC; 21-8-96, 8-11-97, 22-3-97, 4-3-98, 18-4-98
Nunez, Milton, 27-3-00
Nye, Rachel; 27-9-96, 10-5097, 2-5-98, 30-6-00

Observer, The; 25-8-96
Olive; 16-5-97
O'Neil; Martin; 11-9-99
Ord, Richard; 17-7-96
O'Toole, Peter; 11-10-96, 25-5-98
Owen, Bill; 14-7-99
Owen, Michael; 31-8-98
Oxford United FC; 1-9-97, 2-9-97, 28-12-97, 19-9-98, 27-2-99

Parfitt, Rick; 30-7-97
Partridge, Adrian; 25-1-00, 4-1-01, 2-4-01
Patten, Chris; 30-6-97
Patterson, Brian (Taff); 24-8-96, 22-9-96, 29-9-96, 30-9-96, 30-11-96, 31-12-96, 31-1-97, 21-2-97, 19-4-97, 10-5-97, 26-6-97, 28-8-97, 29-8-97, 4-10-97, 1-11-97, 22-11-97, 30-12-97, 21-2-98, 16-5-98, 26-9-98, 1-1-99, 14-3-99, 2-5-99, 4-7-99, 7-9-00, 12-12-00, 9-2-01, 10-2-01
Paulin, Tom; 5-3-98
Perez, Lionel; 29-4-97, 15-2-99
Perry, Bill; 23-2-00
Pescod, Tom; 11-3-00
Phillips, Kevin; 6-8-97, 8-11-97, 3-1-98, 25-8-98, 12-9-98, 15-9-98, 10-8-99, 30-8-99, 2-10-99, 28-10-99, 27-11-99, 5-2-00, 7-2-00, 23-2-00, 6-5-00 22-10-00, 26-12-00, 9-3-01, 31-3-01
Plymouth Argyle FC; 10-2-99
Pollock, Jackson; 6-5-97, 5-1-98
Porter, Tommy; 31-7-97, 4-2-98, 6-2-98, 9-2-98, 12-2-98, 28-2-98, 27-3-99, 29-3-99
Portsmouth FC; 15-11-97, 21-3-98, 26-9-98, 2-3-99, 11-12-99
Port Vale FC; 23-8-97, 31-1-98, 14-11-98, 12-12-98
Powell, Daryl; 26-2-00
Premier Passions; 5-2-98, 6-2-98, 25-2-98, 17-3-98
Presley, Elvis; 26-12-00
Prince; 1-1-99
Prodigy; 8-4-99, 9-4-99
Prokofiev, Sergeii; 16-1-98
Pyle, Denver; 12-2-98
Pythagoras; 20-9-97

Quadrophenia; 25-2-98
Queen's Park Rangers FC; 9-9-96, 6-12-97, 10-4-98, 10-7-98, 8-8-98, 9-1-99
Quinn, Niall; 16-8-96, 15-8-97, 16-12-97, 17-9-98, 27-10-98, 9-1-99, 17-2-99, 9-3-99, 10-8-99, 29-4-00, 1-10-00, 20-11-00, 30-12-00

Rae, Alex; 5-12-97, 27-1-99, 26-2-00
Rasputin; 11-6-97
Ravanelli, Fabrizio; 14-10-96, 19-4-97
Reading FC; 4-10-97, 17-2-98

Red the Hawk; 17-5-00
Redknapp, Harry; 17-2-01
Redknapp, Jamie, 10-10-99
Redknapp, Louise, 10-10-99
Redman, Carl; 15-7-00
Redman, Eileen; 29-6-00
Redman, Paul (Redge); 27-9-96, 26-12-96, 31-12-96, 10-5-97, 3-10-97, 2-5-98, 7-5-99,
29-6-00, 30-6-00, 16-3-01, 17-3-01
Reid, Peter; 25-9-96, 18-2-97, 24-3-97, 2-6-97, 15-8-97, 20-8-97, 21-10-97, 26-12-97,
26-1-98, 29-1-98, 5-2-98, 17-3-98, 28-7-98, 6-3-99, 13-4-99, 29-8-99, 31-10-99, 20-11-99,
4-12-99, 26-12-99, 26-2-00, 20-3-00, 28-4-00, 16-7-00, 14-12-00, 18-12-00, 22-12-00,
17-2-01, 31-3-01, 2-4-01, 9-4-01
Rennie, Uriah; 14-8-99, 31-10-99
Republica; 8-4-99, 9-4-99, 9-5-99, 25-5-99
Rhodes, Cecil; 29-7-98
Rice, Sir Tim; 28-12-99
Richardson, Brenda; 8-11-97
Rickett, Adam; 2-5-00
Riddell, Alan; 6-8-99, 8-8-99
Rix, Graham; 4-12-99
Roary the Lion; 26-9-97, 28-9-97
Robertson, Denise; 26-4-97
Robertson, Peter; 17-5-99
Robson, Bobby; 19-9-99, 5-2-00, 5-1-01, 9-2-01, 19-2-01
Robson, Brian; 11-12-00
Robson, Marcus; 3-3-99, 23-6-99, 25-10-99, 24-6-00
Robson, Sue; 15-3-00
Rogers, Kenny; 27-3-97
Rollin, Jack; 8-7-97
Rollin, Glenda; 8-7-97
Ronaldo; 27-4-98
Roseberry, Matthew; 3-3-01
Ross County FC; 8-2-97
Rotherham United FC; 30-12-97, 2-1-98, 3-1-98, 17-4-99
Rowell, Gary; 11-10-96
Rushden & Diamonds FC; 13-2-98
Russell, Craig; 14-10-96, 22-8-98

Saffron (Republica); 9-5-99
Sampdoria FC; 31-7-99
Samson The Cat; 8-3-97, 14-8-97, 26-9-97, 28-9-97, 24-11-97, 12-12-98, 10-2-99, 26-11-99
Savalas, Telly; 21-1-99
Saw doctors, The; 7-8-99
Saxton, Bobby; 18-11-97, 6-3-99, 24-4-99, 26-2-00, 2-11-00, 2-4-01
Schmeichel, Peter; 8-3-97
Schofield, Philip; 24-3-97
Schwarz, Stefan; 24-3-00, 5-2-01
Scotland football team; 10-6-98, 13-11-99, 17-11-99
Scott, Martin; 7-7-98, 12-8-98
Scottish Opera; 11-6-9, 31-7-99
Seaham Red Star FC; 8-2-97
Sex On The Beach; 12-5-99
Shackleton, Len; 9-7-96, 27-7-96, 10-12-96, 26-12-00
Shearer, Alan; 31-5-97, 30-4-98, 14-8-99, 25-8-99, 10-10-99, 5-2-00, 7-2-00, 25-3-00,
26-5-00, 18-11-00, 9-2-01

253

Sheffield United FC; 10-8-97, 10-1-98, 7-5-98, 13-5-98, 28-11-98, 24-4-97
Sheffield Wednesday FC; 23-11-96, 12-3-97, 19-9-99, 25-9-99, 22-4-00
Shepherd, Lisa; 24-2-98
Shipman, Dr. Harold; 10-2-00
Showaddywaddy; 16-1-98
Sinatra, Frank; 11-7-96, 16-7-96, 7-11-99
Singing Kettle Wild West Show; 28-10-96
Slaven, Bernie; 19-12-98
Smith, Alan; 31-5-97
Smith, Davie; 17-1-98, 25-9-98, 9-2-01
Smith, Gary; 15-4-99
Smith, Helen; 15-3-98, 5-1-01, 12-1-01
Smith, Jim; 26-2-00
Smith, Kerry; 21-3-98, 2-6-98, 13-11-98, 21-1-99, 12-7-99, 1-10-99, 4-1-00, 15-2-00, 14-12-00
Smith, Martin; 20-9-97
Snow, Peter; 31-12-99
Snowball, Donna; 19-5-99
Snow White On Ice; 24-11-97, 26-11-97
Solksjaer, Ole Gunnar; 28-12-99
Sondheim, Stephen; 9-2-01
Sorensen, Thomas; 9-3-99, 21-1-01
Southampton FC; 19-10-96, 22-4-97, 18-12-99, 1-4-00, 11-11-00
Starlight Express; 27-9-96
Status Quo; 30-7-97, 4-1-01
Stenning, Graham; 20-11-00
Stewart, Dave; 25-5-98
Stewart, Paul; 21-4-97, 25-10-97
Stewart, Rod; 25-6-97
Stockport County FC; 1-11-97, 7-3-98, 5-12-98, 1-5-99, 2-5-99
Stoke City FC; 25-10-97, 23-4-98, 25-4-98
Stonehouse, David; 9-9-97, 23-3-00
Storey, Yvonne; 17-5-00
Strachan, Gordon; 29-10-00
Straw, Jack; 20-4-99
Stuart Little; 3-9-00
Suker, Davor; 5-9-00
Summerbee, Nicky; 3-1-00
Sutton, Steve; 30-4-97
Sun, The; 11-12-01
Sweet Female Attitude; 4-1-01
Swindon Town FC; 21-10-97, 3-5-98, 15-8-98, 6-2-98

Taff, see Patterson, Brian
Taggart, Gerry; 1-10-00
Tarzan On Ice; 15-10-00
Tempel Tuttle, Comet; 17-11-98
Tessem, Jo; 11-11-00
Thatcher, Ben; 3-12-99
Thome, Emerson; 28-11-00
Thompson, Phil; 20-11-99, 10-2-01
Tranmere Rovers FC; 29-11-97, 24-1-98, 3-4-98, 22-8-98, 26-12-98, 8-1-00, 10-1-00
Tonka, see Clark, Paul
Tottenham Hotspur FC; 16-11-96, 22-9-96, 4-3-97, 31-10-99, 14-5-00, 15-5-00, 4-11-00, 3-2-01